DAMNED WOMEN
Lesbians in French Novels,
1796–1996

Damned Women

Lesbians in French Novels,
1796–1996

JENNIFER WAELTI-WALTERS

McGill-Queen's University Press
Montreal & Kingston · London · Ithaca

© McGill-Queen's University Press 2000
ISBN 0-7735-2071-6 (cloth)
ISBN 0-7735-2110-0 (paper)

Legal deposit third quarter 2000
Bibliothèque nationale du Québec

Printed in Canada on acid-free paper

This book has been published with the help of
a grant from the Humanities and Social Sciences
Federation of Canada, using funds provided by
the Social Sciences and Humanities Research
Council of Canada. Funding has also been provided
by the University of Victoria.

McGill-Queen's University Press acknowledges the
financial support of the Government of Canada
through the Book Publishing Industry Development
Program (BPIDP) for its activities. It also
acknowledges the support of the Canada Council
for the Arts for its publishing program.

Canadian Cataloguing in Publication Data

Waelti-Walters, Jennifer, 1942–
    Damned women: lesbians in French novels,
    1796–1996
    Includes bibliographical references and index.
    ISBN 0-7735-2071-6 (bnd)
    ISBN 0-7735-2110-0 (pbk)
    1. Lesbians in literature. 2. French fiction—History
    and criticism. 3. Lesbians' writings, French—
    History and criticism. 4. French fiction—Women
    authors—History and criticism. I. Title.
    PQ637.H65W33 2000   843.009'353   C00-
    900134-4

Typeset in 10.5/13 Sabon by True to Type

For Debby and Donna

Francophiles both

Contents

Acknowledgments ix
A Note on Translations and Sources xi

Introduction 3

PART ONE: THE MALE GAZE, 1796–1929
1 Damned Women: The Prototypes 11
2 Contrasting Attitudes: Male and Female Writers 49

PART TWO: THROUGH WOMEN'S EYES, 1929–1968
3 Constrained Desires 97
4 Contrasting Generations: Leduc and Beauvoir, Wittig and Cixous 127

PART THREE: SPECIFICALLY FRENCH LESBIANS, 1968–1996
5 Exploring Lesbian Identity 151
6 Contrasting perspectives: François, Best, and Monferrand 187

Conclusion 211

Notes 217
Appendix: French Quotations 225
Bibliography 253
A French Lesbian Novels 253
B Works Cited and General Works on Lesbianism in France 257
C Sources of French Medical Attitudes to Lesbianism, 1870–1960 264
D Bibliographies of Lesbian Fiction 265
Index 267

Acknowledgments

I wish to thank the Social Sciences and Humanities Research Council of Canada and the University of Victoria for funding and leave time; Arlene Tulloch for obtaining many of the novels through inter-library loan; Sandra McIntyre and Ian Riddell for invaluable bibliographical research; Lorraine Weir, Deborah Yaffe, and Arlene Tulloch for reading and commenting on the manuscript; and Sandra McIntyre for hours of word-processing, patience, diligence, humour, and enthusiasm – without her, this book would still be written in pencil.

A Note on Translations and Sources

All the quotations appear in the text in English translation, followed by the page number of the French original in parentheses. The French originals of all quotations appear in the Appendix, which follows the text. Most of the translations are my own. Where I quote from those few novels with easily accessible published translations, I give as well the page number in the translation, prefaced by the word "trans."

As an example, on page 363 I provide a translation of a passage from Jocelyne Francois's novel *Les Bonheurs*, followed by its page number in the original (12). The original French text appears in the appendix, preceded by reference to the source (Francois, *Les Bonheurs*, 12).

As an example of a borrowed translation: on page 71, beginning on line 15, I quote (for the first time) from Guy de Maupassant's "La Femme de Paul" (Paul's Mistress, 1881), which ends: (1218; trans. 1056)[20]. Note 20 refers the reader to *La maison Tellier* as the source for the French original (page 1218, in this case) and an edition of Maupassant's complete short stories as the source for the English translations from the story (page 1056). The original in the appendix at the back of the book (page 000) begins Maupassant, "La Femme de Paul," 1218.

The Bibliography lists first editions. Whenever these are unavailable I mention in a note the actual edition that I use for the quotations but do not include it in the Bibliography. I do not cite in the Bibliography novels mentioned in the text as having no significant lesbian content.

Within quotations I use ellipses in brackets – [...] – to indicate cuts that I have made in the original text, because simple ellipses – in the form ... – are common punctuation in French, particularly in women's writing.

DAMNED WOMEN

Lesbians in French Novels,

1796–1996

Introduction

Two hundred years ago, in 1796, Diderot's *La Religieuse* (The Nun) was published and for the first time a lesbian entered a modern French novel. Three variants on the character of the lesbian emerged by 1835 – created by Diderot, Balzac, and Gautier – and for the rest of the nineteenth century a variety of male authors exploited the existing prototypes in a variety of ways. Literary lesbians remained products of the male imagination, subject to the male gaze and presented as obstacles to male desire. They were of interest in male terms only as anomalies within a patriarchal hierarchy. Note that I am concerned here with literary history only and not with the history of pornography, in which lesbian characters occupy space in a different context.

As the century advanced, Baudelaire's misogyny added a weight of sin and damnation to the image, and by the Belle Epoque a large number of "naughty" novels had a socio-pathological lesbian in a minor role. Attitudes towards lesbians in novels by men had shifted in concert with those towards heterosexual women. After the French Revolution of 1789, women's possibilities for independence had been severely curtailed by the legal system – the Napoleonic Code. As the bourgeois wife and mother increasingly became an icon of idealized domesticity, images of women polarized and became less varied. On the one hand were desexualized "angels of the house" (to quote Virginia Woolf), and on the other were sexually coded women divided into economically determined strata. At the top were the stylish demi-mondaine mistresses of the rich, aristocratic, and famous, such as Liane de Pougy. Next came working women who could not afford a decent life without a gentleman-protector. At the bottom were multitudes of prostitutes, many of them country girls who had gone to the city as servants and, made pregnant by their employer or his son, had been cast into the streets.

The novels in this study suggest that many of these women, obliged to have heterosexual relations for their livelihood, had affection for and/or made love to other women by choice. "True" lesbians, active and butch, were therefore depicted as the rivals of men, and, with the exception of the ideal wife, all other women are shown as potentially attracted by women. (Beauvoir will call this group "situational lesbians.") Frequently, by 1900, lesbianism was simply added as the last and most titillating characteristic on lists of women's weaknesses, flaws, and vices. The term had become a categorizing label and no more, a mark of woman's inherent viciousness and perverse animal nature. And although the presentation occasionally became more subtle (Proust) or more sympathetic (Lacretelle), male authors perpetrated the same condemnatory attitudes and the same assumptions until the end of the 1920s, when male encoding of lesbians to all intents and purposes died out.

Treatment of lesbians by male authors had been stereotypical, perfunctory, and misogynistic, but, at least as long as men wrote the novels, the novels remained within the margins of literary history. Trailing along behind Balzac, Gautier, and ultimately Proust, they were occasionally referred to, present, and available in library collections. Some were even translated and helped create abroad the perception that Paris was a den of vice and a haven of iniquity – or at least, for women, a place of immoral freedom. This is evinced by the ex-patriate lesbians (English and American) around Natalie Barney. But the tolerance shown to this group was available only to those French women who were highborn and rich or connected to the theatre and therefore *ipso facto* outrageous. (These women – Sarah Bernhardt, Jane Avril, and others remained visible because they were on posters by Mucha and Toulouse-Lautrec rather than because of attributes of their own. The only women in the literary canon to write about lesbian experience and not disappear from sight were Colette and Violette Leduc. Monique Wittig's place in literature has been attributed to her by the feminist community, not by the denizens of literature.)

Half a dozen women produced lesbian novels in the permissive years of the Belle Epoque. If women wrote any between 1910 and 1929 I have not been able to find them. For fifty years from 1930,

Introduction 5

individual women published isolated novels dealing with lesbian experience. One or two – namely, Wittig, Jocelyne François, and Mireille Best – returned to lesbian issues time and again, but it was not until Hélène de Monferrand won the Prix Goncourt in the category of best first novel in 1990 for *Les Amies d'Héloïse* that official, public space began to open up for a variety of "normal" human experiences to be attributed to lesbian characters who neither died at the end of the novel, nor were dead before it started, with their stories posthumously unveiled by more or less judgmental narrators.

My concern in this book is to trace the literary construction of lesbian characters and the social and psychological context in which they are set within the larger frame of the history of the modern novel in France. I hope to make known as many novels as possible and, by presenting them chronologically, to draw a preliminary map of this previously uncharted territory in such a way as to open it up for further study. I am concerned neither with mainstream literary criticism nor with the theoretical debates surrounding Cixous, Irigaray, *et al.*, all amply treated elsewhere by literary theorists in both the French and the Anglo–American traditions. There is far too much published work in either field for me to contemplate offering references here.[1] I have therefore listed in the bibliography only a token number of critical studies, chosen because they in turn have useful bibliographies.

As I discovered to my dismay when I began this project, the lesbian presence in French literary history has been at best ghostly and at worst invisible. It would seem necessary to provide an overview of materials and attitudes on which others can base more developed studies of individual authors or more theoretical analyses of specific periods. I thus intend this book more as a work of feminist historiography than as a piece of critical or cultural theory.

I acknowledge with gratitude Marie-Jo Bonnet's *Les Relations amoureuses entre les femmes du XVIe au XXe siècle* (Love Relationships between Women from the Eighteenth to the Twentieth Century, 1995) which saved me countless hours of fundamental bibliographical research. Her work deals primarily with the history of ideas. Her bibliography lists every French novel that has even a one-sentence mention of a lesbian character; I ignore here all that do not offer a modicum of information. A comparison of my bibliography and hers will save readers who want to read about lesbians a lot of time. I read far too much modish male social chat and gossip masquerading as literature during the course of this research and would like to spare others the frustration that it generated.

The body of material with which I deal falls into two separate traditions: male and female. It fits into three chronological sections, which for convenience I have divided into two chapters each. From 1796 to 1929 the male-created lesbian was depicted unrelentingly and almost without exception as a monster with no hope of redemption; her wickedness could be inborn and inadvertent or deliberately vicious. Subsequently these male-generated attitudes, supported by the work of sexologists such as Krafft-Ebing, Charcot, and Havelock Ellis, became encoded into literature and ultimately into French culture. Although well-known, living women of the Belle Epoque seemed for the most part to escape the punitive application of the new "medical" attitudes (for reasons of wealth, notoriety, and nationality as I said above), later women writers still show their lesbian characters struggling for space, voice, and love against the same misogyny, misconceptions, and homophobia. This struggle is at the core of my second section, which covers the period 1929-68. The third period, since 1968, has produced an increasing variety of lesbian novel writing, which I describe in chapter 5. In chapter 6 I examine three major writers who should take their place in the history of the literary novel in France.

I use the term "lesbian" for convenience throughout to refer to female characters who have or whom, given the implications in the text, the reader may reasonably assume to have sexual relations with women. I am aware that the term was not used in this manner prior to 1867. Marie-Jo Bonnet traces the linguistic and political history of terms used to describe homosexual women in the study I mentioned above: *Les Relations amoureuses entre les femmes*.

Until the appearance of lesbian murder mysteries in France in 1990, there was no evidence of outside influence on the writing of French lesbians/women writing about lesbians in the whole of this corpus, except for Cécile Wajsbrot's novel *Une vie à soi* (A Life of One's Own, 1982) that quotes Virginia Woolf as an inspiration to the narrator. The novelists, when they are not appearing to write semi-autobiographical fiction (which is the case for many of the one-novel authors), respond to trends in the development of mainstream (i.e., heterosexual writers and gay men's) literature. This cul-

Introduction 7

tural self-sufficiency may come as a revelation to 'Anglo' North American readers in particular, who take French thinkers such as Beauvoir, Cixous, Foucault, Genette, Irigaray, and Wittig as authorities in the building of theory in literature, women's studies, lesbian studies, sex and gender studies, and queer theory. It will not surprise scholars of French who know that equally important thinkers have not been translated into French very swiftly, if at all, until recently. (Freud on female homosexuality was not available in French until 1973.) This study is therefore culturally specific: the history of lesbians in French literature in the last two hundred years.

PART ONE

The Male Gaze,
1796–1929

CHAPTER ONE

Damned Women: The Prototypes

DIDEROT: *LA RELIGIEUSE*

Written prior to the French Revolution and published after it, Denis Diderot's *La Religieuse* (The Nun) stands on the cusp between two worlds.[1] Before it came the *romans à thèse* of the eighteenth century, after it developed the nineteenth-century bourgeois novels of increasing social realism; before it, the struggles between churchmen and anti-clerical, atheistic philosophers over moral choice, afterwards the increasing development of psychology and the transformation of the discourse of sin into that of pathology. Before it, "Oriental" novels and convent novels had lesbian episodes incidental to the overriding heterosexual eroticism and choice of sexual partner depended on circumstance and occasion and in no way implied an ongoing state of sexual being; after it came increasing representation of fixed sexual identity, dictated by genetic, physiological, and psychological predisposition, where to be lesbian was to be abnormal, with no hope of contentment or stability. Balzac and Gautier are the first to embody emerging nineteenth-century attitudes in their lesbian characters as we see below.

Diderot's is an eighteenth-century novel in its presentation, yet the way in which the lesbian experience fits into its themes makes it very different both from the male-written novels that preceded it and those that follow for the next hundred years. Madame XXX, the lesbian Mother Superior of the convent at Arpajon, has no possibility of sexual choice and is not represented as a woman in search of a variety of erotic experiences. Neither is she described as a woman with malformation of the sexual organs or with any genetic predisposition to homosexuality or masculine traits – all conditions of lesbianism proposed in nineteenth-century medical literature. The church fathers judge her, but the narrator and the author do not. Diderot presents her as a woman who is out of balance because her social circumstances are not natural. Before looking at her more closely, however, let us examine the context in which Diderot establishes her.

La Religieuse is the story of a young woman named Suzanne Simonin, who is forced to become a nun against her will. The novel is based on fact. A certain Marguerite Delamarre, having spent all her childhood in convents, was forced by her parents to take the veil in 1735 when she was eighteen.[2] In 1752 she took legal action to try to leave the convent. The court action lasted some six years, and she lost her case. When the convent at Longchamp was closed down at the Revolution, she was still there. Diderot took these events and used them as the basis of an exploration of the effects of religious confinement on women who had no vocation.

In brief, Suzanne Simonin considers herself to be more intelligent and more beautiful than her two sisters and sees that these 'advantages' are a source of displeasure to her parents. She suspects that she may not be M. Simonin's child, and this subsequently proves to be true. Her mother hates her because she is a constant reminder of the pain that the father caused her and of her own guilt vis-à-vis Monsieur Simonin. Monsieur Simonin treats Suzanne severely because her mother suffers on her account and because he suspects that she is not his daughter. They send her to a convent initially because the suitor of one of her (half-)sisters prefers Suzanne, who tells her mother this. Suzanne manages to return briefly and extract the truth of her birth from her mother, and although she is transferred from convent to convent, she does not get permission to leave. She finally runs away but does not fit into secular society either, after her years of seclusion.

In the convent at Longchamp she first encounters a mystic Mother Superior, Madame de Moni, who is good to her and whose rule is beneficent, pious, and orderly. Soeur Sainte-Christine, who replaces Madame de Moni at her death, is harsh and sadistic. She victimizes Suzanne and treats her as possessed. Suzanne manages to get transferred to a convent at Arpajon, where the lesbian Mother Superior, Madame XXX, falls in love with her, compliments, kisses, and caresses her, and tries to seduce her. Suzanne confesses this to the Spiritual Director, Père Lemoine, who orders Suzanne to separate herself from Madame XXX. Madame XXX ultimately goes mad and dies, and Suzanne escapes the convent into the hands of a libidinous monk and the dangers of Paris society.

The novel takes the form of a long letter or short memoir to a marquis who has offered help and protection. Its tone is that of many eighteenth-century novels: recounted by a naïve, pure, and innocent narrator, who observes every detail of what is happening but has neither the knowledge nor the appropriate vocabulary to name what she is watching or experiencing – a kind of moral phenomenology. Her precise and simple descriptions are unmistakeable to the reader, who supplies interpretation, analysis, and judgment. This is the technique to which I referred above when I said that the novel is of the eighteenth century in presentation. Montesquieu's *Les Lettres persanes*,[3] Voltaire's *Candide*,[4] and many other texts rely on [apparent] ignorance and innocence as a means of social criticism and ironic commentary. Suzanne's undemolishable purity seems even more unlikely than that of some of the other ingénu(e)s of her period because she states at the end of her tale that she had overheard Madame XXX's confession and had suddenly understood everything that had been happening – and this was some time before she wrote the memoir, so it would have been reasonable to expect this knowledge to carry over and allow her to provide some analysis in her writing. But no.

Georges May, in his multifaceted presentation of the novel in *Diderot et "La Religieuse"*, suggests that Diderot got so caught up in the characters whom he created that he would have 'become' Suzanne as he imagined her during the original experience and written through her as the story unfolded rather than from the vantage point of later knowledge and awareness.[5] Perhaps. The innocent voice is an effective one and has often been used to titillate the reader. Also, Suzanne is supposedly writing to gain the compassion and sympathy of a male protector, and to write with, as she says herself, 'the naïveté of a *child* of my age' (my italics – she is now twenty) is certainly more touching than would be any social and psychological analysis of her misfortunes. Also her apparent naïveté and innocence would lead a male to believe that she herself was not lesbian, despite her experiences.

This narrative tone situates the heroine in a particular circumstance: that of victim, interesting because of her tribulations and suffering. Suzanne spells this out to the marquis, but as we read we realize that this is Diderot's attitude to all the women in the novel. These women are all in the same circumstances: they are all living the monastic life, governed by rules over which they have little or no control. The Mother Superior rules in all minor and internal matters; everyone, including her, must obey the Spiritual Director of the convent in all religious and spiritual concerns.

Diderot sees their condition as unnatural, particularly for those who did not choose exclusion from society and heterosexual commerce. For him, the human being, male or female, is a social being with a right to freedom. He presents the nuns in the novel as victims of physical confinement and emotional deprivation, and he studies the effects of the abnormal circumstances on their physical, emotional, and moral well-being.

Thus at one level the four most important women in the novel are case studies of possible responses to identical circumstances. Suzanne does not want to be in the convent at all, and her one thought is to leave. Among those who have stayed, Madame de Moni has the most appropriate response: she becomes a mystic, thus directing all her physical, emotional, and moral energy towards God. Soeur Sainte-Christine and Madame XXX are opposing figures, the first inappropriately punishing, and the second inappropriately loving. Each turns her energy away from her divine male consort (a nun being a bride of Christ) and uses it to achieve her own material satisfaction in different ways: by the exercise of sadistic power or seductive power over victims and favourites. Diderot shows all three Mothers Superior as being unbalanced and thus obsessive. Sanctity is no more normal than madness for him; both are potentially hysterical states created by abnormal and oppressive circumstances.

Diderot's novel actually offers a controlled examination of female oppression in a particular yet multi-layered pattern of significance. The convent provides the control, but Suzanne's home life establishes the metaphoric structure, and the interrelation between biological family and spiritual family casts interesting light on women's situation within all manner of institutions, thus offering an early feminist analysis of women's situation in general and of lesbians' situation within the larger design.

Suzanne's oppression began with her birth, the circumstances of which separated her definitively from her father. The intermediaries between her and this lost father – her mother and stepfather (see Diagram 1) – enact on her their attitudes to her father, and so the sins of the father are indeed visited upon the children:

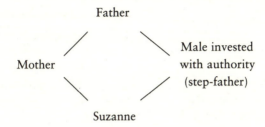

Diagram 1

It is the same pattern that is institutionalized in the convents of *La Religieuse*; It is also one of the major patterns of Christianity (Diagram 2):

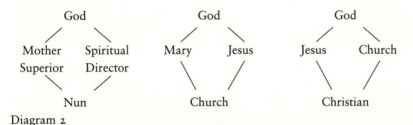

Diagram 2

The problem lies in the fact that the person at the bottom has two different authorities over her, one whom she wishes to please and one whom she must obey. They do not necessarily require the same things of her, nor do they have equal power to oppress or protect her. The one is emotional and domestic; the other, patriarchal and institutionalized. The second has the power of decision, which the first can either subvert or enforce, according to her level of oppression or sense of autonomy. Suzanne, however, has no direct access to the original power that created her place in the pattern and no means of changing it. She can survive through charm, compliance, or obedience (slave behaviour) – no will, no choice, no power to decide her fate, no freedom.[6]

It is now clear that the three superiors in effect provide Suzanne with three versions of her mother: Madame de Moni loves the father and therefore cares for the child; Soeur Sainte-Christine, betrayed by the father, wreaks vengeance on the child; and Madame XXX is the loving and caressing mother for whom Suzanne yearned but who prefers her to her father. The quality of Suzanne's response to Madame XXX is conditioned by her previous relationship with her mother. Diderot repeats the patterns. M. Simonin forbids Suzanne to see her mother because seeing Suzanne upsets her mother and M. Simonin loves the mother. Similarly Père Lemoine forbids Suzanne to accept Madame XXX's attentions and orders her to flee her on all occasions because he is concerned about Madame XXX's state. Monsieur Simonin orders her out of the house, and Dom Morel tells her to leave the convent, but neither takes care of her when she does leave and her circumstances become worse. Symbolically the roles of the two mothers become reversed. Suzanne is repulsed by her mother as she ultimately repulses Madame XXX, and she is solicited and wooed by Madame XXX just as she tries to please and placate her mother. Madame XXX praises and loves her for all the attributes and accomplishments that grieve her mother, and just as Suzanne wants her mother to take her in out of the cold, metaphorically speaking, so Madame XXX implores Suzanne to take her into bed and warm her. Neither Suzanne nor Madame XXX obtains what she desires because of the presence of another sister, jealous of the mother's attention.

Hence at one level Diderot constructs lesbianism as the product of a lack of love – a search for love betrayed, either by a male lover or by a mother or mother figure, a desire for human warmth. Suzanne does not have any active response to Madame XXX because she has not been loved before and so does not recognize what is happening, but she enjoys the attention and the caresses and finds it pleasurable and acceptable to be able to bring pleasure to another. Female socialization has taught her to oblige others, and she has no code of ethics or habit of thought and judgment that would suggest that she do other than comply with the manifest desires of her superior.

It is the nature of the desire that puzzles her – not as desire *per se*, because as a pure and innocent virgin she has no sexual knowledge of any sort – no instruction, no vocabulary, no experience. She observes Madame XXX's periodic physical and emotional disarray with concern and finally concludes that she must have some strange illness that Soeur Sainte-Thérèse has caught and that she herself may catch also. The description that she provides of the Mother Superior's tactics of seduction, increasing arousal, and ultimate orgasm are medical in their precision (and indeed the description of the orgasm is written in much the same style as Diderot's article on the topic for the *Encyclopédie*).[7]

"...finally there came a moment when, whether from pleasure or pain I know not, she turned as pale as death; her eyes closed, her whole body stretched violently, her lips closed at first, they were moistened with a light froth; then her mouth half opened and she seemed to die with a huge sigh" (629–30).[8]

Suzanne is in no way shocked or upset by Madame XXX's behaviour, nor is she attracted by it particularly, although she is increasingly aroused: "I do not know what was happening in me; I feared, I trembled, my heart was pounding, I could hardly breathe, I felt upset, oppressed, agitated, I was afraid, it seemed as though my strength had left me and I was going to faint; yet I could not say what pain I was feeling. I went to her; she signalled me again with her hand to sit on her lap; I sat down. She was as if dead, and I as if I were dying" (630).

Her danger, as Diderot makes clear, is that of victimization, because she has no knowledge, no choice, and no freedom. The sexual behaviour itself is only a problem within the patriarchal institution, and then only because the priest declares it abhorrent to his system. In sum, the man forbids relations between women because their behaviour distracts them from the duty that they owe to the distant father. Similarly Suzanne and her mother were not able to develop a relationship because of the guilt-cult concerning Suzanne's father sustained by Monsieur Simonin to hold power over his wife.

Madame XXX, the lesbian, is out of alignment with the system. She is described as such initially when men are present, particularly when they are describing their (male, dominant) view of circumstances, in which she is implicated. She interrupts, fidgets, and moves about. Her eyes are not at the same level, we are told, and she is a disorderly figure.

She's a plump little woman, yet quick and lively in her movement; her head is never on her shoulders; there is always something wrong with her clothes; her face is not bad; her eyes, of which one, the right one, is higher and bigger than the other, are fiery and dreamy; when she walks, she throws her arms forward and back. Should she speak, she opens her mouth before organizing her ideas; she stutters a little too. When sitting, she squirms in her chair as though something were making her uncomfortable; she forgets all manners, raises her wimple to scratch her skin, crosses her legs. She asks you questions, you answer and she does not listen; she talks to you, forgets what she is saying, stops short, does not know where she is, gets angry and calls you silly creature, stupid, fool, if you do not put her on track. She sometimes uses familiar language to the point of intimacy, is sometimes imperious and proud to the point of disdain; her moments of dignity are brief; she is alternately compassionate and hard. Her drawn face shows how frayed is her spirit and unstable her character; likewise order and disorder alternate in the household. (613)

But as Suzanne gets used to her, and when no men are present, the description changes, and Madame XXX becomes gentle, attentive, caressing, and apparently extremely sensitive to music.

It is when Père Lemoine ruptures the female relations within the convent that Madame XXX is declared guilty, described as sinful, and appears mad. She gradually accepts the image projected onto her by the male gaze, to the point that she voices it as hers. Not until Suzanne hears Madame XXX confess that she is damned does Suzanne understand that the Mother Superior's actions were considered vicious and sinful.

If we consider the book from this angle then, Suzanne's indestructible and obtuse purity, which test the reader's credulity on several occasions, could take on another meaning – that of female trust in female love and community, which is judged disorderly only within male institutions, and from a male perspective.

The lesbianism in *La Religieuse* is only a problem when its expression is inappropriate. Madame XXX is not presented as a monster of deformity, abnormality, or depravity (as she would have been in the nineteenth century). She is injudicious in the expression of her desire, she is obsessive, and she is unstable in her emotions, as people are when they are in love. Diderot presents her as not forcing her "victim" into any act that Suzanne does not willingly accept (although given her position of power over Suzanne, we cannot trust such an assertion, as modern analysis of abuse has made clear). What is important to Diderot is that her sexual activity is inappropriate within the convent because physical, sexual, secular affairs should not be the main occupation of nuns. It is inappropriate also because the women do not have the option of a heterosexual expression of love and so have no choice (Diderot must have written the only convent novel of the eighteenth century where no nun falls in love with her confessor), but Diderot does not present it as a perversity in itself.

La Religieuse is remarkably modern in its tolerance and understanding of the social, emotional, and physical circumstances that might well predispose women to the practice of lesbian sexuality. It is interesting also in its contextualization of the issue within the parameters of women's oppression. Examination of the responses created in each group of nuns shows them as occurring under conditions comparable to those of slavery. The next such analysis is Beauvoir's in *Le Deuxième Sexe*.[9]

Although Diderot's novel presents the first lesbian character in the history of the modern French novel, *La Religieuse* had no influence on the subsequent representation of lesbians. Perhaps this was because convent novels went out of fashion, as a result first of the closing of churches and religious communities during the Revolution and then of state protection of the church. However, anti-clericalists in the late nineteenth century touted the novel as a statement against the church (which is not its true intention). It is also possible that *La Religieuse* was not a model for later male authors because of changed attitudes towards women. Diderot was interested in the condition of women and discussed it from a number of different angles in his writing.

The various issues presented in *La Religieuse* are women's issues, a convent is a female community, and Diderot presents them as such in a woman-focused text. He clearly shows the power that men hold over women to be economic and legal, although he frequently couches them in terms of moral superiority: patriarchal traditions of the right to define right and wrong and thus judge circumstances and types of behaviour. The lines of male power and female powerlessness shape the novel, but male characters do not dominate the book, nor do they have the narrative voice.

Not only does the story unfold from a female perspective, but Diderot also draws the reader's attention to this authorial attitude in a humorous fashion in the scene of Suzanne's arrival at Arpajon.

The "grave Archdeacon," Monsieur Hébert, who accompanies Suzanne begins a speech in her honour to the assembled company; meanwhile Madame XXX interrupts him with comments, whispers in Suzanne's ear how much she loves her, and, when ordered to be silent, fidgets, yawns, and generally disrupts the serious Monsieur Hébert, who plods stolidly on to the end of his prepared declarations. And again later, Suzanne disregards instructions given by Père Lemoine, her spiritual director. Diderot's women may not be able to change the status quo, but they constantly ignore or subvert male attempts to change the way they are in the world. They have a right to social choice, and Diderot is interested in their struggles to achieve it. Diderot is a judicious observer.

BALZAC: *LA FILLE AUX YEUX D'OR*

Such cannot be said of Honoré de Balzac who is the second major influence on the literary presentation of the lesbian in nineteenth-century French fiction. His short novel, *La Fille aux yeux d'or* (The Girl with the Golden Eyes, 1833), together with Théophile Gautier's *Mademoiselle de Maupin, double amour* (1835), set the models of lesbian representation for the rest of the nineteenth century. Balzac is the first to create the lesbian as monster: a mysterious, perverse, jealous, vengeful, and powerful female animal who haunts the decadent male imagination until the end of the Belle Epoque. The entire novel builds to her appearance in the final scene. She has just killed her lover, the girl with the golden eyes. Look at her:

The hair of the Marquise had been torn out, she was covered with bites, many of which were bleeding, and her torn dress revealed her in a state of semi-nudity, with scratches on her breasts. She was sublime so. Her head, eager and maddened, exhaled the odour of blood. Her panting mouth was open, her nostrils were not sufficient for her breath. There are certain animals who fall upon their enemy in their rage, do it to death, and seem in the tranquillity of victory to have forgotten it. There are others who prowl around their victim [...] she was too intoxicated with warm blood, too excited with the fray, too exalted to take notice of the whole of Paris, if Paris had formed a circle round her. A thunderbolt would not have disturbed her. She had not even heard Paquita's last sigh [...] (299–300; trans. 104).[10]

The Prototypes 21

It is for this description that Balzac and *La Fille aux yeux d'or* became one of the major sources and references for lesbians in French literature. The novel contains no scene between the women (who have supposedly been together for a decade), no conversation, let alone a love scene. In this final death scene, Paquita, the victim, speaks only to Henri, Balzac's hero, and Marguerita, the murderess, speaks only to the corpse. (Ultimately Marguerita notices Henri, and they then talk together about Paquita.)

The text is an example of Balzac's exploration of the bizarre and monstrous aspects of the human condition – and he constructs his lesbian character for that purpose. But that she is lesbian at all is both necessary for and incidental to the main development of the novel, as was the case with Madame XXX in *La Religieuse*. Yet it is for the (non-)portrayal of the lesbian character that the novel is famous – and this is a mark of increasing misogyny, homophobia, and male-dominant patterns in literature throughout the nineteenth century.

If Balzac had intended to write a lesbian story with the material in *La Fille aux yeux d'or*, he would have had a tale perhaps five pages long; indeed if his purpose had been to explore the heterosexual relations between Henri and Paquita he would not have had much more. The work is one of three short novels describing destructive and egocentric episodes in the lives of "the thirteen," a group of rich socialite young men who support each other in the accomplishment of their desires, no matter what the cost to others. These novels belong among the "Scenes of Parisian Life" in his *Comédie humaine*.[11]

All three novels are examples of the overriding theme of all of Balzac's writing, which is the study of the multifarious manifestations of self-interest – male self-interest in a hierarchical and increasingly capitalist and individualistic society. To this end, the first third of *La Fille aux yeux d'or* is a disquisition on the physical ugliness and economic ambition of Parisians, presented in layers deliberately reminiscent of the circles of Dante's hell. Paris is described as a place of "excessive movement of industries, interests, affairs, arts and gold" (249; trans. 22), where everybody is driven by the goddess Necessity, which Balzac defines as the desire for amusement, money, and glory. In this turmoil are occasional examples of beauty: women who live in Oriental fashion, hidden and protected like rare plants, and young aristocratic men with "Raphaelesque" faces, which unite an English style of beauty with southern fire and firmness. Thus we are prepared for the meeting of Henri de Marsay and Paquita Valdès.

The next part of the novel is concerned with Henri and his birth, genealogy, and upbringing, at the end of which Balzac sums him up as follows:

Towards the end of 1814, then, Henri de Marsay had no sentiment of obligation in the world, and was as free as an unmated bird. Although he had lived twenty-two years he appeared to be barely seventeen. As a rule the most fastidious of his rivals considered him to be the prettiest youth in Paris [...]

Underneath this fresh, young life, and in spite of the limpid springs in his eyes, Henri had a lion's courage, a monkey's agility. He could cut a ball in half at ten paces on the blade of a knife; he rode his horse in a way that [brought into being (my correction)] the fable of the Centaur; drove a four-in-hand with grace; was as light as a cherub and quiet as a lamb, but knew how to beat a townsman at the terrible game of *savate* or cudgels; [...] Alas, that all these fine qualities, these pretty faults, were tarnished by one abominable vice: he believed neither in man nor woman, God nor Devil. Capricious nature had commenced by endowing him, a priest had completed the work (252–3; trans. 27–8).

Reflection on this long and two-fold prologue suggests that Paris and Henri de Marsay are not unalike in their indifference to the fate of the mass of Parisians.

At this point, after a curious statement that the information is necessary "to render this adventure comprehensible," the reader learns that Henri's father, Lord Dudley, was a philandering (and possibly bisexual) English lord who has left offspring of the same "delicious pattern" all over Europe, none of whom know of the existence of the others, and that Henri has a half-Spanish sister living in Paris. The plot then begins to unfold. Henri is attracted to a beautiful young woman whom he has glimpsed in the Jardins des Tuileries. He is determined to have her, as lover and as possession, despite – or indeed because of – the difficulties posed by a Spanish duenna in constant attendance and by a house with the most complicated system of locks and guards that the postman has ever seen. Henri is bored with women falling in love with him and wants a challenge. Other elements – that Paquita is beautiful, voluptuous, and attainable only with immense difficulty; that she is the prisoner of an unnamed lover; that her servants turn out to be her mother (an ex-slave from Georgia) and her foster father; that Henri is blindfolded and smuggled through a labyrinth of streets and rooms into an unknown location to meet her – all add to Henri's adventure.

He meets Paquita on three occasions, and they make love. It is evident that the lover is due to return soon and that Paquita's fear and tension grow as the date approaches. She expects to be killed as a result of her infidelity and begs Henri to take her away. He makes no attempt to help her and actually disappears for a week. He reappears one night with four friends, presumably to break in and rescue her, but they find her dying in agony, having been slowly killed by her lover – Henri's Spanish sister, who looks exactly like him.

The trail that Balzac lays for the reader begins with the full description of the woman as rare plant: "Nevertheless, there is in Paris a proportion of privileged beings to whom this excessive movement of industries, interests, affairs, arts and gold is profitable. These beings are women. Although they also have a thousand secret causes which, here more than elsewhere, destroy their physiognomy, there are to be found in the feminine world little happy colonies, who live in Oriental fashion and can preserve their beauty, but these women rarely show themselves on foot in the streets,they lie hid like rare plants who only unfold their petals at certain hours, and constitute veritable exotic exceptions" (249; trans. 22).

The juxtapositions in Balzac's text are tortuous and interesting. "Oriental" seems to suggest homosexuality in Balzac's vocabulary.[12] Lord Dudley, he tells us, came to Paris "to take refuge from the pursuit of English justice, which protects nothing Oriental except commerce" (253; trans. 29). This statement is followed directly by a quote concerning a handsome young man: "Ah, it is my son ...What a pity!" (253; trans. 29).

The description of women emerging only at night matches the habits that Paquita will describe to Henri later – namely, that she and her lover went out only after dark, away from other people. The women are described as happy. A comment follows on the existence of true devotion and then a rather ambiguous statement about battlefields of passion and the need for revealed feelings to be "complete" and "sublime by juxtaposition," which could well be preparing the reader for the difference between Henri and Margarita's feelings for Paquita at the end of the novel. Finally comes a depiction of Henri and his like, followed by a statement that such beauty is irresistible to women and that the demonstration of this fact is the prime purpose of the story.

Herein lies the irony of the unfolding tale. Henri does prove to be irresistible, but not directly because of the animal magnetism of which he is so proud, nor of the care that he takes of his person, which, says he, makes a fop the ideal choice of a woman; nor for his daring pursuit of the woman that he fancies, but because he is the male version of Paquita's lover. Paquita has been told that men are to be hated and feared, but she is curious about young men, never having come into contact with any but old ones. We can infer that a male copy of Margarita would be both known and unknown, intriguing and less frightening than any other man.

Balzac plays with this conceit by first having Henri comment on Paquita's great surprise and immediate attraction to him and then having Henri's somewhat naïve country friend Paul remark that Paquita, the girl with the golden eyes, is usually accompanied by another woman whom he finds more striking and who in fact looks like Henri. Henri, who uses Paul (and his money) when it suits him and pays no heed to him otherwise, brushes off the comment with "What has that to do with me, since I have never seen her!" (259; trans. 39) and continues: "Ever since I have studied women, my incognita is the only one whose virginal bosom, whose ardent and voluptuous forms, have realized for me the only woman of my dreams – of my dreams!" (259; trans. 39).

Paquita is indeed the woman of a man's dreams, being voluptuous and ardent, having experience of sensuality and sexual pleasure, and yet being a virgin. However, she is the "woman of [his] dreams," just as she is already the beloved of his sister (as Paul's comment will make clear in retrospect), and he little realizes that his role is to be the chimaera rather than the real lover. Before she will make love with him the first time, Paquita dresses him in women's clothes, and the second time, at the peak of orgasm, she cries out: "Oh Margarita!" Henri is immediately enraged because he is no longer able to blind himself to his situation. He is prevented from killing Paquita only by the arrival of Cristemio (Paquita's

The Prototypes   25

servant and foster father), who forcibly restrains him. He does not abandon his intention, however: "Henri maintained the phlegmatic attitude of a strong man who feels himself vanquished; his countenance, cold, silent, entirely English, revealed the consciousness of his dignity in a momentary resignation. Moreover, he had already thought, in spite of the vehemence of his anger, that it was scarcely prudent to compromise himself with the law by killing this girl on the spur of the moment, before he had arranged the murder in such a manner as should insure his impunity (296; trans. 98).

The situation has now become one of direct competition between a man and a woman for a woman. Balzac wrote that a man uses a woman so that he shall not be used by her, and here the irresistible Henri has incontrovertible proof that he has been used not only by a woman but as a woman, not despite but because of his male attributes and sexual possibility – and that above all is what he cannot forgive. He could perhaps have won Paquita over to heterosexuality, and had perhaps done so because Paquita, having learned lesbianism rather than having chosen it by inclination, had been drawn to him originally as the male manifestation of what she had loved.

He proves emotionally inadequate, however. He has already declared himself unable to leave Paris to save her, and he is too absorbed in his resentment of a rival and his enraged vanity to forgive Paquita and open himself to the love that she offers. True to himself, "inexorable both in his good and evil impulses"(297; trans. 99), his self-interest leaves him indifferent to Paquita's fate except in so far as he controls it himself. He pursued her for sport and she died, victim to his competitive masculinity and to her heterosexual instinct. Paquita's responses give the lie to Henri's beliefs. Balzac shows Henri (and his friends) to be totally self-centred and dangerous in his (and their) obsessiveness. Margarita has to be a lesbian to make Balzac's point absolutely clear. Margarita's visible and fatal passion is the parallel of Henri's murderous response in the bedroom and the reciprocal of his decision to execute Paquita. "The Marquise was a woman: she had calculated her vengeance with that perfection of perfidy which distinguishes the weaker animals" (299, trans. 102–3).

So thinks Henri, but his intention – that if she has anticipated him in his revenge, he will give her up to the law – is thwarted by her peremptory power, and he is obliged to recognize in her not only a sister but an equal in determination and ruthlessness, subject to parallel sexual desire and possessive jealousy.

Both Henri and Margarita want to kill Paquita. Henri's motivation is self-interest: his male ego is affronted by his awareness that Paquita used him as a substitute for and a completion of someone else. He declares that he wants not to assassinate her but to *execute* her. Margarita kills from jealous passion and declares her intention to spend the rest of her days in a convent to grieve "that which has seemed [to us] the infinite" (302; trans. 107).

Balzac contextualizes Margarita as a lesbian, but he does not construct her as one. Her sexuality is a convenience that allows him to use Henri as a lesson in obsessive masculine ego-satisfaction. Balzac creates Henri's sister in her brother's likeness to make his failings more striking and endows her with the passion that he lacks so that in her grief she has a moral superiority. Described as an animal, she is no more untamed than Henri shows himself to be: however, his veneer of self-protective civilization snaps back into place over his brute rage. He decides on cold revenge, whereas she tortures Paquita and revels in the blood. Hence Margarita would seem to be the animal under Henri's veneer. By making her a woman rather than an identical brother, Balzac simply makes a choice for the bizarre, the perverse on the one hand and the ultimately humiliating to the male sense of masculine supremacy on the other. However, this final scene arouses all the latent misogyny in the Romantic imagination. Balzac's bloodthirsty and vengeful lesbian calls to mind all the passionate archetypal women of antiquity – Medea, Circe, Phaedra, and Salome, for example, increasingly depicted by nineteenth-century artists – and with them men's fear of women's unleashed sexuality.[13]

All the years of Margarita's love for Paquita disappear, and she is depicted only in terms of Paquita's fear justified. A sexual woman, when she is not passive, not voluptuous, enticing, and available to a man, becomes monstrous and dangerous. Paquita is the acceptable form of the "femme fatale" – enticing and enslaved, and ultimately heterosexual – available to the male gaze and male desires, shaped to the male ideal by the lesbian experience that she both uses and abandons, a virgin with carnal and erotic knowledge. Margarita, in contrast, is a true "femme fatale," a woman capable of crimes of passion, one who, like a man, aligns sexuality with power and rivalry with ruthlessness. Like her brother, she has the social safeguards that allow her to escape the consequences of her action. But as a woman she has to be punished, and Balzac destines her to guilt and eternal grief.

Both Henri and Margarita are excessive in their attitudes and behaviour, but Balzac contextualizes Henri's self-interest as sufficiently contained to be socially successful, whereas Margarita does not belong in Parisian society: she is foreign in race, and her tastes and behaviour are likewise alien to civilized society. With her begins one of the curious recurrent details in the literary construction of the lesbian character by male authors in the French tradition. She is the offspring of an extremely libidinous parent: Lord Dudley, who leaves progeny all over Europe and who is probably bisexual. Henceforth most lesbians, vicious or victimized, come of overly licentious stock on one side (or both) of their family and as a result have no possibility of living a normal life.

GAUTIER: *MADEMOISELLE DE MAUPIN*

If Balzac provides the model of excessive lesbian sexuality, the third formative influence, Théophile Gautier, offers an alternative in *Mademoiselle de Maupin, double amour* (Miss Maupin, Double Love, 1835) – that of delicate and civilized bisexuality.[14] Curiously, however, both novels have a similar premise and structure. Both have as a first theme a young man's search for his ideal woman. In both, that young man is the chief protagonist, and the first half of the novel deals with his concerns. The second part of each novel comprises an intrigue in which a man and a woman desire the same woman, and by the end of the story each has made love to her. It is here that the similarities cease.

Gautier based his work loosely on the life of a historic woman: Madeleine de Maupin, née d'Aubigny (1670–1707). She dressed sometimes as a man, sometimes as a woman, and had numerous lovers of each sex. She was an actor, an opera singer, and a formidable duellist. In Gautier's novel, d'Albert, the hero, is desperate to get himself a mistress and settles into a delightful affair with a woman whom he calls Rosette. But as a poet, painter, and sculptor, he has an ideal of womanhood and of love that Rosette does not fit. Being a sensitive man, however, he cannot bring himself to cause her pain, so their relationship is still going on when a young man named Théodore de Sérannes arrives in Rosette's family home accompanied by a beautiful, delicate blond page.

Until this point the novel has been narrated by d'Albert in letters to a friend. The author now claims his voice and proceeds to recount scenes between Rosette and Théodore, in which it becomes clear that Rosette has fallen in love with Théodore, who had disappeared abruptly from the house some time previously for irrevocable but unexplained reasons that are revealed later to the readers in a series of letters from Théodore to a friend named Graciosa. We learn that Théodore is actually Madelaine de Maupin. Before being willing to accept any suitor, she wanted to understand more about men, and therefore, being an accomplished horsewoman and mistress of arms, she disguised herself as a man and set off to investigate.

One of the experiences that she recounts to her friend is the tale of having met a band of young men, among them Rosette's brother, who invites him/her to his home; Théodore accepts and charms both his sister and his aunt to the point where everyone is pressing him/her in their various ways to marry Rosette. Finally Rosette arrives in Théodore's room in her nightclothes and ultimately gets into his/her bed. Théodore is trying desperately to get out of a situation that would reveal his/her disguise when the brother arrives and offers the choice of marriage to Rosette or a duel on the spot. Théodore chooses the duel, Rosette faints, Théodore wounds the brother and flees. Now he/she has returned.

The last part of the novel turns around a "mise en abîme" production of Shakespeare's *As You Like It*, with d'Albert as Orlando and Théodore as Rosalind/Ganymede. D'Albert has already been attracted by Théodore and has been writing desperately to his friend about the irony of his perfect ideal woman turning up as a man and about his own horror at his attraction to a man. When he sees Théodore as Rosalind he recognizes him/her immediately as a woman and does not lose that conviction, even though he cannot bring himself to declare love to Théodore except in a letter.

Meanwhile Théodore has been lamenting to her friend that keeping company with men has put her off them altogether and she does not think that she will ever live as a woman again, except perhaps with Graciosa herself. She finds outlets for her need to love (the page is a young girl whom she rescued and "mothers") but wants to have the physical experience of sex. She finds d'Albert more acceptable than any other man whom she has met, partly because he is perspicacious enough to see through her disguise and partly because his treatment of Rosette is sensitive. So

The Prototypes   29

one night Théodore dresses herself as Rosalind and spends a passionate night with d'Albert. At dawn she goes to show herself as a woman to Rosette; she does not reemerge until noon. The next day she has disappeared again, leaving d'Albert instructions that he and Rosette should love each other while remembering her as their ideal.

By creating a set of circumstances in which a sensitive man finds his ideal in a woman who passes as a man and a woman finds her ideal man in a woman disguised as a man, Gautier poses a challenge to social norms, heterosexual behaviour, and gender expectations as they are encoded in most of the novels of the period, especially in *La Fille aux yeux d'or*. Paquita is feminine, erotic, and powerless; Théodore/Madelaine is autonomous and strong – androgynous also. Balzac gives that attribute to Henri, the irresistible young man in *La Fille aux yeux d'or*. (In fact both Henri and Théodore are compared to paintings by Raphael.) In both cases women love androgyny, men femininity. (Camille Paglia discusses both novels at length in the context of androgyny and decadence.)[15]

The piquancy of the love scenes in *La Fille aux yeux d'or* comes from the readers' awareness that Paquita knows love but not coitus and their understanding of why she dresses Henri as a woman. The piquancy in *Mademoiselle de Maupin* comes from the fact that Théodore, the dashing and delicate lover, not only has no knowledge of physical love of any kind but is actively trying to back out of circumstances that his/her charm and pleasure in the niceties of love have got him/her into with a woman who knows more about arousal and desire than he/she does and who is determined to arrive at real lovemaking.

The scenes between Théodore and Rosette are delightful and amusing as a result of Théodore's increasing desperation, which is paralleled by his/her awareness of being increasingly aroused by Rosette. The first time, Théodore muses on the possible pleasure of making love to a woman, "the thought came to me that men were more favoured than we in their love, that we give them more delightful treasures to possess and that they have nothing similar to offer us. – what pleasure it must be to run one's lips over that fine, smooth skin, those curves which seem to anticipate and provoke a kiss! that satin flesh [...] what never ending motives for delicate voluptuousness that we don't have in men!" (296).

And then on the paradox of his/her situation and her response to it:

My situation was becoming very embarassing and not a little ridiculous [...] Enterprising behaviour was not possible and that was the only acceptable kind. I was too sure of not meeting any resistance to risk it. [...] Gallant talk and madrigals would have been good at first but were too insipid at the stage we had reached; – to get up and leave would have been utterly rude; [...] besides, I admit to my shame that this scene, ambivalent as it was for me, did not lack a certain charm that attracted me more than it should have; this ardent desire was exciting my passion, and I was really annoyed that I could not satisfy it: I even wished I were a man, as indeed I appeared to be, in order to crown this love, and I was very sorry indeed that Rosette misunderstood. (299)

The description that Théodore gives of Rosette lying in his/her arms is delicate and sensual in ways quite appropriate to the character that Gautier has created and which are very female in style and perception. The two women are described in a way that allows me, as a female reader, to believe that there is no male gaze present. In this Gautier is as sensitive as he describes d'Albert as being.

The second potential lovemaking scene between Théodore and Rosette has the same components as the first, but more exaggerated. Both characters are wearing fewer clothes, Rosette is more determined to achieve her goal, and Théodore is very concerned that his/her dressing gown not reveal his/her breasts. This time Théodore is clearly conscious of being aroused by the act of caressing Rosette, and the lovemaking has an increasing voluptuousness and passionate energy.

I was moved and I caressed Rosette more tenderly than usual; from her hair my hand had moved down her velvety neck and from there to her round, smooth shoulder that I was stroking gently and whose quivering line I followed. The child was vibrating at my touch like a keyboard under a musician's fingers; her flesh shuddered and gave sudden little jumps, and passionate shivers ran the length of her body.

I myself felt a sort of vague, confused desire whose end I could not fathom and I felt a great voluptuousness in the exploration of these pure and delicate shapes. – I left her shoulder, and, profiting from the gap in a fold, I suddenly closed my hand over her startled little breast, which flut-

The Prototypes 31

tered wildly like a dove surprised in its nest; – from the outer line of her cheek which I touched with a barely perceptible kiss, I arrived at her half-open mouth: we stayed thus for some time [...] Rosette held me more and more tightly in her arms and wrapped her body around me; – she bent over me convulsiively and pressed me to her naked panting chest; at each kiss her whole lifeforce seemed to flow to the place touched and thereby abandon the rest of her person. – Strange ideas came into my head; if I had not been afraid of betraying my incognito, I would have let Rosette's passion have free rein [...] and these spirited attacks, these repeated caresses, the contact of this lovely body, these sweet names lost in kisses disturbed me utterly – even though they were from a woman; – and then, this nocturnal visit, this romantic passion, this moonlight, all had a freshness and novel charm that made me forget that, when it actually came down to it, I was not a man. (326–7)

Gautier is clever and knows his limitations. Again he has Théodore stop before any real sexual event might take place. Then at the end of the novel Théodore/Madelaine goes to d'Albert as a woman – a virgin (as was Paquita), aware of desire and sensuality, as the readers have seen in the scenes with Rosette, but with no sexual experience whatsoever. Gautier describes their lovemaking at length, and when Théodore/Madelaine goes to show herself to Rosette, the author claims not authorial omniscience but rather the author's privilege of ignorance. Rather than attempting a scene between women, he ends with an evasive flourish:

Instead of going back to her room, she went into Rosette's. – What she said there, what she did, I have never been able to find out even though I have searched conscientiously. [...] But one of Rosette's chambermaids gave me this curious piece of information: although her mistress had not slept with her lover that night, the bed was rumpled and unmade, and it bore the mark of two bodies – what is more, she showed me two pearls, exactly like those Théodore wore in his hair when playing the role of Rosalind. She had found them in the bed when she made it. I leave this remark to the sagacity of the reader [...] As for me, I have conjectured a thousand possibilities, all more unreasonable one than another, and so preposterous that I truly dare not write them, even in the most periphrastic style. (368–9)

Gautier leaves the reader to his or her own imagination and thereby avoids several perils – writing an ineffectual love scene after a good one, writing an unacceptably scandalous love scene, and upstaging heterosexual passion with lesbian passion and thereby seeming to give it greater approval. As it is, he carefully does not permit Théodore/Madelaine to make love to Rosette until he/she has proven herself heterosexual by choice, and he leaves Rosette in a heterosexual relationship afterwards – Théodore/Madelaine, again dressed as a man and now considerably more experienced, has ridden away yet again.

Both Balzac and Gautier show the process of access to the ideal love object as a blind advance through psychic threat and danger to the male person. Balzac moves Henri through a physical labyrinth of tortuous streets and darkened rooms – an adventure that leads him to erotic satisfaction but also to symbolic castration, played out in a womb-like space created by a woman for her pleasure. The implied links to what we are told are the terrors of the male sub-conscious are evident and legion. Gautier has his hero face similar complexities by presenting d'Albert first with a love-ideal who appears to be male and then by leading him through an emotional labyrinth created by the gender-metamorphoses of Théodore playing Rosalind in *As You Like It*.

The two novels' explorations of the male psyche are parallel: both heroes take the risk of being unmanned. Henri is made love to as a woman by a woman, used as he uses women, and thus insulted in his male identity; d'Albert, as a man, believes that he loves a man and is devastated by his own potential homosexuality. Both men have an intense need to re-establish their equilibrium in a totally heterosexual and hierarchically gendered context. Henri decides to expunge his shame by killing Paquita. His term is "execute," leaving the reader in no doubt that he feels himself the righteous victim of a heinous crime. To accomplish his self-imposed task, he arrives with a band of male assistants and witnesses. D'Albert, horrified by his own nature, confides in a male friend. Not having been humiliated by his ideal love object as Henri was, he is able to read-just his balance by trusting his own perspicacity and sensitivity.

His reassurance comes, as did his challenge, from a finely attuned response to his emotional surroundings and perhaps to his own feminine side, whereas Henri's is another manifestation of the ego satisfaction that fuelled his efforts to gain access to Paquita in the first place. His "feminine" side is manifested outside and in oppo-sition to himself in the form of his sister. Ultimately both novels are concerned with the fears that heterosexual men have concerning their virility.

BAUDELAIRE: *LES FLEURS DU MAL*

Neither novel would probably have had such a notorious history if there had been no scandal surrounding publication in 1857 of Baudelaire's collection *Les Fleurs du mal*. Six of its poems were banned, and publication of the volume of poetry was forbidden until the offending items were deleted. Advance publicity had announced the title of the volume as *The Lesbians*, but this did not prove to be the case, and only three poems in the book had a lesbian subject. Two of them, "Lesbos" and "Femmes damnées: Delphine et Hippolyte," (Damned Women: Delphine and Hippolyte), were among the six condemned. Both are long strophic poems, one more positively and one negatively inclined in its presentation of lesbianism. "Lesbos" is a defence of sapphic love and a lament for Sappho, but one in which the poet sees the women's voluptuousness as sterile and their laughter too wild. "Femmes damnées" (a poem that had a century-long influence on writers about lesbianism) is set in a context of lesbian lovemaking. Delphine is depicted as an animal with her prey; Hippolyte is tormented by the feelings aroused by Delphine's caresses. She is afraid that she is now on the road to perdition. They debate this possibility. Delphine is scornful of heterosexual love, and Hippolyte chooses her. The women are judged negatively throughout the poem, and Baudelaire describes their relationship in the same language of passion and perversity that he uses in his heterosexual poetry. As a poem, "Femmes damnées" thus adds nothing to the construction of lesbianism per se, but its title provides a label and a judgment that will weigh on subsequent literary representation.[16] Verlaine's poems on the subject, *Les Amies, scènes d'amour saphique* (*Women Friends, Scenes of Sapphic Love*, 1867), published subsequently in *Parallèlement* (In Parallel), are sweetly passionate, sensuous, and non-judgmental vignettes. But they created neither scandal nor counterbalance to Baudelaire's depiction of unassuaged, tormented desire, and it was Baudelaire's view that served as a focus for subsequent generations.

Not only does Baudelaire condemn the women to the depths of hell, where their punishment will be born of their pleasure, but he characterizes their love as sterile in a vivid metaphor of extraordinary aural power: "The harsh sterility of your orgasm / dries out your thirst and stiffens your skin, / and the furious wind of concupiscence / makes your flesh snap/flap like an old flag." Baudelaire calls these women disorderly souls, and his last line recalls Margarita's final words about Paquita. Baudelaire writes: "flee the infinite you carry inside yourselves." Balzac had Margarita say: "There is no consolation when you have lost that which has seemed to you the infinite" (302, trans. 107).

The choice of words is curious in both cases and would seem to imply that a lesbian love has the potential to offer a more extended and positive possibility than that of heterosexual desire. The words that went into literary history as the markers of the lesbian experience were not these, however, but those of the poem's title, which encoded and implied all the sexual sins of which the nineteenth-century male imagination had no experience and did not dare to attempt to express by anything other than innuendo.

BELOT: *MADEMOISELLE GIRAUD*

The most extraordinary example of success by innuendo was Adolphe Belot's novel *Mademoiselle Giraud, ma femme* (Miss Giraud, My Wife, 1870), which Zola reported in his introduction to the 1879 edition as having already sold thirty thousand copies – presumably because the public expected it to be titillating or obscene. The entire plot turns on three factors – on the male narrator's inability to imagine any desire other than heterosexuality, on the juxtaposition in Paule Giraud, the heroine, of coldness towards her husband and a discernible voluptuousness in her general comportment, and on a series of closed doors. Behind one of these, in a rented apartment, Adrien de C ... (Paule's husband and the narrator of the novel) finds black satin drapery, a Turkish divan, and copies of Balzac's *Une passion dans le désert* (Passion in the Desert) and *La Fille aux yeux d'or*, Gautier's *Mademoiselle de Maupin*, Diderot's *La Religieuse* and Feydeau's *La Comtesse de Chalis*. No clue could be clearer to the literary reader, but the obsessed narrator continues to believe that his wife has a male lover until he actually bursts into the apartment and discovers his wife's friend Madame de Blangy in there alone.

The novel is again the story of male desire pursued with no

regard whatsoever for the wishes of the love object – and in a sense
Adrien de C ... gets his comeuppance for his lack of respect and sensitivity. But inevitably, this being a novel by a man about a man,
and written in the middle of an increasingly misogynistic century,
the women have to be punished for their sins against the male
psyche. Paule dies repentant in Adrien's arms. When Madame de
Blangy goes swimming and appears to get into difficulties, Adrien,
who happens to be on the beach, goes out to her and they struggle
– he presumably drowns her, although Belot writes that she is swept
away and drowns. Adrien receives a letter of thanks from her
husband – presumably for killing her.

The book is built on a delayed parallel between two marriages.
Madame de Blangy separated from her husband after six months.
He disappeared, we are told, and she has no inclination to replace
him. She is inseparable from a school friend, Paule Giraud, to
whom Adrien is attracted and who is first described as follows:
"indolent and supple, voluptuous in her slightest movement [...]
Before she spoke, I already heard her vibrant, emphatic, almost
masculine voice. What voluptuousness in her large dark eyes half
veiled by long lashes and surrounded by a bluish circle! What sensuality on her lips, red and generous as though rolled on each other
and covered with an irritating fuzz" (19).

The markers are all present: the masculine voice and hairy upper
lip and dark colouring, voluptuous eyes surrounded with circles of
debauchery, sensuous lips, and seductive body language. Indeed the
description of Paule's mouth suggests vaginal lips, setting her up with
the attributes of the active lesbian, the seducer, possessing the mark
of her sexuality on her face. (Jacques de Lacretelle, in *La Bonifas*
[1925], describes Marie Bonifas in a similar way. See chapter 2,
below.)[17] Her friend is blonde, blue-eyed and (morally) short-sighted.
Also Madame de Blangy plays the required social games with men
and, as she has had a husband, is considered a free (loose) woman in
a rather precarious social situation, who is wise to protect her position and reputation by spending time with a female friend. Adrien
turns to her for support in his desire for Paule, and it is she who ultimately approves the marriage, although she first advises him to go
elsewhere. She mockingly informs him that a husband might not
appreciate the qualities and charms that she herself sees in Paule!

Throughout Adrien's pursuit of her, Paule remains absolutely
indifferent to him. Adrien, intent on the fulfilment of his own

desires only, interprets her behaviour as timidity and marries her without receiving any sign of encouragement whatsoever. He is then surprised, frustrated, and angry when she consistently refuses to let him in to the only bedroom in their home. Seven times he removes the screws of the bolt on the door, and seven times she replaces them. The night that he does break in, she is sitting up, fully dressed, waiting for his intrusion. She opposes her will to his violence. Finally she laughs at him, and he stops trying to get into her bed. He tells his woes to Madame de Blangy regularly, and she shuts herself away with Paule or takes her away for days at a time, ostensibly to convince her to accept her husband.

Finally, convinced that she has a (male) lover, he follows her and discovers the apartment and Madame de Blangy. At this point he packs up and leaves for Nice, where he makes an acquaintance who turns out to be the Count de Blangy. They exchange confidences and plan to separate their wives by demanding that each accompany her husband, as is required by law, and take them to different countries. Adrien takes Paule to Algeria, but as she is ill he makes the mistake of remaining in one place. Madame de Blangy's maid contacts Paule, who returns with her. Later Adrien meets the count, who is glad to be rid of his wife. Ultimately Adrien is summoned to Paule's deathbed.

The male belief in the fundamental heterosexuality of females is supported by conversations between Adrien and Paule when they are in Oran, away from their usual society. Paule describes her childhood sadness at being sent away to school and muses that the first girl to show sympathy to another in such a vulnerable state can take over her mind and soul. She declares herself ready to revert to heterosexual behaviour but will need time to adjust. "I am convinced," she says, "that in most cases it is not men who bring women to perdition, but women who bring each other down" (242). She later relapses into her lesbian way of life, but she dies worn out by passion and by an increasing sense of guilt. The assumptions set up in the first description of Paule have been belied – dark and voluptuous she may have been, but it would seem that Madame de Blangy was the seductress who occupied her body and soul.

In Belot's work, the literary construction of the lesbian continues as the author builds on the encoding established by Balzac and Gautier. Paule has the voluptuousness and sexual knowledge of the girl with the golden eyes, together with the apparent inaccessibility of Théodore/Madelaine de Maupin. The amorous male is thwarted in his sexual designs and suffers in his male pride and sense of masculinity. This novel, however, lacks suggestive scenes, eroticism, and impropriety of any kind. Neither the women in their relationship nor the men in their exchanges of confidences provide any information about what a forbidden relationship between women might entail; they name nothing, describe nothing, evoke no sensuality, no love, no passion. The only voluptuousness lies in the description of Paule's person and movement; the only desire is Adrien's; the only overt indicator is the rented apartment with its oriental décor and specialized library.

Mademoiselle Giraud, ma femme is a *tour de force*: it is an absolutely proper novel that is clearly about perversity and vice. It depends totally on the reader's assumed biases, imagination, fear, and sense of propriety. In a sense, the lack of specific erotic detail functions to frighten and confuse a young female reader, who learns only that relations with other women are fraught with danger, but she does not learn to distinguish where the danger begins, and so all interaction between women becomes tainted for her.[18] The title proposes the admixture of innocence and carnal knowledge that created the attraction generated by Paquita and by Madelaine de Maupin, but the irony of Belot's novel lies in the fact that Adrien's legitimate wife remains a virgin. The only time that she lies in his arms is as she dies. It is true that death has long been a metaphor for orgasm, so Paule is offered heterosexual salvation and Adrien a double and belated sop to his masculine ego, because not only does Paule turn to him at last but he finally gets revenge over Madame de Blangy, who is swept away to her death after being held, in her turn, in his arms.

LESBIANISM AS NEUROSIS

The offended men in Belot's novel triumph in their righteousness just as they do in Feydeau's *La Comtesse de Chalis* (1867), to which Belot refers. *La Comtesse*, again told by an impressionable and amorous young man, is the story of a licentious and frivolous aristocratic socialite with an absentee husband (in Egypt for his health). The young man wants to save her from her shallow pursuits; meanwhile she is deceiving him with a prince who specializes in perversity and vice. The lesbian content of the novel is limited to one inference and one statement: that the countess and the prince frequently visit a dark and fiery demi-mondaine, "la belle Florence," until finally the outraged husband bursts in on them all. He pays off Florence, kills the prince, and has his wife incarcerated in a mental hospital. On his deathbed he charges the guilty young lover with the task of telling the whole immoral tale in order to save other women! As in many other novels written between 1840 and 1914 by male authors, the lesbian element here is simply a damning finale to a list of female vices and has nothing to do with love between women as such.

Only female authors depict women together in a female space, and even then usually with an intrusive male gaze. George Sand first writes a gaze-free passage in *Lelia* (1833).[19] It is a scene of two sisters, asleep together on a river bank. One dreams of being kissed by a man. On waking she finds a likeness to the man in her sister and kisses her arm, at which the sister opens her eyes and looks at her in such a way that she feels immediately guilty, although she had no impure thought, but rather a revelation concerning the nature of love. Her final remark is that her sister looks like a man. This transposition of male and female as object of a woman's love, brief though it is, caused a scandal, even though the dream is spoken of as a lesson sent from God. Clearly women are not supposed to conceive of love in any form when there is no male figure to be its object. Male writers portray women as objects of male desire, and that male desire is the subject of their attention

Increasingly throughout the nineteenth century, as the rise of the bourgeoisie changes the face of Paris and of French culture as a whole and restricts possibilities open to women, the image of the ideal woman becomes that of the idealized bourgeois wife and mother who spends her life decoratively enhancing her husband's social prestige and nurturing him in comfortable and comforting domesticity. He meanwhile frequently seeks passion in the arms of one of the women of whom he officially disapproves. The division between conjugal "love" and lust is almost absolute, because the assumption is that any woman who feels passion gives way to her animal nature, and any woman whose animal nature breaks the bonds of passive propriety is a woman on the direct path to all possible forms of libidinousness. Men of course are able to control their lust through reason. Women's blood feeds either their womb or their brain. Any attempt to use both causes brain fever. In *Mademoiselle Giraud* the doctor declares that a taste for passion causes generalized peri-meningo-encephalitis in young urban women (229).

In *De L'Inversion de l'instinct sexuel* (On the Inversion of the Sex Instinct, 1892), Dr Julien Chevalier sums up lesbianism as described in novels: "As for the cause of perversion, authors agree to blame woman's natural amatory sensitivity, her search for new sensations, her passion for strange pleasures, the attraction of extreme voluptuousnesses, the refinement of the senses caused by excess of civilization and finally and above all social conditions which bring together a large number of individuals of the same sex to the exclusion of the other, in big agglomerations such as armies, prisons, convents, boarding houses and boarding schools, etc., etc." (71). He continues:

Novelists paint these loves, which are against nature, as violent, jealous, terrible, implacable, with all the transports, all the ecstasies and all the pains of real love; they [the loves] absorb the individual they possess and leave only aversion for the other sex. In the depiction of these feminine passions they [the novelists] always give one of their heroines the role of the man, that of command, direction and attack and to the other submissiveness and obedience. The first is often a woman with strong almost masculine features, a violent and uncontrollable nature who dominates her companion, exerting over her a sort of fascination and absolute despotism, conscious of her perversion and when necessary flaunting it. The other, being malleable, lets herself be led without resistance, unconscious and resigned.

In what class of society does this corruption most often appear? The novelists unanimously agree: in the upper classes, in the bourgeoisie, where the absence of any occupation predisposes admirably; never among the peasants and the working classes, whose hard labour offers them effective protection.

Are they debauched or ill, these heroes and heroines in the studies? Believing above all in vice, but glimpsing vaguely an unhealthy weakness of constitution in them, they [the novelists] have mixed opinions, taking a position somewhere between pederasty or tribadism and actual reversion of sexual instinct; *neurosis*, an ambiguous and convenient term, explains everything for them and they abuse it; their heroes are neuropaths, unstable, *unhinged*. They [the heroes] arrive at depravity, the way others become greedy after a loss of appetite. They refine love to be able to love, as others turn to new spices to be able to eat; it is what doctors call *irritable weakness*.

It is necessary to know this side of human nature's defects: warned, one can foresee the danger. As for the remedy, it is obvious: strengthen certain constitutions and get rid of boarding school, that powerful cause of shameful promiscuity during the dangerous age of puberty.

Summarized briefly, such are the main conclusions novelists have come to on a point of mental pathology. (72–4)

His conclusions seem to me an accurate reflection of the main literary attitudes to lesbianism as written by men – women who are not attracted by men are unstable; they can be weakly unstable or aggressively unstable, femme or butch, Hippolyte or Delphine. This is the line that originates with Balzac and Baudelaire. Doctors, using literature as data to reinforce their own speculations, add medical authority to fiction and thereby create social bias and assumptions from bases of fantasy.

MAUPASSANT: "LA FEMME DE PAUL"

The only exception to the presentation of lesbianism as neurosis in this period is Guy de Maupassant's story, "La Femme de Paul" (Paul's Mistress, 1881). A description of an amorous Sunday afternoon on the river in the environs of Paris, this short piece presents class and gender attitudes and needs in all their humanness and complexity.

Paul Berton, son of a senator, has taken his mistress rowing on the river. He is passionately and visibly in love with her. She, Madeleine, is one of those pointy-faced, tiny, vivacious, lower-class women who abound in novels, especially naturalist ones, of nineteenth-century Paris by authors such as the Goncourt brothers and Zola. Such a woman accepts love with a man as a necessity for her survival and is compliant enough to adjust her behaviour accordingly. Maupassant sets the couple up as amusing to others because of their constant embraces. They go to a floating restaurant crammed with crowds in flashy, fashionable clothes: the description evokes tourists with bad taste enjoying themselves in vulgar and

The Prototypes 41

human ways: "The place reeks of folly and stinks of vulgarity and cheap gallantry. Male and female are just as bad one as the other. There dwells an odor of so-called love, and there one fights for a 'yes,' or for a 'no,' in order to sustain a worm-eaten reputation, which a thrust of the sword or a pistol bullet only destroys further (1218; trans. 1056).[20]

This is not a place where the reader might expect to find Paul, and his presence there is an unspoken way of passing comment on the woman whom he loves. There are many boats on the river, and whenever a particularly spectacular one passes the crowd cheers and shouts. One such is a boat occupied by four women. The description already marks them as singular: "A canoe covered with an awning and manned by four women came slowly down the current. She who rowed was petite, thin, faded, in a cabin boy's costume, her hair drawn up under an oilskin hat. Opposite her, a lusty blonde, dressed as a man, with a white flannel jacket, lay upon her back at the bottom of the boat, her legs in the air, resting on the seat at each side of the rower. She smoked a cigarette, while at each stroke of the oars, her chest and her stomach quivered, shaken by the stroke. At the back, under the awning, two handsome girls, tall and slender, one dark and the other fair, held each other by the waist as they watched their companions" (1219; trans. 1057). Someone shouts: "Here comes Lesbos," and the crowd begins to roar.

Maupassant's technique is fascinating. The first description – "a furious clamour, a terrifying scramble" (1219) of overturned table and broken glasses and a "deafening howl" (1219) that sinks and rises again – feels threatening, dangerous to the women in the canoe. the reader expects an eruption of homophobia, yet "[t]he rower, in the face of this ovation, had quietly stopped. The handsome blonde, stretched out upon the bottom of the boat, turned her head with a careless air, as she raised herself upon her elbows; and the two girls at the back commenced laughing as they saluted the crowd" (1219; trans. 1057). The noise is transformed into salutation and welcome as the men raise their hats, the women wave their handkerchiefs, and all shout "Lesbos." It was as if these people, this collection of the corrupt, saluted their chief like the warships which fire guns when an admiral passes along the line" (1220; trans. 1057).

The only negative response is that of Paul, and his attitude provokes a reaction in Madeleine. Against his judgmental "It's shameful! They should be drowned like bitches with stones round their necks" (1220; trans. 1058), she defends the women's right to be as if she were pleading her own cause. Paul's response is violent, however, and, according to Maupassant, instinctive: "But he appeared exasperated, as though borne away by some male jealousy or by deep anger, instinctive and ungovernable" (1220; trans. 1058). As a result of these feelings he forbids Madeleine to speak to the women. She replies that she'll do what she likes, as she isn't married to him.

Given the way in which the couple has been portrayed, these exchanges are unexpected and unexpectedly energetic on both sides. On the other side of the café, the four women are making their entrance, and Maupassant not only takes the occasion to fill the reader in on their situation but, by juxtaposition, in a humorous description of a police inquiry after a complaint destroys Paul's previous threat of setting the police on them.

Having made it clear that Paul is powerless, Maupassant lets the reader see that Madeleine knows the big woman in white whom, just to mark the situation clearly, he calls Pauline. For the rest of the story Madeleine alternates between being with Pauline and with Paul, and all of Paul's attempts to keep her to himself fail. His love and his increasing desperation are depicted sympathetically, yet Madeleine is not real either to the reader or to Paul. She is the cause and the object of his passion, but that passion is generalized as a male response to female sexual power, which in this case takes a mysterious form that is against his will and against his tastes and inclinations:

The fact was that he was hopelessly in love, without knowing why, notwithstanding his refined instincts, in spite of his reason, in spite, indeed, of his will. He had fallen into this love as one falls into a muddy hole. Of a tender and delicate disposition, he had dreamed of liaisons, exquisite, ideal, and impassioned, and there that little bit of a woman, stupid like all prostitutes, with an exasperating stupidity, not even pretty, but thin and a spitfire, had taken him prisoner, possessing him from head to foot, body and soul he had submitted to this feminine witchery, mysterious and all-powerful, this unknown power, this prodigious domination – arising no one knows whence, but from the demon of the flesh – which casts the most sensible man at the feet of some harlot or other without there being anything in her to explain her fatal and sovereign power. (1222; trans. 1059)

She is a body after which he lusts and wants desperately to own. His response to all upsets is to initiate physical contact in order to assert possession.

She maintains her right to choose her own way in the world, quite clearly, saying repeatedly that he cannot control her life and that if he does not like the way things are, he can leave. He tries to cajole her out of going to the ball in the evening by saying (in words usually attributed to women) that he is tired and would like it if they went to bed early. "She, however, understood the ruse, and shot an enigmatical glance at him – *that glance of treachery which so readily appears in the depths of a woman's eyes.* Having reflected she answered: 'You can go to bed if you wish, but I have promised to go to the ball at La Grenouillère.'" (1225; trans. 1061, my emphasis). Again, her response is cast in terms of a generalized misogynistic cliché.

To cut a short story shorter, while Paul contemplates the rising moon and forgets about Madeleine, she slides away and goes off with Pauline. Paul searches for them wildly, and even at the height of his search his desire for Madeleine remains impersonal and idealized: "The entrancing poetry of this summer night had, in spite of himself, entered into Paul, athwart his infatuated anguish, stirring his heart with ferocious irony and increasing even to madness his craving for an ideal tenderness, for passionate outpourings on the breast of *an adored and faithful woman*" (trans. 1063, my emphasis).

When he finds them, his first reaction is a desire to flee. He remembers Madeleine in bed in the morning, then goes closer, hears a moan of pleasure, and sees them: "The couple began to speak again; and he approached, stooping low. Then a faint cry rose from under the branches quite close to him. [A cry! One of those cries of love that he had learned to recognize in their wild moments of tenderness (words omitted in published translation)] He advanced again, in spite of himself, irresistibly attracted, without being conscious of anything – and he saw them. If her companion had only been a man! But that! *that!* He felt as though he were spellbound by the very infamy of it. And he stood there astounded and overwhelmed, as if he had discovered the mutilated corpse of one dear to him, a crime against nature, a monstrous, disgusting profanation (1229; trans. 1064).

Madeleine murmurs "Pauline" as she has so often said "Paul," and this hurts him so much that he flees, jumps into the river, and drowns. But before he leaps he calls "Madeleine." She hears, and the women come to the river in time to see him pulled out, dripping with black slime, stiff and swollen as though long dead. Pauline comforts Madeleine and takes her away.

Then Pauline took the poor weeping Madeleine in her arms, petted her, embraced her for a long while, and consoled her.

"How can you help it? it is not your fault, is it? It is impossible to prevent men from doing silly things. He did it of his own free will; so much the worse for him, after all!"

And then lifting her up:

"Come, my dear, come and sleep at the house; it is impossible for you to go back to Grillon's tonight."

And she embraced her again, saying: "Come, we will cure you."

Madeleine arose, and, weeping all the while, but with fainter sobs, laid her head upon Pauline's shoulder, *as though she had found a refuge in a closer and more certain affection, more familiar and more confiding,* and she went off slowly. (1232; trans. 1065, my emphasis)

So the story ends with the implication that Madeleine is actually loved by Pauline in ways that are gentler, safer, and more trusting and trustworthy than those of Paul – or, in an equal gender generalization, those of the men who do stupid things.

The text raises a lot of questions. Paul Berton is identified as coming from a different class from the rest of the characters in the story. Should his bigotry therefore be attributed to the learned attitudes of his upbringing? He is also coded as sensitive, young, and vibrating with love. Does his antagonism towards the lesbians come from an intuitive understanding of the attraction that they hold for his mistress? Is it the atavistic territoriality of a man in acute lust? Maupassant calls it a deep male jealousy, and certainly at the end, when he sees Madeleine and Pauline, Paul's first wish is that his rival were a man. None of the other men in the story shows any negativity towards the women. Even the waiter, who tells Paul that Madeleine left with Pauline, gives the information with no lascivious, ironic, or disrespectful undertone. The only mockery in the story is attributed to the other three lesbians as they watch Paul in his desperate search for Madeleine. When Pauline dresses him

The Prototypes   45

down in public, she does so in direct response to his insult to her when he insisted that Madeleine not speak to the women.

The two main images in the story are used in a misogynistic fashion. First, Pauline's insults constitute a "downpour of filthy abuse. It appeared to him that the words which came from that mouth and fell on him defiled him like dirt" (1222; trans. 1057). The description of his corpse recalls those words: "A kind of black and liquid plaster covered his whole body. The face appeared swollen, and from his hair, plastered down by the ooze, there ran a stream of dirty water" (1231; trans. 1065). The author thus metaphorically attributes his death to Pauline as well as to the river. And in both instances, he saw the danger and chose to jump in. Second, there is the image of a fisherman, impatient with the hook in the fish that he has caught, who wrenches out hook, throat, and innards all on his line. Paul watches the scene and identifies with the fish when Madeleine is first talking to Pauline: "It seemed to him that the hook was his love, and that if he should pluck it out, all that he had in his breast would come out in the same way, at the end of a curved iron, fixed in the depths of his being, to which Madeleine held the line" (1223; trans. 1057). He has a flashback to the scene when he sees them making love.

In both repeating images the source of pain and humiliation is the woman, and Paul suffers, but he has no sense of why he finds himself in the role of victim, why Madeleine might not love him as he loves her. He is totally oblivious to anything beyond his own desires and class-based assumptions. Madeleine has no reality for him beyond his use of her; deviance is unacceptable in the bourgeois scheme of things, and Pauline is a rival in the Balzacian tradition. What is different here is that it is not Paul the lover who is the centre, but Paul the ignorant, prejudiced, and insensitive male.

It is unusual to find a nineteenth-century male author writing about a woman, let alone a lesbian, with the awareness that Maupassant allows to come through in his story. Other literature and social history make it clear that a woman like Madeleine will be of interest to a man of Paul's age and station for a brief period only. She will then be abandoned to survive as she may – usually in poverty and prostitution, frequently combined with pregnancy. We see that Paul thinks of her as an example of a general category. He can idealize her and make love to her, but her person and personality do not actually suit his real requirements. The rage and despair that he feels are attributed to his instinctive maleness. It is as though he lost a struggle to a humiliatingly inferior opponent and then in shame ends his life. The parallel naming of Paul and Pauline would support such a reading. Again the story is about a crisis of the male ego, but here the almost beardless, refined young man cannot win against the force of nature: Pauline, big, fat, female, loud, and blatantly sexual in her male clothing.

Madeleine meanwhile claims her right to make choices in her life concerning what she does, when, and with whom. She is not cowed by male authority or manipulated by sexual wiles. Her exchanges with Pauline seem more direct than those with Paul, and the reader has the sense that Pauline knows her as an individual. Pauline's words to her after Paul's suicide are ambiguously caring or sexual: she offers to take her to the women's home, so that Madeleine shouldn't follow the corpse back to her lodging, and she says: "we will cure you." But the final paragraph clarifies the tone: with these women, she will be taken care of.

"La Femme de Paul" belongs to neither of the major lineages I am describing here. Maupassant shows his lesbians as human beings, with none of the implications of monstrosity (begun by Balzac in *La Fille aux yeux d'or* [1835]), that come to dominate male writing about lesbians after 1890. Maupassant's story, grounded and sympathetic, offers a different perspective in a different context – one that is not classified by the likes of Dr Chevalier. He sees lesbianism as characterized by love and caring, not as perversion, neurosis, and vice. He also sets it in opposition to the economic reasons for which many women accept sexual relations with men. Maupassant has drawn an interesting vignette of working-class live-and-let-live tolerance of human sexuality in all its forms, of women's need for female care (Pauline becoming an unexpected mother figure), as well as of men's ever-recurrent lack of regard for anything but their own sexual satisfaction and masculine pride of possession.

The line of refined bisexuality that runs from Gautier's *Mademoiselle de Maupin* (1835) follows a different course. It leads on one side to Félicien Champsaur's *Dinah Samuel* (1882) and on to the cross-dressing, role-reversing heterosexual women in Rachilde's novels – *Madame Adonis* (1888) and *Monsieur Vénus* (1889) – and, on the other, to the multitude of theatrical lesbians such as those in Zola's *Nana* (1879–80) and those who have bit parts in the novels of male society gossip such as Willy's *La Môme Picrate* (1903). The last of this lineage is Niquette, the lesbian lover of Monique in Margueritte's *La Garçonne* (1925).

Dinah Samuel has as protagonist a cross-dressing actress and artist who, like Madeleine in "La Femme de Paul," sleeps with rich men for economic reasons and with women for pleasure. She flouts acceptability, mores, and morality and gets away with her improprieties because of her impertinence and her talent. The character would seem to have been created in the image of Sarah Bernhardt (1844–1923). She is mysterious, magnificent, a legend, who, like Bernhardt, keeps a coffin in her bedroom. This novel offers no study of lesbian psychology or behaviour, but like the others it uses sapphic references to suggest an outrageous way of life.

Alice Penthièvre, when cast off by Dinah, calls herself Mademoiselle Sosie and makes a career of imitating her former lover. Just as Alice imitates Dinah Samuel, who is constructed in Bernhardt's image, so Bernhardt modelled herself to some extent on *Mademoiselle de Maupin*, which recreated the life of a real Madeleine d'Aubigny Maupin (1670–1707), who dressed as a man, fought duels, and sang at the Paris Opéra, as did Bernhardt two hundred years later. But this set of parallels produces in effect a closed loop of extraordinary women who, already assumed to be people of dubious morality because of their connection with the theatre and the loss of caste that the profession historically conferred on women, are now expected to be outrageous as an extension of their dramatic talent.

A number of women did fall into this category in fin-de-siècle Paris. Jane Avril and other dancers at the Moulin Rouge, Bernhardt, Colette and Missy,[21] and, more privately, the theatrically inclined group of rich expatriate anglophones that centred around Nathalie Barney. These were, however, lesbian enclaves in a patriarchal and misogynistic culture that generally considered women amorphous sex objects, virtually indistinguishable one from the other.[22] As long as the desired object was available when the lustful male so required, she spent her spare time with another woman. Availability to the male was paramount for these authors, so the lesbian comes into focus only when, as a marauding virago, she enters into direct competition with a consequential male for "his" women. Then she is presented as a monster of depravity and unnatural sexuality because she has and expresses desire, mystery, and danger. The nineteenth century sees the shifting onto the lesbian of all the archetypal fears of the devouring sexuality of women who destroy the virility of men.

CHAPTER TWO

Contrasting Attitudes:
Male and Female Writers

For a variety of reasons archetypal and material, the lesbian became the focus of male sexual fear in the 1890s. These reasons concern power – power embedded in concepts of sexual difference, mental competence, gender roles, and politics, all of which underwent change throughout the nineteenth century in the Western world.

The conditions of women in France differed from those of the Anglo–American world at least in four respects: economic, legal, social, and cultural. Women in France were economically disadvantaged, and those who did not have private fortunes could not earn enough to live alone. The legal system discriminated against women in all possible ways. The Napoleonic Code treated them as legal inferiors, classed with children and criminals as not competent to take civic responsibility for themselves or others. All social occasions were heterosexual, the essential condition being that every adult should be part of an actual or potential couple, legal or illicit. There was little space for women to be without men at any time; there was not place or station for single women at all – let alone pairs of women. French literature in particular was renowned for its immorality. *Risqué* novels were translated and exported expeditiously – Belot's *Mademoiselle Giraud, ma femme* (Miss Giraud, My Wife, 1870), for example, received U.S. publication by 1891 – giving rise to the perception abroad that Paris was a centre of vice. In art and poetry, the Decadents represented lesbians as monsters of depraved appetite, jealous and murderous at worst, outrageously sensual and ultimately guilt-ridden at best.

Until this period, sexual choice in the Western world had been a social and moral issue, with each encounter, heterosexual or homosexual, involving a discrete decision to be viewed in its own context of vice or sin. The sexologists – Charcot, Krafft-Ebing[1] – theorized sexual choice into sexual nature, which they then categorized as normal or deviant. They then pathologized deviance into illness, to be cured rather than punished or forgiven. All the sexologists were male, and their writings show deep-seated misogyny. As their interpretations were disseminated widely, they were absorbed into social attitudes and added to the previously existing layers of constraint, restraint, and potential oppression of women. The sexologists presented woman as other, selected in Darwinian ways for beauty, modesty, and passivity. They classed women with more energetic characteristics as some form of hysteric: overly aggressive, sexual, masculine. With the growth of sexology, the quiet tradition of romantic friendship between women (a term that covered a range of behaviour from delicate affection to an erotic sex life) became increasingly open to reclassification as a pathology.[2] Lesbianism evolved into a neurosis; from being proud, predatory monsters, lesbians become psychiatric cases of instability in French novels at the turn of the century.

The cult of the male, the increasing dominance of the bourgeoisie, and the contexts of all these "scientific" explorations produced the image of the perfect mate for the successful dominant male – that of the compliant, sexually passive, domestic female. This ideal bourgeois wife and mother supposedly spent her days transforming her home, with pillows, embroidery, and other embellishments, into a nest where her husband was protected from the harsh, competitive world of work.[3] In the literature and in the popular press she was opposed to the sexually active prostitute, of whom there were increasing numbers in Paris (some statistics suggest 35,000 to 40,000 in 1900[4]) operating at all levels from the demi-monde concubines of princes, such as Cléo de Mérode and Liane de Pougy, through the legions of flower makers who had insufficient income to survive at best and none at all in the summer season (see Mimi in Puccini's opera La Bohème), to street-corner waifs, starving single mothers abandoned by "respectable" men.

Wife or harlot, sexless or sexual, but always in the service of the male, this was the major nineteenth-century depiction of womanhood. French society is built on the concept of the couple. "Love," love affairs, accommodating marriages, influential mistresses play a visible role in the political and social history of France, with all social and cultural institutions structured around the assumption of heterosexuality. As a result all struggles for female emancipation, civil and human rights, and improved conditions take place from inside the "given" parameters of the family and patriarchal institutions. First-wave feminists redefined women's place as best they could from inside marriage and heterosexual gender relations.[5]

Throughout the nineteenth century there were ongoing struggles to regain some measure of equality for women, some right to autonomy, and some possibility of survival. At issue were questions of economic governance, the right to work and to control earnings, marriage, and maternity – in sum, each woman's control over her own body. As early as 1830 all the most influential social groups accepted that women had useful roles in society and took these into serious consideration in their programs. The general aim of most was to create a society where all sorts of oppression would be abolished (those of sex and class in particular) and all individuals would be free to fulfill their own potential for the good of the whole community. Progressive women in organizations representing a wide variety of religious and political views claimed their rights to education for physical, material, and intellectual strength, to opinions on political and religious matters, and to legal rights over their possessions. They believed that total reform of education, equality in marriage, and sexual liberation would give rise to a new morality. These demands emerged again in the period around 1848, together with demands for universal suffrage. All the demands were still being made in more or less the same form in 1900.

The first Women's Rights Congress took place in 1878; in 1879 reforms in women's education began. In 1880, a normal school for women preparing to teach in primary school opened at Fontenay-aux-Roses, and in 1881 the normal school for secondary-school teachers at Sèvres. State high schools for girls (lycées) started in the same period, although the curriculum for boys and girls would not be identical until 1937. Schooling for children of both sexes became compulsory in 1889. The first woman lawyer was called to the bar in 1900; in 1898 Dr Edwards-Pilliet replaced her husband in the chair of physiology at the Labroisière hospital in Paris.

Women also made legal advances. In 1881 they obtained the right to open a savings bank account, in 1884 the right to divorce was reintroduced, and in 1897 women were recognized as legally competent to be civil witnesses. Married women gained control of their earnings in 1907, and finally in 1912 unmarried mothers could file paternity suits.

The struggle lasted from the institution of the Napoleonic Code to the Belle Epoque, and during that time women reclaimed barely the minimum legal and civil rights necessary for their survival and for some sense of autonomy.

In 1900 the fight continued for the reform of the civil code and for the vote. Male socialists were still including female equality in their program but were rarely precise in the formulation of plans. Feminism was receiving favourable attention: in 1897–98 sociologist Jacques Flach lectured at the Collège de France (a bastion of male scholarship to this day) on the social and political condition of women. Others began to publish on similar issues. Women were being named to local and national committees and commissions alongside the usual male candidates. There were a number of important congresses held in Paris on the rights of women, and numerous women's newspapers – notably La Fronde, founded by Marguerite Durand – were publishing regularly. Things appeared to be moving towards a more egalitarian society.

None the less, the major theme of reform throughout the nineteenth century remained that of woman's role as mother. Whether the attitude be that of the Saint-Simoniens who saw the mother as the saviour of society or, in less exalted terms, as the guardian of the home, teaching her children purity and social values and nurturing her husband; or whether it be described in political terms, in the context of the continued production and raising of citizens; in most cases, the social perception of women – as fulfilling one essential function – was the same. Questions of love, marriage, and motherhood continued to be of central literary and political concern. Obvious in all the writing of the period, though not always addressed overtly, is the inherent contradiction between the apparent value of mothers per se and the social attitudes to and treatment of those mothers who did not fit into the institution of marriage and the rules of bourgeois propriety.

Women in 1900 were still defined by their sexuality and controlled by it. Although they had more legal rights than they had had in 1804, social attitudes towards them were only just beginning to change. Thus, as I have described elsewhere, the politics of gender and the ongoing theme of love in French life and literature remain almost exclusively heterosexual.[6] (And any lesbians in literature written by men, except for Balzac's monstrous Margarita in *La Fille aux yeux d'or* and Marie in Lacretelle's *La Bonifas* (1925), have been bisexual.)

Lesbianism was not on the agenda of first-wave feminism, the nearest approach being Madeleine Pelletier's stand on hygienic education for girls and on the benefits of celibacy in *L'Emancipation sexuelle de la femme* (The Sexual Emancipation of Women, 1911), nor would it be addressed seriously until Simone de Beauvoir's somewhat problematic analysis in *The Second Sex* (1949)[7] and Monique Wittig's theorizing essays in *The Straight Mind* (1992).[8] However, the improved conditions for women created by first-wave feminism allowed an increased measure of female independence, which produced a new, socially acknowledged space for female autonomy. Within this space the lesbian does make a covert appearance around 1900 in the form of the "New Woman," sharing with feminist heterosexual women assumptions of independence and action, diminished "femininity," and habits of riding a bicycle, smoking, and wearing some form of divided skirt. Critics ascribe these intimations of incipient masculinity, which lie at the root of the construction of "butch" lesbians, to all somewhat-emancipated women, who were now open to the charge of harbouring sapphic tendencies – a charge that does not fail to be made continuously, in the press in particular, because, as we saw above, what is at issue is any seeming threat to masculine prerogatives.

All of these various social threads weave together to create bonds and restrictions generally for active, energetic competent women, who find themselves constantly blocked by the social regulation of male privilege, and particularly for lesbians, who, when they are noticed at all, are seen as being in direct competition with men for that most clearly status-conferring of all privileges: a woman as sex object and exclusive possession. This perceived opposition between men and lesbians is crucial to the history of the representation of lesbian characters. This is a crucial opposition, including as it does challenges to male supremacy on many levels all of which, social, sexual, and psychological, are made clear in the literature of the early nineteenth century, as we saw above. The sacrosanct nature of male supremacy is also fundamental to that century's various political ideologies and scientific and artistic misogynies, all of which oppose any female sense of individual identity and refute all notion of reciprocity in male–female relations, as well as any possibility of lesbianism.

The female who, were she to have a sense of self and autonomy, would be the most threatening to male hegemony is the lesbian. Not being susceptible to domestic oppression either economic or sexual, she is thereby much more difficult to control in the public arena. Pleasing men is not one of her concerns, either for her delight or for her survival. But, reciprocally, men have no benefit from pleasing her, because, even should they desire her – and certainly in the novels some of them do – she is not available; she may be made love to on occasion, but she cannot be possessed. Hence it is on the character of the lesbian that falls the virulence of male reaction to any concept of an autonomous, sexually active woman.

Without exception the novels written by men (and by women identified with the status quo, such as Jane de la Vaudère) between 1890 and 1914 vituperate any sign of female control over body or desire as the immediate and inevitable source of carnal perversity, guilt, remorse, atrophy of the soul, and damnation in life or in death. Consciously or not the authors are writing propaganda tracts warning budding New Women of the dangers that they face. Without exception these novels are melodramatic, self-serving, unrelentingly misogynistic, boring, and far too long for their slim and facile plots. None of them has any developed characters, as all are, in one form or another, descriptions of endless sequences of similar and supposedly outrageous salons where socialite women talk and occasionally take off their clothes under the overt or covert gaze of judgmental male characters, or where society men discuss fashionable matters and occasionally sally forth to a café, bar, or theatre to find women for themselves and observe the odd pair of lesbians. In both cases the reader is deliberately titillated and satisfied only if the reviling of women offers satisfaction. Despite their billing as naughty novels, despite the alluring titles, these novels are not erotic, rarely even briefly and mildly sensual. When they are, the scenes are always cut off short either by an interruption or a closed door.

There are two problems at issue, which together preclude the possibility of a novel with engaging lesbian characters being written in these circumstances. First, if the writers' primary purpose is to discredit the way of life about which they are writing, then they cannot allow readers to engage with the characters in any way, in case the said readers might find the characters sympathetic. But a book without characters that catch the readers' interest in some way can neither deliver these characters to a properly dramatic downfall nor engage the readers sufficiently for them to care. And second, given the perspective, it is also impossible for the authors to allow their characters to enjoy or feel passionate about their vices, which might in turn entice readers. Such an attitude does, however, protect writers from having to attempt scenes of love, passion, and sexual intercourse of kinds beyond their experience and very clearly – judging from those unwise enough to try – beyond their imagination.

LESBIAN MONSTERS

With these criticisms in mind, let us look briefly at four novels written before 1900 that illustrate the ways in which lesbians are represented and used to sustain male sexual, psychological, and moral superiority.

Joséphin Peladan's *La Gynandre* (female version of an androgyne, 1891) is the ninth volume in his extensive coverage of sexual sins and perversions. Nothing if not pretentious in his claims, the author begins in pseudo-medical Latin and then writes the following statement: "*The Gynandre* claims to have value, even for the scholar and the confessor, as the only monograph on female sodomy. In it the aberration is studied artistically, and if inferior to *The Girl with the Golden Eyes*, how much more moral!" [page with no number, headed *Rubrique*].

In the tradition of Montesquieu's *Les Lettres persanes* (The Persian Letters, 1721) and other such "innocent" social criticism, the narrator, Tammuz, arrives in Paris with a year at his disposal to study life and the soul in motion (21). His hypothesis is that: "Lesbos can be classed amongst the ways of taking pleasure, not the ways of loving. Lesbos can be catalogued under the subject Lust not Love" (26). He sets out into enclaves of various species of Parisian lesbians to test his premise. He is welcome everywhere; as one of the women informs him: "Lesbos's inferiority is its need of male spectators. If a man is not witness to our trifling carresses, we feel them less keenly" (83). So lesbianism is lust, not love, and lesbians seek the male gaze; the active ones among them also dress or behave in masculine ways. The book is a talking catalogue of the various depravities set out by the author to prove that: "Female sodomy does not exist as a passion; it is a depraved form of dandyism; it is cross-dressing carried over into morals and played out in life" (97).

Lesbians, according to Tammuz, exist in two forms, those who are born with the condition and those who acquire it:

Natives [i.e., lesbians born], tomboys from childhood, play the positive role in the aberration, subject to a perverted ideal, as unsensual as unsexual, aborted boys as women, schoolboy souls in women's bodies; [...]

Newcomers, normal in childhood, still, later on, playing the passive and feminine role in the aberration, this time subject to a false innervation and simply enemies of men by lack of adaptation to voluptuous vibrability, feminine souls in equally feminine bodies, but rebels against sexual orgasm, and whose flesh, to borrow a musical image, suffers from a counterpoint that is definable but requires of the husband or lover a reasoned awareness of the female keyboard and its counterpoint; [...] And this category remains curable by simple vibration successfully given. (190)

All of them, though sometimes sincere in their love games, are in the process of destroying their health and losing their soul. As he leaves, Tammuz sums up their situation as he understands it: "Lesbos, imposture of the body and deception of the soul, nightmare of decadent nights, Lesbos, you will never exist! And you deplorable women, disappointed and in revolt, expect only the pity that is the response to all pain; in the face of attentive intelligence, you have never existed, vain phantoms of an impossible love, actresses in life, actresses in love, hoyden and sick Gynandres!" (340). This is the essence of the male theory of lesbianism: male soul or malfunction of the nervous system.

The other three novels – Henri d'Argis's *Gomorrhe* (Gomorrah, 1889), Catulle Mendès's *Méphistophéla* (Mephistophelia, 1890), and Jane de la Vaudère's *Les Demi-sexes* (The Half-sexes, 1897) – all use the theme of lesbian as monster of depravity in similar ways. D'Argis's *Gomorrhe* is the simplest. Madame Sonnet, the heroine, is always accompanied by two other women and has a black servant, Marie-Antoinette (clearly the shadow side of her mistress as well as the embodiment of the cliché of the lustful Afro-Caribbean), who attends to Madame Sonnet's body and occasionally performs lascivious dances for her and Léopold Desalle, the

Contrasting Attitudes   57

man who aspires to become her lover. D'Argis depicts Madame
Sonnet as a woman sexually abused in childhood by a rich and aristocratic elderly woman and who lusts after young girls in her turn.
(This is the first and only novel to 1920 in which I have encoun-
tered the term "Tribade" [325] to describe a lesbian, although this
was the common term in French from the sixteenth century on.[9])

In exchange for a promise of help in his career, Léopold brings his
innocent young sister to meet Madame Sonnet, at her request: "If
Madame Sonnet wanted him to bring Marthe, it could only be for
[...] immediately he closed violently and forever, the door of his
conscience which had tried to open a little" (312). Madame Sonnet
is hypnotizing Marthe and taking her pleasure on the sleeping girl.
Marthe remembers nothing but is left in a state of nervous over-
excitement. Madame Sonnet is not satisfied with an inert body after
a while, and so she tries to seduce Marthe, instead of hypnotizing
her. Marthe refuses her advances and visits no more.

Mendès's *Méphistophéla* is a more developed version of the
preying-monster story. The book opens with a prologue: a prolonged description of Baroness Sophie d'Hermelinge as an opium
addict, a "mummy of remorse," a woman who goes through the
motions of depravity with no passion or pleasure: "Never had any
human face expressed with such total hideousness the discouragement of having lived, the avowal of an incurable agony. Oh what
self-disgust" (20).

The novel then begins with a lyrical pastoral scene of two sixteen-
year-old girls who may be innocent of their sexuality, but the author
certainly isn't: "A kiss from the mouths of two little girls who are
not kissing on purpose! The beating, breast against breast, almost
not breasts yet, of two chests of those whom sexuality ignores, in a
clasp so pure that the rough tussle of the wedding night will be less
sweet and less fulfilling of their dreams" (33). Flashback to childhood stories of Sophie's excessive passion for Emmeline, including
a mystic and ecstatic kiss given to Emmeline at the altar rail at the
time of their first communion. Then further back into the insalu-
brious past of Sophie's mounther, Phédo. Sophie is the product of
Phédo's calculated union with the semi-paralysed and mentally
incapacitated son of a Russian count for the purposes of forcing an
inheritance. The trick misfired. When he understood that he had
fathered a child, Count Stéphan rose up from his mental and physical paralysis to tell the abominable history of his family, curse the

foetus, and try to kill the mother, before collapsing and dying himself. Deprived of that fortune, Phédo, her aunt, and an Italian manservant steal what they can and return to France. So Sophie, in the fine tradition of nineteenth-century lesbian genealogy, is the product of inappropriate lasciviousness, and the reader is to understand that, sweet, loving, and beautiful though she is at sixteen, she is doomed – and is, in fact, the Sophie of the prologue.

How is she transformed? By marriage to Emmeline's brother, who, frustrated by Sophie's terror on her wedding night finally rapes her and then falls into the heavy sleep of a satisfied brute. Sophie creeps out to find comfort with Emmeline, and standing, watching her beloved friend sleeping, she muses on her feelings for Emmeline, how they are different and yet similar to male desire. Emmeline moves in her sleep, revealing a naked breast, and, her innocence lost in the heterosexual experience, Sophie's desire bursts into consciousness: "She desired that living thing, that's all, she desired her with the madness of a hungry animal. The monster that had always been in her wanted to get out and be satisfied" (138).

Just as she is about to kiss Emmeline's breast, Jean, the brother/husband, bursts in through the window, whips her viciously, kicks her, and leaves, ordering the two trembling mothers, who have also arrived, to attend to their daughters.

That is the end of the marriage. Sophie runs away with Emmeline to an island in the Seine (see Maupassant), but even though little by little Sophie instigates physical contact with Emmeline, paradise is not achieved. Sophie is sexually frustrated, and Emmeline is bored. Finally one day Sophie kisses Emmeline on the lips. They kiss all day, go to bed together, and Sophie has an orgasm, but Emmeline is waiting for more, and Sophie does not know what to do. Here it is evident that the novel is written from a male perspective: Sophie slumps into despair at her incapacity to make love like a man and rails at her inability ever to satisfy Emmeline. (In such circumstances, women writers such as Adrienne Saint-Agen – see below – allow their inexperienced heroines to follow the dictates of their aroused senses and explore the possibilities of two female bodies.) Next morning Emmeline has gone home, leaving a letter for Sophie.

The loss of her "pure" first love puts Sophie onto the downward path. She is seduced on the train by a young working-class Parisian woman (the clone of Maupassant's heroine in "La Femme de Paul"), and this young lesbian, Margalo, teaches her how to make love. Mendès then treats his readers to a discussion on the subject of women's nervous illnesses, remorse, and drug addiction taking place between two male doctors at the theatre. Enter Sophie, superb and proud, now the centre of social attention, a female Don Juan with a beautiful young woman at her side (and in the stalls Margalo crying). Dr Urbain Glaris foretells her downfall.

The rest of the novel tells her story from her waking up with Margalo through her discovery that she is pregnant from her wedding night, the birth, the sending away of the baby, and her abandoning of Margalo because she is the witness of Sophie's fall into motherhood. Then we see Sophie's career: the proud flouting of convention and morality until what remains of her heart is touched by the death of Margalo and she begins to think of Emmeline again. A trip to the house that Emmeline and her husband share with Sophie's husband reveals a plump and satisfied maternal Emmeline surrounded by children, a baby at her breast. Sophie is horrified and disgusted. Deprived of her ideal, she spirals into vice. Finally, she turns to Dr Glaris for help. He suggests that maternal love might save her.

So without hesitation she goes and collects her sixteen-year-old daughter, Carola, from the convent where the girl has been all her life. When the daughter falls asleep – in a pose reminiscent of Emmeline long ago – Sophie realizes that she is sexually tempted by her own child. Instead of taking the girl to Paris, she takes her to the town where Emmeline lives, sends her into the house with a letter for her father, and waits long enough to see that she is taken in. Sophie's last hope gone, she becomes the woman of the prologue. The novel ends with the statement that one day she will end in the Salptrière Hospital in Paris: "A woeful example of Neurosis or of Possession, she will drool [...] she will believe she sees writhing and climbing over her, like an attack by vermin, the anthill of her old sins" (567).

The novel is competently structured: recurrent thoughts of Emmeline punctuate episodes with Sophie's lovers, who come to increasingly bad ends. The presence of Emmeline herself opens and closes the story as the pure ideal love swallowed up by a male-dominated domesticity. All this is in counterpoint to Sophie's own experience with marriage, pregnancy, birth, and the retrieval and loss of her daughter. Approved motherhood is set against perverted motherhood, as the sins of Sophie's mother are visited on Sophie, though perhaps not on her daughter. It is not clear to me whether the author sees Jean's rape of Sophie as a legitimate act of frustrated, legally protected male desire, which will therefore produce a good, compliant heterosexual daughter, or whether it is an act of the kind of inappropriately uncontrolled libidinousness that, to the imagination of nineteenth-century French authors, produces lesbians.

From a woman's point of view Jean's behaviour should be monstrous – and certainly from Sophie's it was – but the final family scene around the dinner table would suggest that Jean has been snugly reintegrated into bourgeois society, even in his sexless and single state. The arrival of a legitimate daughter can only enhance his position. Clearly Emmeline is so ensconced in maternity that reminders of Sophie present no danger to her, and she is the desired model for Carola, who may be young and innocent but who emerges from a place that, in the context of the male-written lesbian novel, is suspect because of the forced containment of women without men: a convent.

The main emphasis of the novel is, however, that Sophie suffered from a hereditary failing from which there was no escape, whereas Emmeline was simply a romantic young girl responding to heightened sensations – pseudo-homosexual, curable by healthy voluptuousness, as prescribed by Peladan. Such attitudes are reinforced by the works of Krafft-Ebing, whose *Psychopathia sexualis* appeared in French translation in 1895 (his *Criminal Responsibility* appeared in French in 1875), and who believed that homosexuality was in some way genetic. Charcot (who was publishing on sexual inversion by 1882), and all his compatriots of the period, saw homoerotic behaviour as a malady of the female nervous system – the over-stimulation, over-excitement, and malfunction of the nervous system that pepper Peladan's text.

Freud's diagnosis of childhood trauma, parallel though it is to Henri d'Argis's story of Madame Sonnet's youth, does not have any influence at this time in Paris. As far as I can discover, the only study by Freud available in French until the 1930s is one on various forms of paralysis – motor, organic, and hysteric, which appeared in 1893. The second volume of Havelock Ellis's *Studies in the Psychology of Sex – Sexual Inversion* (1897) – appeared in French in 1909. The Italian criminologist Cesare Lombroso's *La Femme criminelle et la prostituée* was published in French in 1896. All these studies reaffirm the innate nature of lesbianism and the inevitability of stigma, isolation, frustration, and suffering.

Thus most lesbians were born, but they could also be made. From about 1865 on, the ovariotomy became an increasingly popular surgical intervention, at first for appropriate pathological reasons, then increasingly, in Paris society anyway, as a radical means of contraception.[10] That women should be allowed such control over their own bodies was not to be countenanced, and the practice was condemned both in the novels of heterosexual profligacy, such as Camille Pert's *Les Florifères* (The Flowerbearers, 1898), and of course in novels offering variations on the perverse and perverting lesbian monster, such as Jane de la Vaudère's *les Demi-sexes*.

Les Demi-sexes (The Half-sexes, 1897) opens with a seventeen-year-old girl in a doctor's office. Back in the tradition of Diderot's Mother Superior, Camille has an irregular (i.e., unbalanced) and passionate face, with a strong chin and dilated eyes (caused by morphine or belladonna). To compound this encoded dubiousness of her social behaviour, she is an orphan living with an aged grandmother, who is independent, rich, and opinionated: "What it came down to was that she was one of those modern wrecks who are too highly strung to follow the beaten paths of human mediocrity" (15–16).

How did she find Dr Richard? She has been persuaded to claim her sexual freedom by Nina Saurel, her dear and close friend, a big, dark-haired, impressive woman with orange-gold eyes (shades of Balzac), who is clearly capable of wickedness and even crime. So both women are set up as perverter and pervertee at once, and the story unfolds somewhat predictably. Madame Saurel has several studios, where she practices seduction and vice with women and young girls. After her recovery from surgery, Camille is encouraged by Madame Saurel to take male lovers; she is evidently already her lover although, as usual, we know that only by embrace and innuendo) and joins the group of post-operative, no-longer-female women who meet with Dr Richard from time to time for food, wine, and neurotic erotic exchange: "Cold and corrupting seduction, the morbid complication of all these neurotic women troubled them reciprocally with passions and violent agitation" (147).

The varieties of debauchery continue until Camille becomes interested in a male sculptor, Georges, because he is totally focused on artistic integrity. With some effort she inveigles him into marrying her. She is in love – open to feelings at last, passionate in body and emotions – but with a secret past and now a husband who wants children. Camille refuses to talk about childbearing. Georges is rapidly distancing himself back into his art when they return to Paris at the end of their honeymoon; there Camille learns that Dr Richard and Nina Saurel are being investigated for their joint activities. Nina arrives to propose that Camille leave her husband to begin their life of vice once more. She tries to drag Camille away; Camille retaliates by holding on to her, kissing her so that she cannot make any sound, and stepping deliberately back into the fireplace where a fire is burning. In fine Don Juanesque style, they both go up in flames so hot that their calcinated bodies are indistinguishable and collapse to ash at first touch, leaving the sculptor, his integrity intact, to gain inspiration from his grief. Thus the guilty meet their end in the last of the nineteenth-century, lesbian monster novels.

HAPPY LESBIANS

In a brief story entitled "Don Juan à Lesbos" (1892), Maurice Montegut shows a different punishment: Don Juan arrives on Lesbos and is totally ignored by all the women. As he leaves he is heard to murmur Sappho's name passionately. The author remarks laconically: "The 'one thousand and three' were avenged" (203), in direct reference to Lepporell's catalogue of Don Juan's female conquests in Mozart's *Don Giovanni*. In Montegut's tale, although the women are said to be "damned," they are described as joyful, tender, loving, and happily prosperous. The tone is totally at odds with the rest of the nineteenth century, when non-redemption is the rule. It is also very brief, and the characterizations are stereotypical: the dark-haired women are more "masculine" than the blondes, and the redheads are "hybrid."

Montegut's ironic foray into antiquity leads the way to the work of Pierre Louÿs, whose *Chansons de Bilitis* (Songs of Bilitis), published in 1894 as translations from the alleged works of a female contemporary of Sappho, had great success before and after being revealed as a literary hoax. He was (and is) known primarily for these poems, some of which Debussy set as songs, and for two gracefully licentious historical novels, *Aphrodite, moeurs antiques* (1896) and *Aventures du roi Pausole* (Adventures of King Pausole, 1900), in which sexual mores of all varieties pass lightly, enjoyed, described suggestively with sensuous appreciation and no moral weight. The lesbians in these novels move easily through life, with no particular distinguishing characteristics except the sex of their lovers. Louÿs is as far from the psychopathology of sexuality as it is possible to be.

So is his friend Henri de Régnier, who in 1901 published a story similar in atmosphere to that of Montegut. "L'Amour et le plaisir" (Love and Pleasure) depicts two young married women, friends from convent days, who discover sexual pleasure together one summer while both of their husbands are involved in the country with their hostess, a widow whose lover is away. As we have come to expect, the text itself is chaste. We read about handholding, kissing, and the women looking as though they need sleep – no more, but no self-condemnation and remorse either. It is a slight, eighteenth-century-style summer diversion, which, if it leads anywhere, takes us towards Colette, Willy, and Claudine (see below).

THE LAST OF THE DAMNED

After 1900 lethal remorse goes out of fashion, and the tone lightens somewhat. Lesbian seducers continue to be present in novels of Parisian society such as Jean Lorrain's *Maison pour dames* (House for Ladies, 1908). They tend to be socialites, actresses, or writers – journalists, or mentors to aspiring provincial poetesses – known, tolerated, pointed out, discussed, and observed. They remain predatory, but neither they nor their "victims" come to serious harm anymore, and they all survive beyond the end of the novel.

The new put-down is more subtle; lesbians become their own narrators as mouthpieces for self-serving male authors, in novels such as Charles Monfort's *Le Journal d'une Saphiste* (Diary of a Sapphist, 1902) and Daniel Borys's *Carlotta Noll, amoureuse et femme de lettres* (Carlotta Noll, Lover and Woman of Letters, 1905), both throwbacks with clear links to earlier novels. Monfort's inspiration came from Belot's *Mademoiselle Giraud, ma femme*, Borys's from Mendès's *Méphistophéla*. Our interest in these novels lies in the absence of the apparent male centre, the male gaze. The stories focus on women, as female narrators tell of their lifelong attraction to women. However, as the authors are male, we find the same characteristics as in the earlier, condemnatory novels.

One lover takes ether and participates in orgies, the other dies of seizures, "agitated by some Satan jealous of our passed loves" (10). One narrator is in hospital at the end of the story, struck down by general paralysis, delirium, and possible violence; the other is dead before it starts, having sent her journal to a male friend. Borys's Carlotta has a mother of dubious morals, Monfort's Aline no mother at all and a taciturn father (a pattern repeated by Colette and Jacques de Lacretelle). Descendant of Count Stéphan in *Méphistophéla*, Carlotta's uncle is a hydrocephalic monster who destroys dolls, attacks young women, and finally kills his mother, for which crime he is interned in a mental hospital. Ultimately Carlotta begins to imagine killing her lover, Myrtil, before she herself succumbs to mental collapse.

Le Journal d'une Saphiste is marginally less melodramatic. As in *Méphistophéla*, Aline, who is in love with her boarding-school friend Mireille, is to be married. Hector is a careful lover, but jealous, and forces Aline to choose between him and her friend. She chooses Mireille, and they live together, but they are penniless and have no skills, so Aline becomes the mistress of one of Hector's friends, Gaston, who promises to take care of their financial problems. From the time Aline starts providing sexual services to Gaston, Mireille begins to fade. The doctor says that she is worn out from "boarding school vice." On her deathbed, like Pauline Giraud, she turns against her lover. Aline's heart dies with Mireille, and she goes off to eternal solitude or death, blaming herself for Mireille's demise. Her manuscript ends with a final supplication to all women: "Women, seek as your Love, only the Unique and the Strong he who governs all humanity: Healthy and Honest Love, Comforting and Sublime because the Procreator of Man" (215–16).

All the traditional biases are present in these five novels. The characters are the same, and so are the attitudes, social context, and plots. All that varies is the technical skill of any given author.

WILLY AND COLETTE

Willy (Henri Gauthier-Villars, Colette's husband from 1893 to 1906), or whoever ghost wrote *La Môme Picrate* (That Kid Picrate, 1903) for him, has a light, ironic touch and an eye for suggestive detail. He remains firmly in the lineage of male-centred novelists, however, for whom lesbian sensuality is girlish foreplay to the real business of heterosexual coupling and marriage. Here is the most extended scene between Picrate and Tortille, cut off because they notice a spyhole in the wall and stop to plan what they will do to whomever looks through it: "Naked too [Picrate], she throws herself into the arms of her friend [Tortille, whose real name is Gilberte] who receives her with undisguised pleasure. For a moment both of them embrace ardently (as ardently as they are chaste), like two sisters who are going to part, one remaining in a Latin country and the other leaving for Greece, but not for Lesbos, I hope. But (false start) after contemplating each other with voluptuousness, they clasp each other again. Their loosened hair intertwines. Their lips join. Other caresses are imminent" (309).

La Môme Picrate contains frequent references to the fictional character Claudine, and in 1903 Willy's was still the sole authorial name on the Claudine series: *Claudine à l'école* (Claudine at School, 1900), *Claudine à Paris* (Claudine in Paris, 1901), *Claudine en ménage* (Claudine Married, 1902), and *Claudine s'en va* (Claudine Leaves, 1903), which Henri Gauthier-Villars and Colette in fact wrote in collaboration before their marriage ended in 1906. Colette herself added one more novel, *La Retraite sentimentale* (Sentimental Retreat, 1907) to complete the series.

The attitudes and assumptions inscribed in the Claudine novels represent a shift in the portrayal of lesbians in French literature from the totally male perspective of the previous hundred years. Just as Claudine observes what is going on on both sides of the wall that separates the girls' school from the boys', so Colette and Willy enlarge the possiblity for female identification with their characters, while at the same time maintaining the traditional androcentric underpinnings that structure the presentation of female sexuality within their texts.

Colette writes well, which is more than can be said for any of the other authors in this study since Maupassant. She has an eye for the kind of details that make people, places, and objects spring to life in their particularity and an inherent appreciation of the sensuous variety of the physical world, all of which she evokes with delight, awareness, and a well-honed sense of where the boundaries of scandalousness lie in different social groups. Claudine, her heroine and narrator, takes joy in violating those boundaries at all times and in all her guises. It is her social outrageousness that makes the novels fun. The novels are no more sexually explicit than others, such as Belot's *Mademoiselle Giraud – ma femme*, and despite the apparent focus on women together, the salacious and controlling male gaze is rarely far away.

To begin with, the expected indicators of the lesbian character remain present, though more subtly delineated. All the lesbians are attractive, we are told, but all in the manner of Diderot's Mother Superior, have unbalanced faces, not beautiful, not in the same perspective as the heterosexually attractive women, distinctive because of the unsettling quality of their charm and animation. Claudine herself bears all the major marks. She has the golden eyes of the woman who attracts and desires both women and men (see Balzac); sometimes they are the colour of blond tobacco – havana – and in *Claudine s'en va* they are yellow. Finally Claudine's friend Annie is overwhelmed by their tawny power: "She leans forward and dazzles me with her tawny eyes, suddenly so dominating that I close my own, overwhelmed" (126).

Claudine also has the characteristic family pattern of the born lesbian. She has no mother, and her father is taciturn, is unpredictable, and pays no attention to his daughter. Claudine is cheerfully unloved and appears to thrive on freedom and neglect – unlike Jacques de Lacretelle's *La Bonifas* (The Bonifas Woman, 1925) as we see below – but the pattern created by Colette and Lacretelle is the same, completed in each case by the inappropriate licentiousness of the father, actual in *La Bonifas* and metaphorical in the Claudine novels, where Renaud appears as father figure, husband, and lover combined.[11]

Colette would appear to have had a humanizing role in the writing of lesbian characters. Gone are the monstrous perverts and the totally objectified women found in the masculine writing – but that is more because Colette and Willy situate their bisexuals in a female world where they are given consistency by the particulars of their context. None of them, not even Claudine herself, actually gets a development and a psychology. In *Claudine à l'école* the lesbian focus is two-fold. Claudine herself flirts first with Mademoiselle Aimée (of the ironically chosen name: aimée = loved), the assistant teacher, and then when Aimée prefers the attentions of Mademoiselle Sergent (equally ironic in other ways), the senior teacher, Claudine maintains a suggestive but undeveloped relationship with Aimée's sister, Luce. Once the reader realizes that Claudine is aware of the attraction whereof she speaks, the main focus turns to the two teachers' constant suggestive proximity to each other and frequent extended absence from class, together with the outrageous licence extended to Claudine who, though a student, wanders wherever she chooses and watches her teachers with impunity. She describes tender, romantic attentions only; the reader, together with Claudine's classmates – innocent but sexually curious adolescent girls – and the two male teachers from the boys' school on the other side of the wall infer the rest. The authors titillate their public with the representation of sexual attraction in a girls' school, and also with the overt voyeurism of the students.

The Claudine novels present everyone from the age of fifteen on in a sexual light at all times. Characters observe, speculate, and comment on the activities of others, fantasize, accept, and recount escapades of their own. The maid even finds a suitor for the cat, in heat while she is isolated in a Paris apartment. All the women are bisexual (Aimée and Mademoiselle Sergent both have affairs with the male school inspector), and only Marcel, Claudine's eventual stepson, maintains his homosexuality, despite a deliberate attempt by Claudine (in *La Retraite sentimentale*) to get him drunk and put him into Annie's bed.

Much of the piquancy of these novels comes from the expectation of stories that might be told. Nothing of substance occurs in *Claudine à l'école* except that it establishes Claudine's potential lesbianism; *Claudine à Paris* introduces Marcel as a very effeminate, very beautiful young homosexual, but apart from giving the reader a glimpse of his lover at the theatre and a brief love letter to read, the authors mention only his scandalous taste in neckties and the fact that his father is furious at his behaviour. The rest is left to the reader's imagination. Claudine's sexuality is defined equally vaguely by reminiscences of Luce's unrequited love for Claudine and by Claudine's sudden passion for Renaud, her ex-cousin-in-law and Marcel's father, a man old enough to be her own father, whom she swiftly marries. (See *Gigi* for a further exploration of this theme.)

Claudine en ménage contains the only developed lesbian episode in all five novels. Claudine falls in love with Rézi; both are married, and the husbands of both are constantly present. However, Rézi's spouse is a threateningly watchful figure, intent on preventing his wife's alternative love life, whereas Renaud watches over Claudine and is accommodating to the point of finding them an apartment. Ultimately he too makes love to Rézi; Claudine discovers them (as she is meant to do) and leaves town. In the subsequent novels we see Claudine tempted but never again succumbing to her lesbian tendencies because of the distress that she had caused Renaud (and the way he paid her back).

Claudine's lesbianism is constructed totally within the parameters of heterosexuality, marriage, and a woman's place as her husband's possession. *Claudine en ménage* begins as Renaud and Claudine return from a long, itinerant honeymoon. At Claudine's request they break their journey in Montigny and visit the school. Claudine's purpose is to exhibit Aimée and Mademoiselle Sergent to Renaud – lesbianism as entertainment for the male – but instead the authors create a dormitory scene where Renaud and Claudine tempt the young girls out of their beds to claim chocolate. This creates an extraordinarily suggestive metaphor, which moves on three levels simultaneously within the novel – that of Claudine's past and how Renaud wooed his very young bride-to-be with chocolate, desire leading to desire; the deliberate enticing of young girls to sexuality by older men, which leads to the story of Luce and her uncle; and the separate and mutual involvements of Renaud and Claudine in sensual and sexual games as participant and observer of the other, which prepares the episodes with Rézi. And all this with the tacit approval of the schoolmistress.

Once in Paris, Claudine meets Rézi; their connection is fast, close, and suggestive. We see the daily habits of middle-class women, one visiting in the morning as her friend dresses; visiting again at five o'clock to talk about their day: the round of social engagements, obligations, and preparations that occupy them. Next Claudine informs the reader that, because she has short hair and is not interested in any man besides Renaud, everyone, male and female, thinks that "she *is* for women" because: "If I don't like men I *must* seek out women, oh the simplicity of the masculine mind" (113).

This apparent negation of Claudine's lesbian tendencies is but the prelude to a discussion between Claudine and Renaud as to why Renaud is not displeased by the idea that Claudine could have made love to Luce – "an overly tender friend" (122) – or might even hope that Rézi might be treated more kindly, whereas all question of Marcel's homosexuality makes him angry. We read that what women do between themselves has no importance, for it is a diversion that consoles women for the absence of men and some women need women in order to maintain a taste for men:

– No, it's not the same thing! You can do everything, you others. It's charming and of no importance ...

  – Of no importance ... I don't agree.

  – Yes, I tell you! Between you pretty little creatures it's a ...what shall I say? ... a way of consoling yourselves for our absence, a restful diversion ...

  – Oh?

– ... or at least one that compensates you, the logical search for a more perfect partner, with a beauty more like your own, where your sensitivities and failings are mirrored and recognize themselves ... If I dared (but I don't), I would say that some women need women in order to keep a taste for men. (122–3)

Renaud treats women as little animals – much as he treated the schoolgirls in the dormitory. Claudine comments that his explanation is a cover for voyeuristic tendencies – and thus Colette and Willy introduce the rest of the story. But Renaud's attitude to lesbianism was one of several typical male views of the period. Women who were seen as primarily heterosexual tacitly received "time off" with women – Zola's Nana being an early case in point – as long as the arrangement inconvenienced no man.

Renaud is a voyeur (as is Claudine). He also gives Claudine more than the usual amount of freedom, partly so that he can share in her escapades – he expects her to tell all – and partly because he, as a considerably older man, is somewhat afraid of appearing old and thereby losing her love, desire, admiration, and attention (as indeed we learn that he does in *La Retraite sentimentale* when he returns, ill and older, from the sanitorium). As a result he is a complaisant husband. When Claudine asks for help in finding a place where she and Rézi can be alone together, he obliges swiftly. However, as it would not be morally appropriate for two women to go there alone, says he, he accompanies them and keeps the key. This means that he has control over their meetings. Indeed, to Claudine's annoyance and discomfort, he sits and chats with them longer and longer each time before leaving. Finally, Claudine in desperation borrows Marcel's apartment, but she does that just once, because there it is Marcel who keeps watch.

So the authors draw a parallel between the watchful negative control exerted by Rézi's husband and the equally watchful positive control present in the help provided by Renaud (as well as in the blatant, gossip-driven curiosity of Marcel.) And when Claudine becomes too involved with Rézi for his liking, Renaud beds Rézi in his turn – from curiosity, he tells Claudine – thus bringing Claudine back to him and to her role as wife for the rest of the series.

The shift in moral codes is interesting. Earlier in the novel Claudine comments that for Renaud adultery is a question of sex – that is, if she takes a woman lover rather than a man it does not count as adultery (146) – but this proves not to be the case. Women are allowed homosexual desire, but not the freedom to pursue it to a point where it might displace heterosexual duty. Claudine must exercise her sexuality for and with Renaud. The difference in power structure between Rézi's husband's sneaking back silently to disturb the two women and Claudine's walking in on Rézi and Renaud is clear. In both instances it is Claudine who leaves. And the pain that she feels is not for the loss of or betrayal by Rézi, but for the infidelity of Renaud, the fear of which keeps her sexuality under his control thereafter.

There is no construction of a lesbian here from a woman's point of view, in terms either of social analysis or of gender relations. The female touch comes in the scenes of seduction and mounting desire between Rézi and Claudine, which are not unlike the descriptions of Claudine's increasing awareness of her desire for Renaud in *Claudine à Paris*:

Her whole body follows my game with a willingness that betrays her [...]
– Yes, Claudine, we shall get there!!
– Where??
– Bend down and I'll tell you very quietly.
Credulous, I obey. And it's her mouth that I encounter. I listen, for a long time, to what her mouth says to mine ... She didn't lie, we are getting there ... My haste equals hers, dominates it and brings it into subjection. Revealed to myself, I push away the caressing hands of Rézi, who understands, shudders, struggles for a brief moment, then stays still, arms hanging ...
The thud of a distant carriage door brings me to my feet. Vaguely, I distinguish the pale shape of Rézi sitting in front of me, who presses her warm

lips to my wrist. An arm around her waist, I pull her to her feet, crush her against me, I bend her back and kiss her randomly, on her eyes, the bush of her hair, her damp nape...

– Tomorrow!!

– Tomorrrow ... I love you ... (157–8)

It is this knowledge of the female body and of its expressions of desire, pleasure, and satisfaction that separates the Claudine novels from the male tradition and makes Colette a bridge to female lesbian novels such as Liane de Pougy's *Idylle Saphique* (Sapphic Idyll, 1901) and Adrienne Saint-Agen's *Charmeuse de femmes* (Woman Charmer of Women, 1906), examined below in this chapter.

Claudine has female sensual responses and a feminine social life, but, as she herself comments in *La Retraite sentimentale* (the only novel of the series that Colette wrote alone), she is isolated from other women. Claudine has no trace of a mother or any other female relative, except one paternal aunt who appears briefly in *Claudine à Paris* in her role as Marcel's grandmother. Claudine has possible and rejected lovers, but no friends. Even as a girl in school, her only interest in her companions lay in either shocking them or talking with them to tell or hear stories of their own or other people's sexual exploits. Even the servant, who concerns herself as much with the cat as with Claudine, has as her main aim getting each of them a suitor. That done, she disappears again back into her life at Montigny with Claudine's equally insubstantial father. (Both have very particular ways of speech and a couple of mannerisms that recur as leitmotifs, but they have no real substance as people in Claudine's world.)

Claudine is a voyeur, an observer, and an extractor of other people's stories. She appears to keep her own secrets but increasingly has none to tell, for she herself has decreasing substance as the novels unfold. She reaches her peak as a developed female character, with a life, presence, attitudes, sexuality, and desire, in *Claudine en ménage* and later becomes a gradually diminishing caricature of herself, with the low point occurring when she puts Marcel into Annie's bed and listens at the door (*La Retraite sentimentale*).

Deprived of the right to explore her sensuality and sexuality by the role attributed to Renaud and the exclusive relationship – filial/paternal, spousal, and amorous – established between them,

Claudine loses her charm and interest. What she had become was profoundly subversive of male heterosexuality and marriage. It is possible that Willy was unwilling to condone such female freedom in literature (or in life, given that he and Colette separated in 1904). A wife who feels free to love a woman, to tell her husband about the relationship, to expect his assistance in achieving her sexual ends, and to become irritated by his attempts to remain part of her new life – while expecting and accepting from him financial, domestic, emotional, and sexual support – has very thoroughly reversed the roles of the usual bourgeois French marriage of the period. That she should also react to his infidelity with anger and immediate departure shows moral indignation, strength, decision-making, and energy, which women in 1900 were not supposed to possess and certainly not to exercise against their husbands.

In a much more threatening way than their predecessors, Colette and Willy were on the way to creating a real lesbian monster. Not for them a dysfunctional, self-destructive, non-socially [re]productive woman, but rather a smart, autonomous, sexy "New Woman," whose outrageous behaviour charms and tempts all the women around her. In that sense *Claudine en ménage* is effectively feminist in its influence. Also, although Claudine is stopped in her development, she survives, as do all the actual and potential lesbian characters who pass under her appreciative yellow eyes. It is the libidinous patriarch with a taste for little girls and a voyeuristic interest in lesbianism who is killed off for the first time in the hundred-year tradition of male-authored lesbian novels. Colette gives Claudine neither shame nor guilt – and this is revolutionary. Claudine savours sexuality, and in giving her heroine this taste for pleasure Colette remains alone until Clarisse Francillon publishes *La Lettre* in 1958. To find lesbian characters who enjoy their sexuality and are not violently separated from each other, we have to wait until the novels of Jocelyne François, writing in the 1970s.

FEMALE PERSPECTIVES:
VIVIEN, POUGY, AND SAINT-AGEN

Liane de Pougy and Adrienne Saint-Agen write more emotionally woman-centred novels than Colette, but their heroines are still trapped in guilt, shame, and social opprobrium. Free of the male gaze they may be in the circumstances of their personal lives, but they are not free of the homophobic attitudes of society in the way that Claudine is, protected at all times by her underlying hetero-sexuality (I found reference to another woman novelist by the name of Henriette Willette but have been unable to trace find a copy of her apparently lesbian novel *La Femme et la faunesse* [The Woman and the Female Faun, 1910].[12] Her name suggests to me yet another manifestation of the ubiquitous Willy (Henri Gauthier-Villars) and his team of ghost writers – or perhaps someone wishing to benefit from his success.

Liane de Pougy's character Annhine de Lys, heroine of *L'Idylle Saphique* (Sapphic Idyll, 1901), dies an apparent martyr to her virtue and to the tensions between financial and emotional self-suf-ficiency, work, and love. Hélène, the protagonist of Saint-Agen's *Charmeuse de femmes* (1906), almost commits suicide, then dis-covers that she is pregnant. She sees herself as "saved" by the prospect of giving maternal love, which leads her to life and hope. Maybe. In 1906 the future of a single mother with neither money nor prospects is hardly an improvement over the social condition of a lesbian who has only one mouth to feed.

Renée Vivien's *Une Femme m'apparut* (A Woman Appeared to Me, 1904) does not fit into the same category as Pougy and Saint-Agen because she does not deal in any way with the material world. It is rather a French, female *Bildungsroman*, tracing the poet's search for self and her art, a search for love of self and self as another whom one can love. Narrator, muse, and love are female figures in a female world – an *art nouveau* world of irises, lilies, violets, and vaporous spirituality, where the aspiring poet suffers, is consumed, and is reborn onto the higher plane of art, where she will survive. The concepts that Vivien uses are the accepted nineteenth-century ones of woman as muse, as impossible love, as body, and as death. She presents them, however, from a woman's perspective, trans-forming them into the elements of a female psychology of love and female spiritual quest. For Vivien, physical love is unsatisfactory and true love unattainable.[13]

Vivien constructs this apprenticeship to poetry from autobio-graphical elements of her own love affair with Natalie Barney, just as Liane de Pougy did in her novel of 1901. There is also a novel published much later, in 1930, by Lucie Delarue-Mardrus called *L'Ange et les pervers* (The Angel and the Perverts), in which the

74 THE MALE GAZE, 1796–1929

androgynous hero/heroine lives a double life as male and female, both sexless and both living as invisibly as possible while trying to choose between monastic solitude and maternity. Delarue-Mardrus did not succumb to the seductions of Barney, and her novel throws more light on the perception of the single working woman before 1914 as an unnatural being than it does on the role or situation of the lesbian, except where both are identified as "New Women," breaking the rules and expectations for women in a patriarchal, hierarchical, and gender-driven world order.

Within the paradigms of this study, however, the novels that are revealing are Pougy's *L'Idylle Saphique* and Saint-Agen's *Charmeuse de femmes*, because they are the first to show a female perspective on sensuality, sexuality, and relations to other women and offer psychological and physical descriptions that will touch a female reader. These novels, unlike all the other French novels about lesbians thus far, are not written for male consumption, and when the lesbian lovers do happen to come under the male gaze, the observation is not gratuitous voyeurism but a functional part of the plot structure. Though not surprising, the extent to which this single shift in authorial attitude changes the tone of the whole work is quite remarkable.

In Liane de Pougy's novel the interest lies in the acute sensitivity attributed to the narrator. From this comes a perspicacity of analysis born of the not-unusual mixture of profound narcissism, frustrated desire, and irritated conscience. Indeed the more famous male-centred novels – *La Fille aux yeux d'or* and *Mademoiselle de Maupin*, for example – have much the same tone. What is unusual is to find this combination in a woman and then to find it directed towards another woman. The result throws light on social interactions from a peculiar and revelatory angle, especially because Annhine de Lys, Pougy's protagonist, lives a life similar to that of Odette de Crécy in Proust's *Un Amour de Swann*.[14]

Annhine de Lys in *Idylle Saphique* has a permanent lover, Henri, who pays her bills and generally plays the discreet "husband." The stability that he provides is complemented by passionate encounters with her current "sin" – some young man whom she finds attractive – and by occasional men whom she picks up for an evening's entertainment. Her friend Altesse has a similar life, although she is older, more business-like, and less sensitive. Ernesta is the faithful maid.

Into this household comes Florence (Flossie) Temple-Bradfford, a rich young American who throws herself at Annhine's feet, declares her love, and begs to be allowed to serve as her page. Annhine accepts Flossie's presence and becomes fond of her but will not make love with her, and the resultant nervous tension between refusal and desire kills Annhine (as it killed Alyssa in *La Porte étroite 15*). Twice Annhine agrees to let Flossie make love to her. The first time, having reached a pitch of acute desire, they are about to dash off together when the woman whom Flossie left for Annhine stabs herself before their eyes. Annhine collapses and is thereafter taken away from Paris by Altesse and Henri. The second time they get as far as the bedroom, but Annhine cannot bring herself to go through with it, much as she now loves and wants Flossie.

Two paradoxically opposed factors inhibit Annhine – she sees lesbian love as a vice, and Annhine's own commerce with men makes her body unclean and not worthy of Flossie. In a bourgeois novel the husband might well take mistresses but would not go to a prostitute because of the danger of moral and physical contagion; Annhine's code is parallel. Sexual commerce with men is normal and right – moral, one might say – but similar relations with women are dangerous to one's health, vicious, and addictive. Altesse talks about lesbian lovemaking in the same terms as those used to discuss masturbation in other books of the period: those who practise such a vice get old before their time, and risk being paralysed, losing their hair, and going mad. Annhine is therefore afraid of succumbing to Flossie's "perverse embraces" even while finding her friend ever more enticing and desirable.

The ambiguous treatment of lesbian love and sexual expression lies in the contrast between the tone of the descriptions of intimate moments between Annhine and Flossie and the judgmental vocabulary employed at other times. Given that this novel is autobiographical, it would seem safe to assume that Pougy's own memories, reticences, and internalized homophobia have marked her style very clearly. She immediately establishes the sensuous nature of the physical intimacy between the two characters and shows it to be a source of pleasure to both of them. Flossie helps Annhine to dress, shares her bath, kisses and caresses her at all times. Such behaviour is quite acceptable to Annhine, as long as the sensuality of the embrace remains polymorphous, because if the contact is not genital she can deny its sexual nature and remain free of vice.

Any discussion of lesbianism in the novel refers to it as perversion – even Flossie, who is trying to convince Annhine of its charms, does so. It appears that Pougy enjoyed her escapade with Natalie Barney to the full, but in retrospect she either thinks that she should not have or, being prudent, fears that her friends and admirers will not approve of the episode. The result is a rather eighteenth-century mixture of licentiousness and prudery that manages to be at the same time suggestive and proper – the story of a courtesan who has her moral standards.

The novel is neatly constructed, believable, and written well. It does not suffer from the excesses of self-indulgence that spoil Pougy's other novels, and it does give some insight into the period – the quantities of jewels that pass through Annhine de Lys's hands, for example, are quite breathtaking – although that is not of course where its main interest lies. It is certainly fascinating to discover the underlying relationships between the various characters after all the circumstantial details and decorations have been stripped away.

Flossie's proposal of herself as Annhine's page sets the scene for the insertion into a heterosexual context of lesbianism as sensual androgyny. A reminder of Théodore/Madelaine's return in Gautier's *Mademoiselle de Maupin*, when she brings with her a young girl disguised as a boy, it sets the tone of devotion, service, romance, and impermanence, as well as theatricality. Even in medieval stories the lady does not go off to live happily ever after with her page. Nor does Annhine, for, supportive as the people around her may be (and she has two supportive men and three women in her immediate environs), they take care of Annhine in her role as the heterosexual courtesan who is permitted to enjoy the sensual attentions of another women as pleasurable leisure. They do not condone any disruption of her primary role and sexuality.

So all the characters in the novel, except for Flossie and Annhine, are exclusively heterosexual, and all the characters, including Flossie and Annhine, have heterosexual relationships. The text, which contains one explicit scene of sensuous pleasure of one kind or another in every chapter, is constructed on a series of parallels that make comparisons between male and female attitudes quite inescapable. Although the moral rhetoric of the novel defends heterosexuality, the actual message transmitted is that men are crass and undependable and thus cause women to suffer. Any dealings with them should therefore be well remunerated. For affectionate love and dependable help, women must turn to each other.

Annhine dies not from the vice of lesbianism, frustrated or otherwise, but from being taught that she was wrong to love Flossie. Such an autonomous female relationship is forbidden by society, because it interferes with male desire. Altesse, as a professional courtesan in the world of male desire, plays by the rules, and even though in very real, material, and practical ways she is a friend to Annhine, she does not acknowledge the possibility of lesbian love, and so her support becomes paradoxical, and she is one of the causes of Annhine's death.

On the surface of the novel, Annhine dies a martyr to her virtue. The underlying structures, however, suggest that she is caught in a network of financial and sexual exchanges from which she cannot escape as long as she has to earn a living. Even Flossie needs Willy to pay for the home that she offers Annhine.

There is no satisfactory solution for women here, especially not for lesbians. Women in France in 1900 cannot survive without male financial support. The entire economic system is male-dominated. Women, and lesbians are no exception, must perforce support the system or struggle against it from within. Neither choice provides the opportunity for a satisfactory life. Annhine actually dies of the tensions between them. Whether Liane de Pougy was aware of the profundity of what she had written or not (and I would say not), by its polarization of male and female, heterosexual and lesbian roles, her book offers material for a very clear analysis of the reality of lesbian life in 1900.

Although the structures within which lesbians live are universal in French society during this period, conditions of life varied enormously according to class. Pougy's lesbians are rich and protected, but this is not true of the characters in the next novel that I discuss. Pougy's novel takes place on the margins of the upper class; Adrienne Saint-Agen, in contrast, writes about a woman who barely makes ends meet. It is interesting to compare the discrepancies and similarities between the attitudes of the various women whom she describes. Saint-Agen is also concerned with the economic realities of women's lives, as well as with the social realities of lesbian love. Hélène, the heroine of *Charmeuse de femmes*, at twenty-five lives in a sixth-floor room, alone and poor because of the rates of pay for women and because she is exploited. To earn a little extra she sells stories to a man who publishes them as his own work. She is in love with someone who is unattainable and who, the reader gathers, must be a woman. The first inferences situate lesbianism as a vice: "O you whom I have made divine, sovereign idol who rules my soul [...] tell me to be vile and I shall be vile!" (17).

Hélène had been married to a man who did not treat her well. She is avid for love and companionship. A good friend, René, suggests that her secret love is a woman. She denies this but does admit to a passion for a writer, Reine Delagloire, whom she goes to see and admire at a banquet. There she meets René again; he proposes that she go away with him as his mistress, and she does so, in the hope that he will make her forget all her other loves. In their hotel is a very young woman, named Reine also, who wants desperately to be married because she dreams constantly of love and caresses (and marriage is the only legitimate way to fulfill her desire). She connects herself with Hélène because unconsciously she sees her as an intermediary on the way to René, the male potential lover. But to Hélène she offers acute temptation, for she is a means for Hélène to express her feelings for the ongoing secret love whose portrait she carries.

When the occasion arises, René watches the two women together and is tempted by the voluptuousness of the one and the youthful freshness of the other. After various scenes of mounting desire on everybody's part – in which Hélène withstands the temptation of Reine, only to be taken by René, or does not withstand the temptation, only to see Reine go to René – René, at Hélène's insistence, proposes to Reine. Hélène leaves, knowing that for her Reine was a substitute for the other Reine and that the young woman was so ardent only because Hélène was for her a substitute for the morally as yet unavailable male. Hélène considers suicide, is distracted from it, becomes ill, and then realizes that she is pregnant. Immediately her desperation fades in the prospect of a new and socially acceptable love to fill her life: mother love.

At the end of the novel Hélène considers herself no worse off than at the beginning, although she has no more prospects, less chance of work, and one more mouth to feed in a society where unmarried motherhood and illegitimate children are anathema.

In terms of the traditions of the novel, she is indeed better off, as she is alive, healthy, and unpunished for her sexuality. Nor has she died of her inclinations, "which are fatal, which upset and kill" (101) though in her loneliness she fears falling again to "irresistable temptresses [...] debauchery [...] vice [...] foul compromises" (255). At the end of the novel, just before she is redirected into heterosexual normality if not social acceptability by her pregnancy, she has reached a point not of guilt and sin – the usual pattern – but rather of pain in the injustice of her situation: " – Oh! God! she sobbed, since you have allowed me to love Reine ... allow me to tell her so, give me the right by giving me the courage!" (264).

This cry by itself makes this work the first realistic and poignant writing about the lesbian condition in the history of the French novel. Through her awareness of the conditions of women's lives, as well as through her female perspective on love and sensuality, Saint-Agen situates her book not in the male-authored tradition of the lesbian as monster preying on victims who belong by right to men, but in the growing school of feminist novels examining various aspects of the female condition.

Like Liane de Pougy, Saint-Agen sees men's attitudes as very different from those of women. Despite the enormous class difference between the heroines of the two novels, each depicts even the well-disposed and sympathetic men as unaware of women's needs, both emotional and economic, because they are enclosed in their male egoism. Saint-Agen reveals the situation succinctly in her protagonist's words, not without irony: "'She forgot herself for me, you forgot me for yourself'" (71).

In both novels the less well-disposed men do the women deliberate social, financial, and physical damage. Hélène does not have the female support that Pougy gives to Annhine, but she does everything she can to prevent young Reine from being hurt by her position between Hélène and René, either by being turned into a lesbian by Hélène's embrace (251–2: "What if I had done something irreparable without meaning to? [...] certain kinds of initiation get into the blood") or by being seduced by René and then left by him. (It is Hélène who persuades René that he should marry Reine.)

Both Adrienne Saint-Agen and Liane de Pougy describe explicitly the sensuousness of female desire in their scenes of caresses between women. Annhine, the uninitiated older woman, does not ever make love to Flossie in *L'Idylle Saphique*, but *Charmeuse de femmes* reverses the roles. Here the older woman is already lesbian and suffering from frustrated passion. The younger woman is burning with adolescent desire that is searching for expression; she is avid for caresses and innocently focussed on the unattainable man while prodigal with her embraces to the apparently socially acceptable female. The result is a high level of physical attraction between the two, exacerbated by their frustrated desire for each other – and Saint-Agen meets the challenge in the first love scenes since Gautier's *Mademoiselle de Maupin*.

Hélène has avoided physical intimacy with Reine until she is about to leave. Reine offers her a memento, and Hélène asks for a kiss: "'Kiss me with all your soul, your kiss will be the last one that I shall have from a human being'" (235). And this kiss arouses them both: "A secret instinct had just warned them that an extraordinary and blameworthy feeling had made them accomplices in forbidden voluptuousness, new and with a savour so intense that it had left them quivering still" (236). That night Reine returns, saying that she wants another kiss, even if she should die of it: "'Reine!' [...]" The burned down candle went out at the last syllable of this name, doubly dear to Hélène, and darkness – accomplice of all shame, inciter of all voluptuousness, faithful guardian of all ignominious secrets and pure ecstasies, protector of all immodesties – wrapped in its tempting veils the couch where the silken tresses of the the two heads of brown hair intertwined" (240). The language here is a delicately balanced mixture of all possibilities, open to any eventuality that the reader's imagination might provide.

Next morning, compulsory propriety is re-established by Hélène's remorse that her will and morality failed her because of her loneliness and love of beauty. Saint-Agen situates herself here in the same cultural context as Marcelle Tinayre, who, in novels such as *Avant l'amour* (Before Love, 1897), explores the way in which young girls are raised to expect and exalt feelings of love, almost as a divine mystery, so that they are completely vulnerable to expressions of love in any form. They then become dangerously open to exploitation when bereft of someone onto whom they can pour their feelings and need for attention, particularly if the person listening is both apparently acceptable and of a caressing nature – a pseudo-mother figure. The cause is over-stimulated imagination together with culturally fostered expectations set in a context of sexual ignorance.

Within the parameters of Saint-Agen's world a woman needs a man for financial survival. A man expects to obtain love whenever he so wishes. His aim is erotic satisfaction, and his behaviour is frequently unseeingly abusive of the women in his life. A woman needs love also, and her imagination leads her to voluptuousness. This may find expression directly with a man, or sometimes with a woman, as interposed body between the woman and her imagined male beloved. A woman hurt by men might find love with a woman as an alternative, but always the newly discovered pleasure and emotional comfort are mixed with guilt and a sense of falling into vice and perversity. A woman's need for love can also be fulfilled by a child.

Some of the attitudes here are similar to those found in the Colette–Willy novels. Renaud's attitude in *Claudine s'en va* – that female homosexuality is part of the supportive structure of hetero-sexuality – is one example, with another being the representation of an active sexual imagination in adolescent girls. But whereas Colette–Willy create salacious voyeurs and gossips, Saint-Agen offers a picture of burgeoning sexuality searching for a physical outlet. Colette shows her adolescents titillating themselves and the reader, whereas Saint-Agen engages with her characters in ways that are socially and psychologically in accord with other women-centred perspectives on the female condition in the Belle Epoque.

I was able to find only one novel by Saint-Agen and no others by women writers of the period. Indeed until 1930, she remains, with Liane de Pougy, the only novelist to cast a female eye on lesbian women. Her writing shows them as complex figures, caught in the many different constraints of a social system that oppresses all women, but particularly those who exist outside its phallic economy. She is the only writer since Diderot to show awareness of the real traps set for women by patriarchal institutions and expec-tations.

EMANCIPATED BISEXUAL WOMEN

Curiously, and perhaps because of the upheavals caused by the 1914–1918 war and the breakup of Belle Epoque society, there are no lesbian novels – or none that I have discovered – between the writings of Adrienne Saint-Agen and Colette in the early 1900s and the likes of Charles Rivière, Victor Margueritte, and Proust (who is examined in the next section) in the mid-1920s. By then, the trap-pings of society have changed significantly, though not its basic assumptions. The main issue now in those novels, still bearing the nineteenth-century subtitle "roman de moeurs" (novel of

THE MALE GAZE, 1796–1929

manners/customs), is money and the marriage of daughters across class lines for very crass financial reasons. Daughters are pawns of their father's fortune in undisguised ways.

In the novels that I take as my examples – Charles Rivière's *Sous le manteau de Fourvière* (Under Fourvière's Mantle, 1926) and, perhaps the most famous novel of the 1920s, Victor Margueritte's *La Garçonne* (The Tomboy, 1922) – the heroine is an emancipated new woman, with a taste of lesbianism as one of her liberating experiences, but the authors still encode lesbianism in the same ways: either as foreplay to the world of heterosexual marriage or as a rebellion against it.

In Rivière's *Sous le manteau de Fourvière*, the character Marguerite de Vieux has discovered her lesbianism at boarding school: "Helped by a dear companion, escaping all supervision, she had studied the ways first of arousing the senses and then of giving them the approximate satisfactions within her powers" (43–4). The reader learns that her father is aware of her tendencies and is not troubled by his awareness, because – in the traditional pattern – he is a débauché of long standing and gives little thought to any possible moral role that he might have as a father.

Marguerite is therefore free to arouse the sensuality and sexuality of Irène Vimel, a young woman whose rich parents desperately want entry into Hector de Vieux's class of society. This she does first by profiting from close proximity during a bumpy car ride to initiate fleeting but intimate physical contact with Irène: "The light touches are swift ... furtive ... , quite natural. But when the car stops [...] Irène feels all funny, all red ... no doubt from laughing so much ... Skirts and blouses are all rumpled and creased" (57). Then she setts up a trying-on session, where, once they have both undressed, Marguerite caresses Irène to orgasm: "Her [Irène] half-open lips are closed by Marguerite's. At the same time an unknown excitement thrills her flesh under her friend's caress [...] Without her realizing, little by little deep inside her a string vibrated. A new feeling comes over her ... [...] Soon she pants, tenses, contracts in on herself ..., then ..., all at once ..., relaxes, anguished, moaning and shuddering, all shaken in short waves by a delicious discomfort in whose claws she is suddenly held" (69–70).

The writing here is much more sensitive to female response than the male writings of the earlier period, but the male gaze is not so easily relinquished, so, at the end of the scene between the two women, the reader finds out that Marguerite's brother Paul had been watching the interaction. He subsequently requires, as the price of his silence, that Marguerite help him to seduce Irène. She is passed from the sister to the brother: "And in the evening when Irène, wounded, trying not to cry out, groans from pain and pleasure, the new and complete intensity of this voluptuous climax is necessary to show her that, almost without suspecting it, she had passed from Marguerite's hands into her brother's arms" (88).

The vocabulary of the description is revelatory: first, the archetypal image of the sexual wound inflicted by the male, and second, a new and more complete and more intense voluptuous experience. The result of course is that Irène, having tasted the superior (though more painful) pleasure of heterosexual intercourse, converts forever to desire for men.

Victor Marguerette's *La Garçonne* attributes Monique's lesbian phase to the opposite but still understandable and acceptable cause in a heterosexual society – revulsion for unfaithful, untrustworthy men. Her fiancé lied to her about a mistress, so, in distress and as an assertion of equality, she allows herself to be picked up by a strange man for one night. Then she breaks off the planned marriage. This leaves her father in some considerable financial embarrassment, as he deals with the prospective son-in-law, so he throws his daughter out of the family home. When she resurfaces in society she has her own business and also a famous, theatrical female lover. Clearly, the author uses the lesbian lover simply as a motif to indicate Monique's freedom and change of fortune. There is no interest in the relationship *per se*. The author does not use it to stir prurient interest and certainly does not choose to portray female sensuality, for as soon as he has established the relationship between Monique and Niquette, he creates a pseudo-infidelity: Monique dances a passionate and physically arousing tango with a male friend. Soon thereafter Monique is again taking male lovers.

The novel's other lesbian episode, between Monique and Elisabeth, a friend with whom Monique had an adolescent fling, who reappears for a time in Monique's life, is also sketched very briefly and serves only as an indicator of Monique's emotional state. Both of the scenes are there to show Monique's lost innocence, first as an adult and retrospectively as an adolescent.

By the 1920s lesbianism had ceased to be monstrous in the ways that prevailed throughout the nineteenth century. French society was changed profoundly by the 1914–18 war and much of the old moral order crumbled, together with some elements of patriarchal hierarchy. In *Sous le manteau de Fourvière* and *La Garçonne*, fathers' interests in their daughters' moral and sexual behaviour take second place to the financial deals that surround their marriages. Discretion, compliance, and the appearance of propriety until the wedding day are the watchwords of most of the novels set in the 1920s. The books, though centred on the female characters, continue to be told from a male perspective. No interaction between women receives attention, except in so far as their behaviour affects the concerns of the male protagonists.

This is also true, though with a somewhat different twist, in Jean Binet-Valmer's *Sur le sable couchées* (Lying on the Sand), published in 1929. The title, taken from the first line of Baudelaire's poem "Femmes damnées" (Damned Women), imposes on the reader all the weight of the nineteenth-century tradition of domination and torment, which does indeed prove to characterize Mabel Waybelet, the novel's American protagonist. The action takes place in Eze (a picturesque village in the south of France) in the height of summer, the excessive heat serving as a metaphor for the tormented sexuality present in all four characters. Mabel seduces Martine and gets her to an acute state of arousal and the brink of lovemaking before Mabel dashes off, apparently because she is never able to act on her desire.

Martine's mother, Yvonne, is having an affair with Hubert. When he admits to wanting to be Martine's lover also, which would make him Yvonne's most recent lover and Martine's first, Yvonne and Hubert break off their relationship. Mabel is invited to Hubert's farewell lunch. She meets Hubert as she crosses the garden and decides to leave with him. Her intention in so doing is two-fold: to break Martine's heart, while saving her from herself, and to see whether she herself can be "cured" by sex with a man who is very good at lovemaking. Both abandoned, mother and daughter become friends, whereas previously Yvonne had ignored Martine and then come to see her as a rival.

The result of this convoluted storyline is very interesting in terms of focus and social values. The pattern opens with two pairs of lovers: Mabel and Martine in a passion that is beginning, Yvonne and Hubert in a waning relationship. Martine and her mother are in parallel circumstances, and, as we ultimately realize, the putative lesbianism of Martine would not have been a problem for Yvonne, because then Martine would not have been a rival. But then the focus of desire settles on Martine, throwing Mabel and Hubert into direct competition with each other. The lesbian is the rival of the male suitor for the desired woman, as was the case throughout the nineteenth century. It is highly symbolic that Mabel is unable to consummate her passion, while Hubert has no such problem. The act of lesbian desire is thereby coded as unacceptable, and the licentious male claims both available women (Yvonne and Martine). In traditional heterosexual fashion the older of the two women loses her status: Yvonne breaks with Hubert

Diagram 3

and the male move restates the heterosexual rules of the game (see Diagram 3). This shift is consolidated by Mabel's departure with Hubert. By this action Mabel gives up her status as opposite and equal to Hubert – with similar desire and right to choose her woman/lover – in an attempt to assimilate into the heterosexual structure as a woman. Hubert accepts her because she is a greater challenge than Martine. Mabel sacrifices herself to conformity, and they both walk out of the novel.

The reader is left to decide which of three tensions characterize the novel – first, perversity (Hubert's lubriciousness and Mabel's lesbianism) versus normality (Yvonne and Martine); second, the height of sexual passion and prowess (Mabel and Hubert) versus age and immaturity (Yvonne and Martine); or third, pain and sacrifice (Mabel saving Martine from both herself and Hubert) versus friendship and support (Yvonne and Martine in their new relationship as abandoned women). However we label it, the author transforms the situation from one where it looks as though Martine might get both lovers to her getting neither but connecting finally with her mother (see Diagram 4).

Diagram 4

Mabel, who is the emotional centre at the beginning of the novel, has been totally eclipsed by the male, who is given all the prerogatives. Women are there for the male to choose and use. The only sanctioned relationship between women, when the male is not present, is that of mother and daughter, who can be friends whenever they are not the objects of male desire. Female desire for anyone has no place, no rights, and no status. This novel is as openly heterosexist as its nineteenth-century counterparts. Male gaze, male desire, and male ego remain central to the value structure of the masculinist and usually male-authored novel.

NEW SENSITIVITY: PROUST AND LACRETELLE

Marcel Proust's *A la recherche du temps perdu* (In Search of Lost Time [published in translation as *Remembrance of Things Past*], 1917–27) establishes a somewhat different perspective while retaining, and indeed tightening the focus of the male gaze. The main preoccupations of Marcel, the narrator, concern the delicate nuances of his sensitive feelings and his acute social perceptions. Marcel Proust, the author, creates a vast, semi-autobiographical panorama of Parisian high society in which male homosexuals play a prominent role and lesbians are visible as part of the context of male activity. In that respect the women are present as part of the social fabric, and their lesbianism is commented on or judged in the same way as any of the other personal foibles and eccentricities by which the characters relate to their surroundings. A lesbian from the right family who has good taste and powerful friends is as acceptable as a virtuous or a discreetly adulterous wife in similar circumstances. Any lesbian who lacks one or more of these attributes, and so is in some way marginal, runs greater risks of exclusion from society on the basis of her sapphic behaviour.

Three lesbians belong within Marcel's network of connections: Esther Lévy, cousin of Marcel's friend Bloch, Bloch's sister, and Mademoiselle Vinteuil, daughter of the musician whose composition runs as a leitmotif through the work. All are attributed bad reputations, and each is shown in one slightly extended scandalous scene. Bloch's sister creates a disturbance by making visible and unashamed love with her actress friend (who of necessity is suspect because of her association with the theatre) on a sofa at the casino in Balbec (II, 842). "They were no more restrained than if they had been in their bed," but they avoid expulsion from the building because Bloch's sister is under the protection of her uncle, an old, rich, family man, who eats lunch every day in the casino-hotel where he has a young male lover. Thus Proust indicates the presence of complicated networks crossing homosexual and family lines, including implicitly all the complex currents around Jewishness and the Dreyfus Affair in French society. This Jewish network includes Esther Lévy, as does the network of lesbians who recognize each other's tendencies and make preliminary eye contact in the many mirrors of the casino.

Esther Lévy, in the only developed description of lesbian behaviour, is described connecting at speed with another young woman: "Bloch's cousin went to sit at a table and looked at a magazine. Soon the young woman wandered vaguely over and sat down beside her. But under the table one could have seen their feet worrying at each other, then their legs and their clasped hands. Words come next, a conversation began, and the naïve husband of the young woman, who had been looking everywhere for her, was astonished to find her making plans for that very evening with a girl he didn't know. His wife introduced Bloch's cousin as a childhood friend with an unintelligible name, because she'd forgotten to ask her what she was called" (II, 852).

The role of Mademoiselle Vinteuil is somewhat more curious. Early in the novel, she has a female friend of bad reputation. This woman moves in with the musician Vinteuil and his daughter and throughout the novel is considered an evil woman, responsible for causing Vinteuil considerable unhappiness until his death, because of the stories told about his daughter. In one famous scene, the narrator, Marcel, watches and listens through a window as the two women indulge in preliminary love play around a photograph of Vinteuil, on which the friend threatens to spit. This scene is used to substantiate the wickedness of the women; much later in *A la recherche du temps perdu*, however, we suddenly see her as a musician with a good heart who spends untold hours deciphering and copying out Vinteuil's music in order to ensure his continuing reputation as a composer. With the rehabilitation of this woman, the last "evil lesbian" disappears from the French novel. Male authors will shortly cease to write about lesbians at all, and women writers create "bad" women of a different kind.

Lesbians are present in Proust's novel, but even more present is Marcel's anxiety that his beloved Albertine may make love with women. Marcel's worry is created by a remark that Cottard makes as he watches Albertine waltzing with her friend Andrée.

A girl I didn't know sat down at the piano, and Andrée asked Albertine to waltz with her, [...] I remarked to Cottard how well they danced. But he, from the particular viewpoint of a doctor and with a bad education that did not take into account what I knew about the girls, to whom, none the less, he must have seen me say good day, replied "Yes, but parents are imprudent to let their daughters develop such habits. I would certainly not let mine come here. Are they pretty at least? I can't make out their features. Just look," he added, pointing out Albertine and Andrée, who were waltzing slowly, pressed against each other, "I've forgotten my eyeglasses and I can't see clearly, but they seem to be at the climax of pleasure. It is not widely enough known that women reach it mostly through their breasts. And, look, theirs are touching each other completely." Indeed, contact between Andrée and Albertine's breasts had not been broken. I don't know whether they heard or guessed what Cottard had said, but they detached themselves slightly one from the other while still waltzing [...] Albertine looked as though she was showing, as though she was getting Andrée to affirm some voluptuous and secret shudder. (II, 795–6)

From this moment on Marcel worries, watches, and questions Albertine, who is friendly with Esther Lévy, Bloch's sister, and Mademoiselle Vinteuil and who claims at one time, only to deny it vehemently at another, that she was in part raised by Mademoiselle Vinteuil's lover. What is at issue here is not Albertine's or Marcel's sexuality, but rather Marcel's jealousy, possessiveness, and need to control everyone in his personal world. His physical gaze is on

Albertine whenever she is present, and his mental gaze never leaves her for a moment, even long after she is dead.

Proust's inscription of the lesbian grows out of the literary patterns and attitudes that prevail from Balzac to Colette. Because women together are a mere social curiosity for Marcel, with the interest that they might offer lying, as it were, beyond the range of self-centred preoccupations, they do not get enough of Proust's attention to be re-created by his particular perspective. Similarly, the focus on Albertine's possible lesbianism has virtually nothing to do with her and everything to do with Marcel's obsessive introspection. Proust's main theme is identical to Balzac's and Gautier's: the struggle which takes place within a male ego when it is faced with a desired and unpossessible woman. They all use lesbianism to intensify the focus of men's attitudes towards women in personal and social circumstances. After a hundred years of writing, it still has no existence in itself.

Jacques de Lacretelle's *La Bonifas* (The Bonifas Woman, 1925) is very different from Proust's novel because Lacretelle focuses totally on his heroine and writes about her empathetically. He tells of a woman with lesbian tendencies in the period from about 1870 to 1920 who never expresses her sexuality in anything other than tender, caring attentions, yet is persecuted cruelly by small-town prejudice until the moment when the townswomen need her help – she being the nearest thing to a man available in wartime. This is a careful, sensitive piece of writing, in which the author attempts to analyse individual and group psychological make-up. He centres on the woman, the causes and manifestations of her marginalization, her feelings, and her social context. In the history of lesbian characters since 1796 (apart from Maupassant's short story), this is the only novel written by a man that portrays a lesbian as a human protagonist, rather than as a symbolic pawn in a male game.

Lacretelle does not escape tradition entirely. Marie Bonifas (like Claudine) has a curmudgeonly, undemonstrative father and an absent mother, who, as we learn towards the end of the novel, was a nightclub singer in North Africa. She is thereby not only situated as one of the overly lascivious parents whose legacy is lesbianism in their daughters but is also tainted with eroticism. Marie is physically ugly in somewhat masculine ways that are not unexpected and, in one curious way, reminiscent of Paule in *Mademoiselle Giraud, ma femme* and equally designed to suggest excessive sensuality: she has double lips: "Visible in the middle of the pink and fleshy part was a line which traced the outer contour of the lips – a strangeness rather than a deformity, but it added to the unattractive impression" (12).

So far the author does not challenge the basic literary construction of the lesbian character, but he does give Marie attractive eyes, which show "integrity and a naturalness of thought" (12) and he maintains as her central characteristic a direct simplicity in thought, in emotional response, and in action, so that she can affirm with truth at the end of the novel, when, after a lifetime of persecution, she is suddenly honoured for her wartime activities: "But I haven't changed. I could always do these things." Lacretelle's point is indeed that small-town attitudes swing around according to the self-interested susceptibilities of those who dictate the norms of fashion, taste, and social acceptability.

The actions that Marie Bonifas took at twenty, when she first ran the sewing workshop and then tried to "save" from illness and overwork the woman she loved, are characteristically parallel to those she took at forty, when she ran the town and impulsively rode out to negotiate with the German soldiers to "save" the town. For the first she was pilloried as a lesbian pervert for ten years or more and then ignored totally. For the second she was honoured as a patriot and heroine. In each case Marie expressed her love – for the individual and for the group – in the most direct way possible, to help improve dire circumstances. Whether it was a question of the health of her beloved colleague or the health of her beloved country, Marie listened to her heart and responded to the need with all the resources at her disposal.

The author builds his picture of Marie carefully and sympathetically to make clear the origins of her need to feel and express love and her capacity for decision and action, although he does present her as a slightly defective child, in her ugliness and also in the primitive, animal-like violence of her emotional responses. (The vocabulary is his.) Marie forms strong and exclusive attachments to those whom she loves; she has a will to dominate, protect, care for, and serve her beloved; and she protects her love object, and therefore her own territory, as best she can against any rival.

Her first love is a gentle, loving serving girl who looks after her from the age of six. It is from Reine that she learns to feel and express tenderness and affection, and Reine's caresses arouse her

Contrasting Attitudes   91

first sexual and sensual responses. Her father becomes her rival; Reine gets pregnant, throws herself out of a window to cause a miscarriage, and dies as a result. By this time Marie has definitely come to dislike the physical presence of men and to choose women as desired love objects. This is presumably because her father is not communicative, not affectionate, and not attractive in himself and because he took away the first woman whom Marie was aware of loving. (Today we would link her loss of Reine with the earlier loss of her mother, but Lacretelle makes no such connection at this point in the story.)

Marie is then sent to boarding school, and her next love is an older student. By now she is old enough to conceptualize the love that she feels and to fantasize a future life together with Geneviève built on the closeness of their friendship and the caresses that she gives and receives. This time two rivals emerge: a fiancé for Geneviève and also a rival female friend. One day, already upset by the loss of her future dream life, she is irritated by the remark of Marceline, her rival, to Geneviève: "'Is it because her lips are fatter than mine that you let Marie Bonifas kiss you more often?'" (57). Marie then beats up Marceline and is expelled. Her friendship with Geneviève does survive, however, until the end of the novel.

At this point the author takes care to validate Marie's feelings as feelings of passion, while suggesting that she should have received psychiatric attention for them:

Marie's love passed through all the detours and defeats of a great love. There's no difference between the feelings that dawn in our hearts when we're children and those we feel later. The sum total of our joy is the same, we endure the same pain, we try the same remedies. They are judged differently, the first are diminished, because the immediate reactions that they provoke are most often without importance. But are all the effects of a passion immediately visible? Do we know what slowly developing seeds it leaves in the organism? The psychologist who disdains the souls of children is comparable to the doctor who observes his subjects without paying attention to their history; and a novelist who wants to draw a personality without starting his character from the egg always seems to me to have omitted the primordial task. So, as this story advances, it will be decided whether Marie Bonifas' innocent love for her boarding school friend should have been neglected. (56)

The author then moves Marie's education and condition to a new level by setting her in a progressive and female environment for the rest of her adolescence. At the Cité Blanche, on the other side of France and far from home, she learns to live comfortably in her body – she is (of course) big and somewhat masculine – to use her strength, enjoy physical activity, and express her independence; she is also exposed to feminist and atheistic discussions concerning issues of women's autonomy. The conclusion of these discussions is usually that an independent woman must choose to live a life without love because love leads to marriage and servitude and also because love takes up too much of women's thoughts, thereby precluding intellectual pleasures, explorations, and success.

Marie learns that love and autonomy (or even self-respect, for women) are not compatible, but she refuses to conceive of a life without love. It is the contradiction between her learned unfeminine behaviour, her desire to love and be loved, her antipathy for men (born of very limited experience), and her need to take care of the weak (usually women) that generates all the grief in her life. The irony is that, although she is vilified as a sexual pervert, she never expresses her love in anything other than caresses and tender attentions. Her "perversion" is defined by her attitude towards men as much as that towards the woman whom she loves. She is considered unnatural in her refusal to marry. She creates enemies by her active and energetic discouragement of Claire's male suitors. And it is one of these frustrated men who, with a gang of helpers, threatens her with physical harm and harasses her to the point of impaling her cat, with a poster round its neck, on the railings of her house.[16] The final assault comes from a German soldier whom she has found drinking wine in her cellar. At her angry, "Yes it is a woman, a mere woman, who is throwing you out, you wretch" (297), the soldier turns on her and tries to rape her. She kills him – and then is prepared to turn herself in to the Germans to prevent reprisals by them against the town. On the one occasion when she is tempted sexually and knowingly by a young woman measuring her for a corset, she realizes that she is emotionally and morally unable to take the step into physical sexuality.

The first section of the novel shows Marie's upbringing; the second tells of her love for Claire, devotion to Claire, semi-rejection by the dying woman (who does finally thank her and kiss her from her deathbed), and then total rejection and persecution by the townspeople. During her years of solitude, Lacretelle has her read about lesbianism and permits himself some oblique comment on the damage done by sensational fiction that passes itself off as psychological study, while having Marie reflect on her desires, attractions, and behaviour. He shows her coming to the conclusion that although her actions have been blameless, she deserved the blame laid on her by her neighbours because her subconscious desire had indeed been impure. Curiously, having brought his heroine to this realization, Lacretelle does nothing further with it. He does not submerge Marie in shame and guilt in the tradition of lesbian characters in the French novel. It would seem that he expects his readers to make the connection between Marie's realization that she is a mixture of pure and impure intentions and his own statement of the same earlier in the novel. Later Marie becomes aware that it is not she who has changed and so moved from a state of being persecuted and condemned to one of being celebrated and praised, but rather that circumstances have made people appreciate certain of her characteristics rather than criticize others.

Lacretelle's interest lies in the group process that creates marginality. His novel is a study of bias, rumour, innuendo, and the cruel process of social isolation in the face of self-protective self-righteousness – small-town small-mindedness. Did he choose lesbianism as a simple exercise after his study of the marginalization of a Jewish child in *Silbermann* (1922)? Did he construct La Bonifas on a model he had known? Whatever his reason, Jacques de Lacretelle created the only sympathetically and sensitively described man-made lesbian in the modern history of the French novel.

Marie Bonifas does remain, however, like many of her lesbian predecessors, in a category that might be called "substitute men." Her rivalry with an individual man for the female beloved is a minor part of her story. She is not loved as she deserves to be because of the heterosexual morality and attitudes bred into Claire, which poison the end of their life together. Also, and particular to this novel, is the author's clear awareness that Marie Bonifas is free to live as herself, to function at the level of her true capacity, when she is surrounded by women only. She is encouraged to be herself at school, and she comes into her own in the war.

When there are no "real" men available (i.e., those fit to fight) then Marie Bonifas is the next best person available. She runs the town, negotiates with German officers, and shows herself to be

94 THE MALE GAZE, 1796–1929

intelligent, resourceful, decisive, well organized, far-sighted, and so on. But she is allowed to occupy this traditionally male space only when the men are away occupying even more archetypically male space – that of the battlefield. When Marie rides out on to the battlefield to negotiate with the Germans, surrounded by all the symbolic trappings of a (male) hero of historic and literary proportion, and carries out her mission with panache, we are being told by the author that she is more male than many men. Her reaction to attempted rape is to kill the rapist, which is not a usual feminine response to male sexual violence in French literature – and yet these "masculine" reactions are counterbalanced by her gentleness and lifelong refusal to give up the possibility of love.

Hence the author does not encode Marie as a sexual rival to men, nor as a pervert and degenerate; in this way he situates her outside the traditional characterization of the literary lesbian, although the supposed causes of her lesbianism directly evoke the nineteenth-century novels. Marie is, however, clearly a misfit within heterosexual social structures, which allow women no place for autonomy, independence, and extra-domestic competence. The book is set before and during the 1914–18 war. It would have been interesting to see Lacretelle's view of the situation of lesbians in 1925. As it is, he and his heroine change the parameters of lesbianism and act as a bridge between the male assumptions and perceptions of the nineteenth- and early-twentieth-century novels and those established by female authors publishing after 1929.

PART TWO

Through Women's Eyes, 1929–1968

CHAPTER THREE

Constrained Desire

In 1929 the writing of lesbian novels shifted abruptly from male to female authors, the only exceptions being André Gide's *Geneviève* (1937), a sensitive exploration of adolescent attraction of one young woman for another, and Philippe Sollers's *Une Étrange Solitude* (A Strange Solitude, 1958), where the egocentric narrator begins by telling the reader that he has been abandoned by a lesbian girlfriend whose lesbianism is never of account again. These two, like the majority of male authors before them,. used lesbian characters for the most part in novels of exploration of the male ego, and the male–female–lesbian triangulation showed their argument more clearly than would a more usual male–female–male conformation.

The women, in contrast, explore the lesbian–female–male space from a different perspective. Rather than the lesbian's being the intruder in male homo-social space, as in all the novels examined in chapters 1 and 2, which portray female desire as unimportant in all realms except that of heterosexual sex and subordinate female relations to male interrelations of all kinds, novels by women tend to situate the lesbian as an outsider in hetero-social space or as an element, comfortably integrated or not, in female homo-social space. Troubled she may still be in the period covered by this chapter, but no longer constantly vilified with Baudelairean rhetoric directly or by implication. For the most part the authors' sympathies lie with her, and the depiction of a lesbian way of life and psychology becomes less extreme and less ambiguous as time goes on.

My attempt here to trace lesbian characters across the history of the modern and contemporary French novel is unlikely to be totally comprehensive. It is, however, as complete as I have been able to make it, given that I have found no bibliography of French lesbian writing, apart from Jeannette Foster's *Sex Variant Women in Literature* (1956), which includes no French titles after 1950; Lilian Faderman's *Surpassing the Love of Men* (1981); and the admirable bibliography to Marie-Jo Bonnet's *Les Relations amoureuses entre les femmes* (1995). Also, presumably because of the profoundly heterosexual nature of French culture, and perhaps therefore of publishing practices, most of the authors cited (if they have written more than one novel) intersperse one or two novels about lesbian concerns among a sometimes-extensive heterosexual output, so I may well have missed relevant works. My desire for completeness may militate against certain kinds of analysis, but I have chosen to make as many novels known as possible and to draw an approximate map of the territory that will I hope open it up for future explorers.

All of the above I offer in justification for my finding only four novels of interest published between 1929 and 1934 and then nothing at all until 1946. The 1950s produced novels of hopeless love, and the 1960s novels of greater sexual freedom, albeit almost entirely bisexual. I leave to chapter 4 the major literary figures of this period – Violette Leduc and Simone de Beauvoir, of the generation born around 1900, and Monique Witting and Hélène Cixous, who reached adulthood in the 1960s.

This chapter is full of unknown novels and little-known authors, with only Françoise Mallet-Joris and Christiane Rochefort having achieved some measure of renown, although a number of the authors, Jeanne Galzy and Irène Monési in particular, are career writers. Three of the very early novels here are by Jeanne Galzy, the other one by Claire Cahun.

1929–1934: UNRESOLVED ATTRACTION

Cahun's novel, *Aveux non avenus* (Declarations Not Made, 1930), is explained fully by its title. She deals in the ambiguous variability of desire while maintaining that same ambiguity in her own book. The novel is made up of a series of letters and meditations on love and other topics in which gender indicators go back and forth, creating deliberate confusion for the readers: "Jumble the cards   Masculine? feminine? but that depends on the case. Neuter is the only gender that would suit me always. If it existed in our language, one would not see this indecisiveness in my thoughts. Once and for all I would be the worker bee" (176).

The ambiguity that interests Jeanne Galzy concerns not gender but rather her characters' process of realizing that their feelings are indeed those of love for other women. Her protagonists have no models and no language for what they are experiencing and no place to situate themselves socially. Heterosexuality and motherhood are the only modes of love publicly available in their world. As a result it is not surprising that Galzy sidles up to the issue of lesbian desire gradually. By 1929 she was already an established writer with five novels, a play, and a life of St Theresa of Avila published and three literary prizes to her credit. The first novel that interests me is *L'Initiatrice aux mains vides* (The Empty-handed [female] Initiator, 1929). The book carries the dedication: "To the memory of Mademoiselle Germaine Normand, teacher of the first grade at the Montpellier High School, I offer this book with the heart of a child," which, given the story, suggests an autobiographical seed at the very least.

The novel tells the story of a single woman, a schoolteacher, who is drawn to a little girl in her class. Marie Pascal's days are illuminated by the presence of Annette; the girl responds with rapt attention and little gestures and behaviour of fondness. Gradually Marie Pascal's thoughts come to focus more and more exclusively on the child. She realizes the dangerous level of her feelings, manages for a long time to justify them as mother love, and then tries to restrain them and curb Annette's attentions also. When Annette writes to her during the vacation and shows her love, Marie forces herself not to reply, but as soon as term begins and she sees that the child is marked by suffering caused by the waiting and disappointment, she suffers in her turn.

All is more or less under control until Annette falls ill with pneumonia. Sickbed scenes are a staple in novels by women writers, because, in this pre-antibiotic period, the strain of watching a loved one hover between life and death for several days can serve to precipitate the revelation of true feelings. Galzy has Marie Pascal replace Annette's weary mother for the crucial night when the child's fever breaks. Thereafter there is a jealous hostility directed at Marie by the mother, who manages to force Marie's transfer to another school and also to take Annette away, without letting the child and the teacher meet again. Marie is left only with Annette's school overall, which remained in the classroom, and the knowledge that Annette had carved "Marie" inside her desk. The choice of the first name is used to suggest that Annette dreamed of her teacher in more personal ways than as "Mademoiselle" and to make clear to the reader the tone of Marie's feelings as well. The implicit message of the novel is that these two loved each other.

Galzy's next book approaches lesbian desire even more clearly. In *Les Démons de la solitude* (The Demons of Solitude, 1931), Clarisse Soubeyran and her widowed father both project their fantasies onto Sabine Fédière who owns the neighbouring property and spends summers there. Galzy makes it clear that throughout high school Clarisse has had a constant companion and intimate friend named Eva, and she suggests their awareness of their possibilities by having them read Proust. They graduate at the beginning of the novel, and Eva goes to university, finds new friends, and ultimately becomes engaged. Clarisse's father owns vineyards, his aunt keeps house, and the two of them want Clarisse to take an interest in the property, marry, and carry on the family line. Clarisse is not really interested in anything at first, so she does not object when her father forbids her to go to university. She stays at home for a year and is very lonely.

During that time she concentrates her attention on Madame Fédière. Clarisse is furious that her father is attracted by Sabine and that there are rumours that he might marry her. Gradually that anger transforms itself into jealousy. Clarisse sees herself as being in competition with her father, who is indeed attracted by their neighbour but is too shy in her presence to make his feelings known and risk both rejection and the loss of her companionable friendship. Both he and his daughter wander out secretly at night and hover under Sabine's windows – sometimes they encounter each other.

Clarisse, having heard Sabine play the piano, sets herself to work at her music. Finally she gets the courage to visit Sabine, play one or two of her compositions, and ask for the older woman's opinion. When they do meet, Clarisse is perspicacious enough to realize that the real person bears no relation whatsoever to the image that she has created in her daydreams. None the less Sabine does serve as a catalyst: her intervention leads Clarisse's father to allow her to go to Paris and study music. But at the very end of the novel both father and daughter are having doubts.

The novel disturbs a lot of the reader's assumptions and resolves none of them. Does Eva love her fiancé or prefer Clarisse's father? Is the father attracted by Eva, or was she just a distraction for his lust? Does he really lust after Sabine, or is he lonely? Two things seem sure: Sabine has no desire to marry again; Clarisse is not interested in men.

Galzy's next novel is more explicit. *Jeunes Filles en serre chaude* (Girls in a Hothouse, 1934) is reminiscent of Gabrielle Reval's *Les Sévriennes* (The Students of Sèvres, 1900) but contains more latent sexuality. Set in the Sèvres Normal School, the novel turns around the shifting relationships between the young women, their teachers, and the young men to whom they are connected and with whom they spend their spare time. The central figures are Isabelle Rives and a red-haired, perfumed professor by the name of Gladys Benz, who makes very subtle advances to her. Nothing is ever said, but they spend time together in implied tenderness and possible sensuousness. Miss Benz, who fascinates everyone, gets included into the wider, heterosexual group and eventually seems to form a relationship with Marien, a young man to whom Isabelle was somewhat connected also. (The various links and relationships are both ambiguous and highly charged – hence the "hothouse" of the title.)

The night before her exams Isabelle panics when she suspects that Gladys is with Marien at the house they all frequent in the country. She goes to the house, returns to Gladys's room, tears up a dress, and, failing her exam of course, flees to Paris. There she reflects on Freud and Baudelaire: "She remembered Baudelaire and his artificial paradises and immediately afterwards the divine dialogue of sadness that passes between the women who were damned. And all at once an iron blade pierced her heart" (274). She rages that she didn't even fight Marien for Gladys, but now both are lost to her.

A philosophical friend suggests that she return home to her "terre natale" – symbolically a return to her own beginnings to rediscover herself. She broods in the train about her anger and despair and then, when darkness falls, reflects on her own face in the window behind which she "discovered this secret and dependable witness, this soul that was not part of her upset and in whom she could trust in order to go on living" (286). End of the novel.

It is a troubled book that Gladys Benz haunts like a wraith of the nineteenth-century lesbian monsters, fascinating, perverted, and doom-driven. She is more benign in form but still devastating in effect, and her origins are made precise by the reference to Baudelaire, even given the lesbian-positive choice of words – "the divinely sad dialogue" – rather than the emphasis on damnation, with the stress being on tenderness and pity for the pain and unassuaged thirst for love that the damned women suffer.

POSTWAR DISILLUSIONMENT

The novelists published in the late 1940s – most notably Suzanne Roland-Manuel and Celia Bertin – deal in repression, denial, and lack of energy. It is as though the restrictions and cautions of life in wartime and under Nazi occupation have seeped into the very sentences of the novels and drained the life and possibility from them.

Suzanne Roland-Manuel constructs *Le Trille du Diable* (The Devil's Trill, 1946) overtly on the premise that adolescent girls have a need for love and sensuality that they express between themselves, especially when they have too much imagination and no education. We have seen this already in Saint-Agen's *Charmeuse de femmes* (1906), in the way in which Reine responds to Hélène. In *Le Trille du Diable*, Florence and Augustine begin to kiss and indulge in sensual play and exploration at fourteen years of age and continue to do so until they leave normal school at twenty. Their unchallenged cover for all this time is that Florence has a crush on a famous violinist, José Soline, and they are enacting scenes between Soline and his wife. Augustine first suggests the game, but thereafter it is Florence who invents, suggests, and encourages their caresses: "At night in bed she [Florence] constructed extravagant sequences. Her extreme nature made her invent things that made her blush the next day" (93).

During their student years they meet in a hotel room on their free afternoon. Never do they question or analyse what they are doing, and the novel provides no explanation either. Nor is there any description of lovemaking beyond kissing and hugging, although the text certainly suggests more sexual and erotic activity: "'Take me by force!' [Florence] whispered very softly. The girls didn't hear the loud bell of an alarm clock" (257).

Their "love affair" continues until Florence becomes engaged. She writes to Augustine: "You understand ... *I've got a man*. It's marvellous" (294). After her marriage she misses Augustine and, one must suppose, their clandestine activities: "It was still possible to have fun with Augustine!" (392), but when she reads about two lesbians in a novel, she dismisses any thought of having been in love with Augustine. It is clear to the reader that Florence's behaviour was the expression of lust, fuelled by adolescent hormones: "Florence had just read a novel about two women in love and who had shameful relations with each other. Florence hadn't long known that such things existed. After informing herself of all the details, she thought about them for a long time and came to the conclusion that she was not in love with Augustine! Absolutely not! The very idea actually gave her the giggles!" (392).

The implicit message of the novel is that Augustine *did* love Florence and continues to do so, although she makes no protest at Florence's defection. At thirty-three, she marries a man of forty-five in order to stay in their home village and not be separated from Florence. Florence leaves, however, and after many complications in the long novel (667 pages) returns a widow, and Augustine helps her find a house. Nice symbolism of the true homecoming, that we can choose to interpret as a return to Augustine if we so wish!

The fact that the two girls playact through "literature" – that is that they invent an ongoing heterosexual love story – is supposed to be a mark of Florence's overheated imagination and body, but it is also the only model that young, inexperienced lesbians have to permit their expression of feelings. Here is the first of the elements that we saw in Saint-Agen's novel, in which an unattainable love, fired by imagination, is acted out between two women, one of whom is a lesbian and the other is "aimante" – of a loving and sensuous disposition and therefore easily led into shameful activities by the lesbian, although she is actually practising for heterosexuality.

Saint-Agen makes her lesbian character acutely aware of the situation and burdens her with guilt. Roland-Manuel makes Augustine's lesbianism clear but does not focus on it. The central theme of the novel is Florence's ongoing self-indulgence and its results. Augustine fades quietly into a marriage of convenience and respectability. Her only gesture of self-defence is to write an anonymous letter to the woman already engaged to Florence's man, Jean, denouncing his behaviour. She feels remorse at her action, and it has no effect on Jean and Florence's plans to marry.

The lesbian love in *Le Trille du Diable* is less voluptuous, less affectingly written, and less touching than the similar pieces of writing in *Charmeuse de femmes*. However, the scope of this novel is much broader, and its focus lies elsewhere. It does not explore Augustine's feelings except in direct connection with Florence. Her pain is rendered invisible by the lack of a context in which it can be examined. Roland-Manuel seems to acknowledge the reality of lesbianism but then to set it aside as being of less interest than heterosexual lust, self-interest, and thoughtless self-indulgence.

Celia Bertin's novels also include and even focus on lesbianism but repress it at the same time. *La Parade des impies* (Parade of the Impious Women, 1946) centres on a long-established lesbian couple: Ginger, rich, devoted, and possessive, and Marine, an actress. Marine is attracted to a mysterious dancer, Delia, who leads her on, but the affair does not seem ever to really come into being. Marine has no decisiveness and no energy. She ends by returning to Ginger. Around this non-adultery move a crowd of theatre people and some artsy women. The whole story takes place in wartime Paris. The character with the most presence is a Jewish actress who has been forbidden to work under the German occupation. She is afraid of being taken away one night. But even that fear is not developed sufficiently to touch other characters, or even Valérie Meyer herself, who seems fatalistic and uncaring.

I spent my entire reading of the novel thinking what a waste it was of potentially interesting material and wondering whether the author was so careful of her own lesbianism that she could not allow herself to evoke the feelings in fiction. The book contains no tenderness, no physicality except Marine's awareness of the first time that Delia touches her hand, no sensuality, and ultimately no feelings except Marine's boredom with Ginger and her obsessive thoughts about Delia.

The author puts no energy into the representation of lesbian life; she puts none into the fears, tensions, and complexities of living in wartime in an occupied zone either. It is as though Bertin is numb.

Constrained Desire 105

(A much more interesting novel set in the same period is Jeanne Galzy's *La Jeunesse déchirée* or Torn Youth, 1951. In this long and complex work the reader feels the struggles, shifting or divided loyalties, and passionately held views of a wide range of characters. The author concentrates mainly on young people, many in the Resistance, among whom is Lucienne, a young woman who had a lesbian relationship while in a sanatorium and at least one subsequent lesbian love affair with a Spanish dancer, Dolores Segara. Her current lover in the novel is a Jewish man; he is betrayed to the authorities by Dolores because she is jealous. This is the only lesbian episode in the novel but fits well into the context, and despite Dolores's action, she is not set up as vicious in the traditional way. Galzy is a compelling writer, and this novel catches the excitement and peril of the the the times.)

Bertin's next novel, published the year after *La Parade des impies,* was *La Bague était brisée* (The Ring Was Broken, 1947). It uses Ginger and her actress friend as constant reference for the taboo of lesbianism to which the young members of the family and their friends constantly refer. It is a curious book because many of the multifarious women in this busy but again rather pointless novel are set up to appear to be lesbian couples, but nothing ever develops, except perhaps between the English women, Olive and Sheila, who are in Madagascar and therefore doubly "foreign" and more free.

Bertin was beginning to hit her stride, however, and published a novel for which she received the Prix Renaudot in 1953 – *La Dernière innocence* (The Last Innocence). This time she offers a more engaging, though equally complex tale of an extended family, a story that turns around a dead poet and the suicide some years before of his sixteen-year-old daughter Françoise. One of the daughters, Paule, is lesbian, and her difference is made clear from the beginning. This does not prevent her from being loved by her brother-in-law, and the complications continue.

Paule is accepted for what she is within the family. She is marked as different, but she has no reality of her own. She is not like the family, but she is given no life that grounds her for herself. Her real life is secret and is disdained/scorned by the family, we are told. The only scene of her with another lesbian – a breakup of their relationship – has nothing specifically lesbian at all about it, except that the conversation takes place between two women and includes the odd cliché such as "a girl like you with a man ... "(190).

Bertin uses Paule as a destabilizer of circumstances, an unpredictable addition to the patterns of desire. She observes things clearly and more sensitively than the other characters, but she has no developed role. True to type she gives thought to suicide but chooses life. The novel ends: "She had already got a taste for happiness, she had to go home" (293).

Not until 1977 does Célia Bertin publish another novel with lesbian undertones. *Liens de famille* (Family Ties) is the story of the complicated emotional intertwinings of three women. Maria is a professional singer reaching the end of her career, and Anna is her widowed daughter-in-law. Anna lives with Maria, takes care of most of the details of their shared life, and is Maria's accompanist. The two women live in comparative harmony, united by their passion for music and somewhat ambiguous memories of Jacques, their son and husband, who was killed in the war. Into this regular pattern erupts Clarice. Young, rich, beautiful, married, and Brazilian (often accompanied by a sad little daughter, Alice), Clarice sets out to seduce Maria and indulge her every whim. Anna, feeling more and more excluded, withdraws in pique and possible jealousy. She reflects intently on her relationship with Maria in an attempt to see whether it is more possessive and emotionally complex than she had thought.

Meanwhile Maria finally goes to bed with Clarice. The violence of her reaction to her own act and previously denied desire is such that she finally turns on Clarice physically and throws her out: "'Every day I regret the mistake I made in going to bed with you. I lost my freedom'" (176). Marie claims that she has lost her freedom. Instead of being a unique and beautiful experience, her final love affair has instead become a series of increasingly unpleasant scenes from which she wishes to escape. Clarice's rebuttal is that Marie loves her but sees their love as sinful and that is why their relationship has soured:

– Go away! I could kill you! Marie's violence no longer surprised me and I could imagine the scene clearly [...]
  – Because you love me! yelled Clarice again [[...] Had she not read in

Marie's eyes all the love-hate that inflamed her. There was nothing left to do but she couldn't accept it. Never had she felt such pain [...]

– There, it's over! murmured Marie as she felt me approaching. We shall not speak of it again because there is nothing to say. It's the saddest story of my life. The one where I behaved worst. And it is ending badly... One has no right... No right. (178–9)

All of this seething emotion erupts in the context of family life, which focuses on Anna's niece Brigitte, a child of the same age as Clarice's Alice, whom Brigitte finds antipathetic. In retrospect, the lesbianism in the novel seems clear. As the story is actually unfolding, however, sexuality flows as an ambiguous undercurrent between the women.

At the end of the novel, long after the death of Marie, Anna has remarried, and Alice reappears in Anna's life. She becomes close to Brigitte's brother Julien, and then commits suicide. Julien reports Alice's perspective on the past to Anna and Saad (Anna's new husband). According to him Alice felt that as a child she was often taken out with Marie and Clarice because they felt that two women accompanied by a little girl would not give the impression of being lesbian. Her view was that such camoflage should not have been necessary: "To love a woman when one is a woman and has the taste and capacity for it, offends no one" (310). Her father had taught her that everyone is free to love and that the notion of sin denies love.

In a retrospective reflection before her death, Alice tells Anna that Clarice's love for Marie was the greatest love of her life. Anna concludes also that Marie's life was diminished by the loss of Clarice: "I was totally preoccupied by Marie, obsessed by Marie's emotional life, which stopped completely after the break with Clarice. And Marie died of that rupture! ... She needed to vibrate, to share with the beloved the life that flowed in her. That was how she was, and living without love had no interest for her. I'm telling you: Clarice was right to proclaim that Marie loved her! I understood too late!" (359) Thus everything becomes apparent, if not clear. The central message is that neither Marie nor Anna is open to a sexual and passionate relationship between Marie and Clarice. Neither woman is aware of the roots of their resistance, but neither can deny the intensity of her feelings.

Celia Bertin's *Liens de famille* is, in sum, a novel of cultural homophobia. It categorizes the lesbian Clarice in the traditional way as a dark, foreign, exotic seductress who tempts Marie into the paths of sin. Anna is Marie's guardian – her accompanist on all symbolic and practical levels – who keeps her bound to the regular practice of her art and to the regularities of her respected (and respectable) life as a heterosexual diva. Only at the end do we have these expected codes challenged and see Anna not only as having been diminished in her own life – choosing to tend to Marie rather than having a career as a concert pianist – but as having curtailed Marie's possibilities in ways that proved fatal.

This novel has much more power and energy than Bertin's earlier works. It is a good and fascinating read, full of well-constructed characters and interesting twists and turns. It is also the product of a later time. Its intensity brings to mind the writings of Mireille Best and of Jocelyne François, and its world is one in which lesbianism is not the taboo that it was in the years before 1968.

Apart from Bertin, the novelists of the immediate postwar period examine the process and progress of love as experienced by the central female character. About love that is intense, obsessional, and destined not to last, these stories are reminiscent in tone of the psychologically focused, analytical tradition of Benjamin Constant's *Adolphe* (pub. 1816), André Gide's *La Porte étroite* (1909), Raymond Radiguet's *Le Diable au corps* (1923), and Colette's *Chéri* (1920), all of which belong to a French tradition of semi-autobiographical first-person narratives in which the young male protagonist agonizes over his first heterosexual love affair.

THE 1950S: HOPELESS LOVE

Violette Leduc's *L'Affamée* (The Starving Woman, 1948) is both the first of these lesbian self-reflective, self-reflexive novels to appear and the most avant-garde in its writing style, resembling as it does the early work of Nathalie Sarraute in the way in which it is based on assumptions associated with the Nouveau Roman. It is, however, a long lamentation of hopeless, one-sided adoration, where the lover subsists on minimal kindness, incidental encounters, and much obsessive imagining.[1]

The next to appear is Françoise Mallet-Joris's *Le Rempart des Béguines* (Beguine's Rampart, 1957, published under the title *The Illusionist*). An accomplished piece of writing and a good read, this novel, Mallet-Joris's first, published when she was twenty-one, has a clearly calculated shock value, which is underlined by the irony of the title, the Beguines being a medieval community of women who lived as secular nuns. Hélène Noris, motherless since she was eight and very lonely, is seduced at sixteen by her father's mistress, Tamara, a wild Russian rebel. Their stormy affair lasts for two years until René Noris proposes to Tamara, who, to Hélène's disgust, accepts him. The novel ends on their wedding night – Tamara succumbs to small-town bourgeois security, and Hélène declares herself free of her obsession.

Tamara, at first a businessman's exotic mistress, gradually changes into a modern version of the nineteenth-century mannish, cruel, dominating lesbian. She is dressed in pants, then a suit, then jodhpurs and boots. She has a lost woman lover for whom she pines. As her story is filled out, she reveals a past in which she was married to a fifty-year-old rich Jewish husband. He loved her sufficiently to accept the presence in his house of her female lovers so that she would not leave him. He also paid her a stipend that allowed her to live independently but obliged her to go and request money from him. She had control of him in one way; he had control of her in another.

These patterns of power and control recur in various ways in all the relationships in the story. Hélène is a willing slave to Tamara, in exchange for attention – kissing her hand in secret the first time they meet in public – but Tamara's care and attention rapidly turn to domination, violence, and cold cruelty, alternating with love-making in which she accepts total sexual pleasure from Hélène: "This cold expression, suddenly upset, coming apart, scattered itself in half smiles, in half smiles, in very gentle, hardly perceptible moaning, in glances sliding out under her eyelids and as if immediately drowned in liquid tenderness, this internal cry that I felt rise, this purring ending in groans, and these pointed canine teeth biting the oh so pale lower lip, no longer able to hide an ecstasy, wicked and carnivorous, that was the centre, burning poignant and rending, of my love for Tamara ... this burning light: the love-face of Tamara" (81–2, *Livre de poche*).

In terms of lesbian lovemaking, this novel is no more explicit than Saint-Agen's evocation of lovemaking between Reine and the other Hélène. But Mallet-Joris's writing is more audacious because of the tone and intention of what is implied. Tamara and Hélène both enjoy being in bed, revel in the sensations of erotic sensuality, understand and use the power relations between them.

What sickens Hélène in Tamara's decision to marry is not that Tamara will be her stepmother, sleep with her father, or be in her house. She has neither moral nor sexual scruples. Rather, Tamara seems to her diminished by the decision. No longer imperious and heedless of the consequences, Tamara treats Hélène with circumspection. She needs her as an ally, complicitous in the new triangulation of sexuality in the household. Hélène, no longer the slave and victim, now on her own territory, is in a position to denounce and destroy Tamara (though at some risk to herself as a delinquent minor, as Tamara points out).

The nineteenth-century triangle in which man and lesbian struggled to win the female is here turned on its head. Both Hélène and her father love Tamara, so that the lesbian is the centre of desire, though remaining marginalized as outrageous in the social context, just as before. Rather than man and lesbian struggling for supremacy, they both capitulate into a conventional marriage, in which Tamara suddenly becomes banal, feminine, and socially almost acceptable. Just as surely as Mallet-Joris constructed a traditional lesbian in the virago role, she deconstructs her utterly, leaving the reader with Hélène, laughing in disbelief at what she sees.

So after 1945 the Belle Epoque–style mature lesbian collapses into the security-conscious wife more appropriate for the postwar period. Meanwhile the young self-discovering lesbian characters, intense and anguished, relate to ambiguous objects of desire, who lead them into unhappy non-relationships.

The simplest versions of hopeless love come from Nicole Louvier in her two novels *Qui qu'en grogne* (literally: "Who grumbles about it," 1954) and *L'Heure des jeux* (Playtime, 1955), and the most idealistically hopeless from Irène Monési's *Althia* (1957) and Eveline Mahyère's *Je jure de m'éblouir* (I Swear to Dazzle Myself, 1958). Clarisse Francillon's *La Lettre* (The Letter, 1958) is a very different story.

Louvier's *L'Heure des jeux* begins with a sister, Pat, and a brother, Dominique, who are both fond of the same woman. This woman marries the brother. Then one night there appears Fabienne, a mysterious woman who carries off Pat, the sister/heroine, after her show (she is a popular singer), and it is clear that there is a sensual tenderness between them. After the main plot – Pat's affair with Dominique – is almost over, Fabienne reappears. But no sooner is it implied that they have built a relationship than Fabienne collapses with a brain tumour and dies. Curiously, there are only two places in the novel where it is contextually clear that Dominique is a man. Louvier has crafted the text in such a way that there are no grammatical clues to gender for him; the subsequent ambiguity – noticeable for someone reading, as I was, looking for possible lesbianism – gives a subtext that evokes a power relationship similar to Tamara's with Hélène at times and gives a twist to a relatively ordinary love story of a young woman and an older man.

Louvier's other novel, *Qui qu'en grogne*, relates in the first person the evolution and dissolution of Adrienne's love for Gabrielle over the period of about two years. It is a very symmetrical story: one summer holiday Adrienne begins to think of Gabrielle, and she dreams of her as the perfect love, perfect because of the parallel nature of their situation, which permits her not to be "in love" but to "love." (The distinction seems to be that being in love is more distant and more unequal a situation than loving.) Adrienne sees them as equally new in the world, equally idealistic, equally ready to explore. The long list of equivalences ends as follows: "I don't have to teach you about the world any more than you have to teach me. I am as ignorant as you about that joy that we have been searching for since birth, as clumsy, as incapable of defending myself against suffering that would come after an excess of happiness, as vulnerable in the face of someone irreplaceable, as new. I desire neither a master nor a servant. I want an equal" (14–15).

However, when Gabrielle returns, Adrienne realizes that she is still a little girl, a schoolgirl. Adrienne herself has failed her exams and is to prepare for them again at home. (The failing of exams, deliberately or not, seems to be the mark of lesbian disturbedness in the 1940s and 1950s. Whether the instability appears to be temporary or an indication of the non-conforming failure of the life to come varies according to the symbolic and deliberate nature of the choice. It appears to be the mental equivalent of asymmetrical features.)

Throughout a school year Adrienne engages, encourages, and forms Gabrielle to be her love and, when Gabrielle herself so demands, her lover. The midwinter break is marked by their spending Christmas night sleeping in the same room and then, in contrast, by Gabrielle's first ball and subsequent illness, which precipitates their first struggle with Gabrielle's incipient heterosexuality. The year ends with exams, two passionate nights together, and separation for the holidays – end of part I.

Part II begins with Adrienne again waiting for Gabrielle and receiving a brief letter from her – but this time she is in Cannes. Gabrielle has fallen in love with a young man, and the rest of the book details her vacillating attitude to heterosexuality and to Adrienne. This time Adrienne is ill. She gradually realizes that she invented and created Gabrielle and, having seen the situation lucidly, works and actually passes her exam. But Gabrielle does not allow a clean break between them. Afraid of being alone, she returns to Adrienne every time men are unavailable. Adrienne realizes the situation and in an odd passage – which makes a distinction between lesbian and woman that Monique Wittig will later theorize – she classifies Gabrielle: "Little by little I felt immense pity. Gabrielle seemed no worse, no better than the others. She was a woman. And what can one expect from a woman? I scorned them all for being so incapable of firmness, value, creative intelligence, and no doubt for those very reasons I couldn't detest them ... And I felt great pity for Gabrielle" (151).

Adrienne sees that the relation that she has to Gabrielle is similar to that between Claude and herself. Claude is an older, more experienced lesbian who comforts and supports Adrienne when necessary and is kind to her whenever she appears, without reproaching her for her unexplained absences.

Towards the end of the novel Adrienne and Gabrielle have a conversation in which they talk through all the betrayals and cruelties of Gabrielle's behaviour in Cannes the previous summer. Shortly thereafter Adrienne recognizes that Gabrielle feels desire for her – no love, just desire. She does not act on it, but Gabrielle does and comes to Adrienne's bed. Adrienne resists and recognizes her resistance and how she has never allowed herself to open totally to lovemaking. She would like Gabrielle to be the first with whom she does that: "I wanted to offer myself to her so that she would at least be the first: for the first time to abdicate everything, and in *her* hands" (180). When Gabrielle looks at her "with a hard smile, mocking angry eyes ... her gaze which took hold of me without flinching, without faltering, without any indulgence" (181) she suddenly gives in. Gabrielle has of course changed roles; from being the weak, protected beloved woman, she has become the dominant and desiring lovemaker. (The ghost of Tamara hovers.) Adrienne abdicates all control, all self, and floats free, "that she should read not only on my body and my shivers, but also on my face, to what degree I become her will, to the point of shame, indecency, lewdness, total annihilation: only after that could I become malleable again. *Only at this price.* And wanting to cry aloud to her the words of my surrender, I shattered in moans of pleasure" (182).

The choice of words is important; it indicates a certain covert homophobia, the shame attached to female sexuality and the open expression of desire, the affront that is total vulnerability. Certainly in the subsequent passage Adrienne is treated either thoughtlessly or, as she believes, with deliberate cruelty, as Gabrielle evokes the time in Cannes to other people.

The novel ends with a reference to Antoine de St Exupéry's story *Le Petit Prince* (The Little Prince, 1943), which is also mentioned at the beginning. In the conversation between the prince and the fox, the fox explains how, once he has been tamed and adopted by the prince, many things that were of no importance to him as an animal will take on significance as they remind him of his friend – wheat, for example, is of no use to a fox, but now its colour will remind him of the prince's hair and so will be a symbol of love. Thus the feelings between them enrich his world. Likewise Adrienne claims a gain, despite the failure of the love relationship. Her ruefully positive attitude and the fact that she passed her exam mark her as a survivor.

This is not the case for Eveline Mahyère's *Je jure de m'éblouir* (1958). At the end of the novel, not only is the heroine in hospital, neither eating nor sleeping and drinking whisky in secret, but she is waiting for a sign from God. Her one desire is to fly away and disappear. There is no direct mention of suicide, but there does not need to be, as the author killed herself in 1957.

Je jure de m'éblouir takes place over an even shorter period than the three previous novels. It begins in February, when seventeen-year-old Sylvie has been expelled from her convent school because she expressed in a letter her passion for Julienne Bressner, her twenty-five-year-old teacher of mathematics. It ends in July. Julienne, having now entered the convent as a nun, has returned Sylvie's letters unopened. Sylvie engineers one last meeting at a gathering given by Julienne's friends from the time when she was an architecture student. Sylvie is deep in despair and blasphemy; Julienne affirms her choice of belief and religion to Sylvie and, more articulately, to Claude, Sylvie's dear and equally cynical friend and cousin with whom (very unexpectedly, given her character until then) Julienne dances a tango before leaving the party. Next morning Sylvie goes to find Claude, who tells her that there is nothing like deep despair to save one from despair. He sends her away because he is sleepy. She leaves but then buys and takes a stimulant, wanders out into the street, provokes an accident, and wakes up in hospital ...

During the intervening months Sylvie writes constantly ever more deliberately provocative letters to Julienne, always requesting meetings and declaring her love. In various and distant ways Julienne increasingly accedes to the requests; she meets Sylvie, but they never connect in any satisfactory fashion. Both Sylvie and the reader are often left wondering why Sylvie and Julienne met at all, in the light of the palpable levels of discomfort and frustration on both sides.

Gradually it becomes clear that the book is set up as a struggle on two levels. Sylvie is trying to tempt Julienne into loving her and thus becoming as painfully human as Sylvie – who, when the moment finally arrives for her to kiss Julienne and perhaps prevail, cannot bring herself to do so. Sylvie is also struggling to survive despite her bitter cynicism; she is a soul on the edge of despair, challenging and begging Julienne to save her and give meaning to her life. Julienne has chosen faith, hope, and the structures of the Catholic church. Her desire for order is made symbolically clear by her choice of fields of study: first architecture, then mathematics, and finally God. Is her attention to Sylvie an act of charity? is it the last pull of human love? or sin and sexuality? Whether she sees Sylvie as a lost sheep, a lost soul, or the face of temptation is not possible to tell with any certainty. Her final conversation with Claude goes like this: " ... I would like to avenge my cousin. She set out after you as though searching for the Holy Grail, and you have betrayed her. 'What you call my betrayal will perhaps remind her that God suffers no sharing. I am weary of sharing myself between this studio and St. Theresa's [school and convent], Sylvie and my duty, your tangos and my Gregorian chant ...'" (192). She will pray for Claude and Sylvie, she says.

Sylvie claims to see Julienne as the way out of the disorder of her life, whether into sexual love or into love of God, but she pushes Julienne ever further in the demands she makes of her. First she asks that they meet first in a bar and then in Claude's apartment, a seventh-floor walk-up, in the evening. (Julienne outdoes Sylvie by asking to meet her there at 10:30 one night.) Julienne urges Sylvie to aim to pass the *baccalauréat*. Sylvie says that the exam is no use to her and she has no intention of simply conforming to social expectation. When Julienne accuses her of backing off from what is difficult, Sylvie forms the perverse project of failing all the subjects in which she can do well and passing only those for which she has to struggle and work very hard. She sees this as a gift of effort offered to Julienne; Julienne sees the result as grotesque perversity, and it is then that she withdraws from Sylvie, away from the deliberate creation of failure and disorder. She does not know that Sylvie has taken the precaution of checking that she does not need the baccalauréat in order to get into art school and that Sylvie intends to follow Julienne's path at least in its earthly manifestations.

Claude's comment to Julienne would seem to serve as epilogue to the possible futures of Julienne and Sylvie: "You live in your renunciation, I die in my refusal, but the burial will be the same give or take a symbol or two" (195). Eveline Mahyère traces the intensity of the struggle for survival. What is implied by the initial situation – Sylvie's expulsion from the system – but never explored is that the root of Sylvie's disorderly life – her desire for love, for salvation through a woman, and her determination to prove herself unworthy again and again – lies in her lesbianism. To win the love of a nun would demand the ultimate answer: either that she be accepted as she is into God's world or that the nun step away from God into hers. Mahyère does not allow a positive outcome; we must suppose that her own death is the result of the internalized homophobia and despair that mark Sylvie. If this is so, then the novel bears witness to the struggle for the right to be lesbian and a practising Roman Catholic – the right not to be damned. And this struggle is lost as the characters separate into soul and body.

Just as Julienne is unpredictable in her responses to Sylvie, so is Mademoiselle Althia to the narrator of Irène Monési's *Althia* (1957). The intensity of the feelings that Monési invokes makes her novel resemble Leduc's *L'Affamée* and Louvier's *Qui qu'en grogne* and *Je jure de m'éblouir*. However, Monési's narrator is a twenty-eight- or twenty-nine-year-old married woman, mother of two little girls, who, having fallen in love with their dancing teacher, reflects more consciously and differently on her situation than do the adolescent narrators. "I intended to love her in secret. It went without saying that even if she learned about this love one day she would give me no return: she must have been so loved by better loving people than I, who was already married, had children, and, *it just occurred to me, who was a woman*. A shared love seemed to me to be impossible" (28). We see that this narrator is thinking as a heterosexual and assumes her love to be impossible, whereas the other novels approach the possibility from the other side, struggling against the supposed heterosexuality of the beloved.

The narrator tells her husband about her new love, and he remains supportive to her throughout the period of her connection with Althia, so that even when she does have thoughts of suicide she sets them aside and makes a decision not to despair.

Throughout the novel there is no suggestion of any thought of a sexual connection between the narrator and Althia. Tenderness is the major mode, and there is much kissing, touching of face and arms, burying heads in the other's shoulders on the days when Althia is welcoming. She is absolutely unpredictable, alternating between coldness and gentle sweetness and concern – much like Julienne Bressner. And just as behind Julienne stands a vigilant elderly nun, so in the background of Althia's life is an older woman, described as having been her only friend for thirty years, who seems to determine Althia's responses and to control all access to Althia. The implication is that she is a jealous lover who has not received love or sexual response from Althia either and who, while protecting Althia for her art, guards her from any other possible love.

The underlying structure of the novel carries reminders of the patterns of *La Fille aux yeux d'or*, except that here the would-be lover is also a woman. Indeed, at the very end of *Althia* the narrator sees the colour of her beloved's eyes for the first time: "the sun made them transparent, they shone, golden, sweet and tawny like a honeycomb" (186). And they are golden. The reader is now free to assume that Solange Dechauvry has been holding Althia prisoner to her desire for many years, that Althia's tendernesses towards the narrator were not feigned but that Althia could see no way to escape and so ends their relationship. The novel draws to a close with a curious reference to "physiological or glandular instability. Any psychiatrist will fix that" (181), which appears not to be ironic but rather to show the numbed state of the narrator, who sees herself separated from her life.

Unsatisfied and unsatisfactory passion is the mark of these novels of hopeless love. The unspoken undercurrent is that the loves are unacceptable and also that the lovers have no right to them. There is no analysis or explicit contextualization by the authors, however, to show whether this unacceptability is social and cultural or internalized. Most of the novels do not name it as homophobia or even identify it as difference. They are stories of intensity, passion, and pain that fit into our historic understanding of the postwar, post-occupation period in France but that are not marked in any specific way as lesbian, except by the sex of the lover and beloved and by the unrelenting awareness – an inheritance perhaps of literary tradition – that these loves cannot flourish.

When the love does flourish, as in Clarisse Francillon's *La Lettre* (The Letter, 1958), the heroine is dead at the beginning of the novel and her love is told in retrospect. Such a narrative strategy is safe in a way that the others would not have been, because the reader knows that a dead lesbian is not a threat to heterosexuality and she may thus be allowed a little more space and more sexual satisfaction.

La Lettre rings true in a way that the previous novels do not. Rather than creating high drama with little material context, *à la Racine*, Francillon presents a life that has been lived, and the reader feels the difference in the rightness of the emotional, physical, and material details that are gradually revealed.

The novel begins when Renée has been drowned in Spain and her family – brothers, sisters, sisters-in-law – are dividing up her belongings. One of them finds a letter written the last night she was alive: "There's a wild wind blowing so hard that the house might fly away. I'm thinking of you all the time, I want to take you in my arms and I love you. Renée" (19). They destroy it. The story goes into flashback, and we learn about Renée's past in Paris. It is interspersed with memories of Spain and her love for Monserrat, which was full of ups and downs until Renée's sudden departure for Spain because "I don't think I shall make it without her" (262).

There is an epilogue in which Monserrat goes to Paris to see Jacques, Renée's favourite brother. After her visit the family discusses various subjects, including the problem that their father has in dealing with Renée's lesbianism and the letter again. The novel ends with an affirmation: "She loved her" (280).

Francillon's is the first modern French novel to include lesbian lovemaking that has real physical components. The author breaks new ground with descriptions such as: "putting off the moment of touching, separating the lower lips with her fingers, going further, searching, finding a damp point, following the secret furrow then penetrating gently with infinite precautions into even more secret places and staying there and reaching the far depths which offer her their warmth, their sea anemone magic" (201).

The author gives no sign of internalized homophobia in either the presentation or the content of her story. (Renée's father has a problem understanding her way of life, and there is one reference to the attitude of French society.) It is the first novel to have real lesbian couples where both lovers know and accept their sexuality. None the less it is clearly not yet conceivable to create an ongoing lesbian couple in a novel, nor can the freedom to love be situated in France, so the events occur in a holiday place, surrounded by an unexpected complicity on the part of the parents of Monserrat and her previous lover, Trini. Renée's family and work friends know that she is lesbian, but they know nothing about her life, and nobody meets her lovers. All the information becomes known only after Renée's death, so that in some sense she is exposed like a specimen in a laboratory or a little piece of history, rather than being offered as a social possibility.

La Lettre is the first French novel that gives a clear sense of being focused on specific lesbian experience lived in a real human, material, and social context, written by an author who understands that lesbians have lives and who can transmit that sense of actuality to her readers. Francillon's lesbians are not stereotypes, clichés, or obsessives in crisis, nor are they living in fantasy. This integration of lesbian experience into human experience in a moderate, sensitive, and realistic way marks a huge step in the depiction of the lesbian in the French novel. It is a step that will not have a sequel until Jocelyne François begins to publish in the 1970s. As far as I have been able to determine, it is the only one of Francillon's novels with a lesbian theme.

THE 1960S: BISEXUAL FREEDOMS

Reading chronologically, as I am for this study, I am quite amazed at how utterly tones and attitudes shift from one decade to the next. The novels of the 1950s were passionate, intense, and despairing. The (unlabelled) lesbian heroines focused completely on one (impossible) love. Then, from one year to the next it would seem, solitary hope and persistence are exchanged for serial sexual relationships, only some of which are between women, and for power relations in which implied lesbianism is only one of the contextualizing factors. Perhaps the pain and turmoil of the postwar period in France were characteristic also of lesbian writing, and with the coming of the 1960s lesbians, like everyone else, began to think in terms of sexual freedom and refusal of authority.

However, cultural time was not yet ripe for the exploration of lesbian sexual freedom, free of the repressive authority of a heavily heterosexual society. So, just as in 1890, when the ferment of first-wave feminism in France had to be contained within the structures of marriage because no woman could earn enough to live alone and survive with time to spare for activism, in 1960 the sexual revolution for lesbians had first to find expression in terms of bisexuality and triangular relationships.

Thus traditional forms are used to sanction new possibilities. Lesbianism has been acceptable in the French novel as long as the women are together either under the eye of some male observer or waiting for a male (be it that he is absent or that the females are not yet old enough for him to be present). Triangular relationships are also a staple of these novels of the 1960s. However, in traditional heterosexist novels the male has usually kept his two females apart – husband and wife, adulterer and mistress – whereas these novels from the 1960s are essentially bisexual, with two women making the primary sexual connection, which includes a man either directly or indirectly. Setting the works of Violette Leduc aside for the moment, I have found no novel, until *Les Guérillères* (Female Guerrilla Warriors, 1969), by Monique Wittig, which offers as a possibility for the literary imagination a lesbian space or even a female space free of the male gaze.

The first novel of the decade, Claire Vallier Hatvany's *Solitude à trois* (Three Alone, 1961) is a sparsely written tale, and in that way it resembles its predecessors. As its title makes abundantly clear, however, it is a novel with a triangular structure and energy flow, if not precisely a triangular love affair. Anne, the narrator, engaged to Pierre when the story opens, is attracted to Simon, who shares a living space with and looks just like his sister, Maria. Maria attempts a low-key seduction of Anne, who is seduced by Simon. While she is staying at their country house she realizes how close the brother and sister are and that she has no real chance of getting either of them. She also comes to the belated realization that although she desires Simon, she loves Maria.

It is clear from the beginning that Maria is lesbian. She wears pants (still not usual for women in 1960), she runs her own business, and she looks just like a very attractive man – so much so that she is taken for her brother. (There is no suggestion that he might be taken for her.) She touches Anne in meaningful if not truly suggestive ways and tries to persuade her to take her bathing suit off as they lie by her private lake. Underlying possibilities are implied. The novel is built on Anne's feelings as she pivots between attraction, confusion, denial, and desire. The singlemindedness of the emotional focus and the triangular love relationship make this piece a bridge between the intensity of the 1950s and the sexual promiscuity of the 1960s.

Constrained Desire

Anne Huré's three novels, *Les Deux moniales* (The Two Enclosed Nuns, 1962), *En prison* (In Prison, 1963), and *Le Péché sans merci* (The Unforgivable Sin, 1964) are all built around characters who were in or on the edge of lesbian relationships in their youth, and this is stated quite clearly. The novels then turn to quite different concerns: aspects of the abusive use of male power, discussed quite abstractly and philosophically for the most part. *Le Péché sans merci* is about father-daughter incest. *En prison* is set in a women's prison and includes dealings with male lawyers and the whole androcenric justice and incarceration system in France. Women are seen to be wholly in the power of an institution and of certain men. (As neither of these topics is directly pertinent to my study, I do not discuss these novels here.)

Les Deux moniales has a similar structure to *En prison*, but here the institution is a convent and the men with decision-making power are priests within the Roman Catholic church. In some ways the novel inevitably recalls Diderot's *La Religieuse* because it is set in a misgoverned convent. It would seem that the current abbess, Mère Hildegard, had once been (overly) fond of a younger nun, Mère Stanislas. The latter, an intellectual much in demand by church scholars in Rome, cannot travel without express permission because she is in an enclosed order. Her abbess systematically blocks her opportunities for scholarship and research. It is clear that in Mère Hildegard love has turned to hatred and her governance is overly rigid because of her pride. In short she misuses her power. A young novice, a philosopher trained by and fond of Mère Stanislas, instigates inquiries into the running of the convent. Contrary to the events in *La Religieuse,* however, Soeur St Jean de la Croix comes to admire Mère Hildegard's misguided nobility, and harmony is restored between Mère Hildegard and Mère Stanislas.

The whole novel is built on the concept of love in the wrong context, homophobia, and guilt. The resulting misuse of power creates an intimacy of anger and hatred that compensates for the loss of a tender and positive relationship. And it does serve to maintain an intense connection between the two nuns over many years – and the reader's knowledge of *La Religieuse* adds a level of intertextuality to what is otherwise a rather cerebral novel.

The rest of the novels of the 1960s that have lesbian characters are physical in focus. They include works by a number of new names – Irma Dupont, Albertine Sarrazin, Emmanuelle Arsan, and Anne Vilmont, as well as by known authors Christiane Rochefort, Suzanne Allen, and Irène Monési. Descriptions of lovemaking abound now, but lovers are merely named and their characteristics listed. For the most part they have no role outside the bedroom and are not around long enough to develop in any way. The lovemaking itself is recorded in much greater detail than before – high on sensation and low on sentiment.

Irma Dupont's *Le Cheroub* (The Cheroub, 1962)[2] tells the story of a young woman who wants to be a boy. She has her first sexual experience at fourteen. The novel opens on the morning of her wedding day when she is in bed with a woman lover. It then unfolds as a sort of female *Bildungsroman*. "Sensuality was not yet something I chose but the very essence of my activity" (103), she states at one point. Then again: "I bent towards her, close to the nape of her neck, as though the temptation to plant my lips there made me dizzy. Habit had created in me the reflexes of a seducer that it didn't occur to me to control. I gave in to them quite naturally, hoping to find at the end the climate of passion that I believed to be absolutely necessary to my life" (154). And there we have it – the novels of the decade concern themselves with "the climate of passion that [the heroine] believes to be indispensable" if she is to feel alive.

Christiane Rochefort's *Les Stances à Sophie* (Stanzas to Sophie, 1963) offers the most interesting development of the theme. Céline, the narrator, has energy, perspicacity, and humour. Her descriptions of bourgeois attitudes and life are ironic in the extreme. Married against her (subconscious) will – she realizes as she walks into the church for the wedding that she is dressed in an outfit suitable only for a funeral – she tries to fit into her new middle-class context, then rebels, and finally escapes. In the midst of all the hollow platitudes, facades, and emotional void, Céline connects with her husband's best friend's wife, Julia, the only character who is not playing a role. They warm each other with support, fun, laughter, outrageousness, and lovemaking. Then Julia dies in a car crash because her husband is trying to outdrive everyone in his new vehicle. The novel is mostly a criticism of middle-class, upwardly mobile male attitudes, ego, competitiveness, and insensitivity.

The short scenes in which the women are alone together serve as contrast. They show an alternative way of being in which women can flourish. The hope that it offers is immediately denied by the death of Julia before she and Céline can come to the (obvious) conclusion that they are much better off together than they are in their marriages, despite the manner in which they have trained themselves to be professional wives in terms of strategies of self-protection, active exploitation of their husbands, and material gain for themselves. Julia and Céline have the most complete lesbian connection of any in these triangulated novels, although it is not in any way named as such. Their passion is for life in all its richness.

Suzanne Allen sets up a different triangle in *Le Lieu commun* (The Common Place, 1966). This novel, recounted by the wife in an "open" marriage, focuses primarily on sex. After much reflection on her marriage and her husband's mistress, much reminiscence over her own male lovers, the wife decides that she will find passion in joining her husband and his mistress in their lovemaking. Instead of offering Geneviève to Pierre by her acceptance of the relationship, she will actually prepare and offer the young woman and take physical part in a triangulated relationship. Two women there may be, but this is not a lesbian connection. Both women – wife and mistress – are interested only in the relationship between the husband and the mistress.

The connections between women in Albertine Sarrazin's *L'Astragale* (The Anklebone, 1965), the semi-autobiographical story of a delinquent teenager, with survival as its theme, centre on men in a similar way. Even more so do the women described by Emmanuelle Arsan. In *Emmanuelle* (1967) (and all her subsequent novels) Arsan certainly describes lesbian sex, but she writes purely for titillation of any and all readers. As in licentious novels of the eighteenth century, encounters between females serve simply as variations on the unchanging theme of seduction and conquest. The women thus displayed are objects for voyeuristic pleasure and have no existence outside the sexual experience described.

Anne Vilmont's *Les Drosères* (Venus Flytraps, 1968) is similar; it begins as a slightly less deliberately scandalous and better-written version of *Emmanuelle*. Then suddenly, towards the end of the novel, the narrator, Suzanne, settles with Ariel (the woman whom she has compared to a venus flytrap), and they become a couple. Suzanne claims to love Ariel as a man loves his woman, and questions of budget, projects, faithfulness, and a "wedding" ring are raised. Heterosexual as these words may be, the statement they make is important, because this is the first time in a French novel that two acknowledged lesbians see themselves as a couple and an author depicts them as such: "We were an authentic couple, indissoluble, imprudently formed, whereas we should have fled, made as we were too well for each other" (213). The text then shifts into psychological analysis of the type mentioned briefly at the end of Monési's *Althia* (1957).

The attribution of bad heredity to the lesbian character was a staple until 1926. In writing by women the same assumption recurs occasionally, as for example in *Le Cheroub* (1962). A troubled childhood is the more modern alternative to "bad birth," and it, together with social homophobia, appears unambiguously at the end of *Les Drosères*: "I had to admit ... that I was in a couple with a woman; that troubled childhoods had caused it, and that now that we had finally emerged from the blind quietude in which our love had kept us we would face, perhaps for life, the weight of our deformity" (213).

Les Drosères offers a lesbian couple as a possibility for the reader. Both women survive the end of the book, together, with plans for a joint future. Disadvantaged they may expect to be, but not destroyed. The author uses the term "the weight of a deformity," thus marking her characters as different and limited in some respect, in a relationship that requires explanation and social tolerance, but not as objects of persecution or victims of some mortal or divine punishment. They may not be made quite like other people, but they are not sinners damned by nineteenth-century expectations.

Une tragédie superflue (A Superfluous Tragedy, 1968), by Irène Monési, is also the story of couples – but couples that do not last, in part at least because of Florence's inadequate childhood. Florence, married to an older man and mother of two young children, is asked by her employer to write the biography of a famous actress,

Lili Leventis, whose career is more or less over. Florence becomes so fascinated by Lili (whose real name is Georgia) that she neglects her family and moves out of the family home in order not to be distracted from her increasing obsession. She seeks in Georgia the mothering that she never had.

Georgia is interested not in Florence, but only in her project. She continues to see her but finds her boring. Georgia's only experience of love and desire is sexual, and she does not see what Florence wants from her, because she assumes that the younger woman must be feeling sexual attraction. Georgia talks at first in the negative – that she has no intention of making love with Florence. Then she does make love to her. The sexual contact breaks Florence's fascination with the older woman. She does not want a lover, she wants a mother substitute who will give her permission to claim and grow into her own life. As Georgia wants more connection with Florence, Florence draws away. At the end Florence is alone. The tragedy of the title is hers; she created it, and she lived it. The lovemaking between the women is an important part of Florence's journey, but it has as its purpose the negating of any lesbianism and therefore any possibility of life as a couple for Georgia and Florence.

CONCLUSION

As the 1960s drew to a close, most writers still considered reciprocated lesbian love in a stable relationship inconceivable. In 1946 Célia Bertin had postulated a long-term relationship in *La Parade des impies*, but there was no equality of love in it. No author followed in her footsteps. The novels of the 1950's are full of adolescent fervour, impossible love, and very little physical contact. Those of the 1960s offer liberated sex and little love. The fervour moves from emotional to physical sensation, and the writing comes to include descriptions of passionate lovemaking, but there is still no sense of any space where women can love together as partners and complex human beings, living within a context where they can sometimes be alone and can expect to survive unpunished for avoiding male presence, gaze, and control. The step of being oblivious to the male gaze is as yet inconceivable.

The only writer besides Clarisse Francillon (*La Lettre*) who transmits a real sense of lesbian existence in the period from 1929 to 1968 is Violette Leduc. She is interesting for her life, her autobiography, her literary situation, and her writing style. The challenge that she poses leads directly to the theorizing of Monique Wittig and Hélène Cixous and the beginnings of contemporary attitudes to lesbianism in French literature as we see in the next chapter.

CHAPTER FOUR

Contrasting Generations:
Leduc and Beauvoir, Wittig and Cixous

The authors discussed in this chapter are writers of greater sophis-
tication and skill, in purely literary terms, than any of the women
presented to date, except Colette. As a result, my analysis of their
novels is more developed. The comparisons that I make situate the
texts within the literary history of the French novel, as well as
within the history of lesbian issues in French. The two lines of
development intersect a little more frequently as time goes on, but
really good writers, male or female, are always rare. In fact, the
generation born early in the century was remarkable, giving us, in
order of birth, Yourcenar, Leduc, Beauvoir, Galzy, Audry, and
Aurivel. That born just before the 1939–45 war was also extraordinary, including as it did Wittig, Cixous, Best, François, Monferrand, Causse, and Eaubonne, and producing second-wave feminism. In part III of this book, Audry, Aurivel, and Galzy figure
again in chapter 5, and chapter 6 deals extensively with Best,
François, and Monferrand. The present chapter makes visible connections between two important groups of women from the different generations.

LEDUC AND BEAUVOIR

Five years younger than Marguerite Yourcenar,[1] one year older
than Simone de Beauvoir,[2] Violette Leduc (1907–1972) is in many
ways the shadow side of both of them. She is the voice of what they
refuse to make audible in their own works, and yet without Beauvoir Leduc would have remained perhaps silent and certainly
unheard. Beauvoir encouraged her, edited her writing, and arranged

for Gallimard to publish her works and pay her a small stipend. I find myself thinking that Beauvoir, at least subconsciously aware of the denials and suppression in her own writing and the rationalization of her own life in her autobiography, helped Leduc take on all the elements of unreason so that they should not vanish, but yet remain separate from Beauvoir, embodied in the material form of her disturbed and disadvantaged friend and *doppelgänger*.

Beauvoir and Yourcenar grew up in a climate of respectability and taboo. They were marked by family silences; their lives and careers manifest their struggles to take a place in the world. Yourcenar (a pseudonym) published her works in France and wrote about historical Europe and homosexual men, while living in North America. So far distanced from her roots was she that she and her female partner lived for years on an island off the coast of Maine, in literal as well as metaphoric isolation. To her dying day she denied that her feelings for her friend were those of lesbian love. Meanwhile she explored and depicted male homosexuality in those cultural periods when such relationships were common and accepted for men who wielded real power. Clearly, for Yourcenar, female homosexuality was not respectable in the same way, and it had to remain distanced from all aspects of her public persona and her creative work. When her archives are opened, it will be fascinating to see whether in her intimate exchanges she did indeed express a love that was lesbian or whether she was homophobic and constrained. The question to be explored is whether the transfer in her creative imagination from lesbian experience to male homosexual narrative frees or impoverishes her writing. The circumstances remind me of Proust's creation of Albertine.

Beauvoir's posthumous papers and Bianca Lamblin's memoirs have revealed clearly Beauvoir's bisexuality.[3] Thus her love for Zaza and the implicit lesbian relations in *L'Invitée* (She Came to Stay, 1943), which antedate the androcentric triangle that dominates the novel, come into fresh focus. In all of Beauvoir's fictional writing the female characters have presence, colour, and energy, while the males are flat, grey, overly discursive, and rhetorical: living bodies and talking heads. It is obvious to the reader that Beauvoir observed what was going on around her with the rational and precise interest of a sociologist but that she was also an avid watcher of women in their specificity.

In *Le Deuxième Sexe* (The Second Sex, 1949)[4] she presents lesbianism as a choice and acknowledges the potentially political nature of that decision as a choice against women's domination by men in ways that foreshadow the separatist lesbian feminism of the 1970s. She writes, as a true existentialist, that every choice is a new one to be measured according to its authenticity, not according to its "normality": "Homosexuality can be for woman a mode of flight from her situation or a way of accepting it. The great mistake of the psychoanalysts is, through moralistic conformity, to regard it as never other than an inauthentic attitude" (II, 172; trans. 453).[5]

In true French tradition she sees female homosexuality as "a stage, an apprenticeship, a girl who engages in it most ardently may well become tomorrow the most ardent of wives, mistresses, or mothers" (II, 174; trans. 455). For Beauvoir the lesbian becomes lesbian when her taste for women is exclusive – and such a definition would eliminate just about every novel in this book so far!

What Beauvoir does make very clear is that whenever a woman behaves in ways that are considered normal human behaviour in a man she is said to be unfeminine/non-female and identifying with the male. No one before her had analysed the extent to which the requirements of femininity mutilated women. The crucial question, according to Beauvoir, as she turns the discussion from lesbians to heterosexual women, is why most women put up with the limitations and degradations involved in being a heterosexual woman. She sees it as quite understandable that some women find lesbianism a more relaxing choice: "Among women artists and writers there are many lesbians. The point is not that their sexual peculiarity is the source of the creative energy [...] it is rather that, being absorbed in serious work, they do not propose to waste time in playing a feminine role or in struggling with men. Not admitting male superiority, they do not wish to make a pretense of recognizing it or to weary themselves in contesting it. They are looking for relaxation, appeasement, and diversion in sexual pleasure: they do better to avoid a partner who appears in the guise of an adversary" (II, 178; trans. 459).

Lesbianism is relaxing, according to Beauvoir, because women's love is "contemplative," as each seeks to re-create herself rather than gain possession of the other. There is a total lack of boundaries, and identities meld as "each is at once subject and object" and "duality becomes mutuality" (II, 184; trans 465). The lesbian is similar to the mother "in the degree to which both are narcissistic, enamored respectively in the child or the woman friend, each of her own projection or reflection" (II, 185; trans. 465).

Beauvoir goes on to look at environmental circumstances and other factors in choice, deciding that one should not distinguish sharply between lesbian and heterosexual because heterosexual women often return to the loves – platonic or not – that have enchanted their youth. "The truth is that homosexuality is no more a perversion deliberately indulged in than it is a curse of fate. It is an attitude *chosen in a certain situation* – that is, at once motivated and freely adopted" (II, 192; trans 473).

Beauvoir thus presents lesbianism as an ever-open option chosen from a place of basic heterosexuality, because although she sees it as a choice and woman as a social construct – "One is not born but rather becomes a woman" (II; 13, trans. 301) – she does not challenge heterosexuality or analyse it in any way. Is this another of these moments, with her theories coming too close to those parts of her life that she does not wish to examine, when Beauvoir ceases to think like a philosopher and veers into blindness caused by denial? The book is full of such moments, having been written, I am quite sure, as a way of distancing her own mid-life crisis. Instead of analysing herself, Beauvoir found it easier or more acceptable to write a description of the condition of womankind. (Most of us work on a smaller scope!)

So Beauvoir dissociates herself from her own lesbianism, much as Yourcenar does, by writing from a distance. She does, however, theorize the possibility of lesbianism as an authentic choice. Meanwhile she presents herself as a heterosexual who gives a higher priority to a partnership of the mind than to sexual relations. It is only after her death and Sartre's that the extent of his philandering and her lesbian engagement with younger women find confirmation in their posthumously published papers and in Lamblin's writings, mentioned above.

Yourcenar hid in another culture, Beauvoir hid behind Sartre, and both maintained a silence in their fiction. Social acceptability and a desire to take their places in the androcentric traditions of French literature and thought no doubt shaped their choices. Meanwhile Violette Leduc embodies all the taboos, and Beauvoir supports her in the struggles that she herself has chosen not to take on.

When I think about Violette Leduc's position with regard to those writers contemporary to herself, with whom she was acquainted, the pattern presents itself in the conformation in Diagram 5.

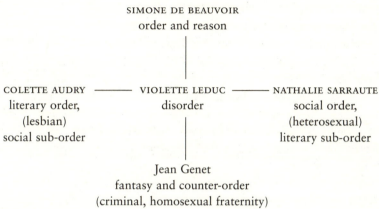

Diagram 5

Beauvoir represents containment and reason, work, discipline, facts, accuracy, clarity, and the absence of sex. She is a mentor, model, and love object for Violette Leduc, a good but distant "mother" to the growing author. She expresses both intellectual and social order. Audry, by her lesbianism, subverts social order but does not write about it at this time.[6] As a philosopher, like Beauvoir, she represents reason and rationality, as well as silence.

Nathalie Sarraute is Audry's counterbalance. Socially acceptable in terms of her heterosexuality, Sarraute writes about all the sub-order, counter-order, and disorder that lurk under silence and behind the façades of social intercourse.[7] Her writing resembles that of Violette Leduc both in style and to a degree in context. Leduc, like Sarraute, sees the subtext in any situation, and that is what they both express in language. They write about everything that order, reason, and social respectability seek to contain. Sarraute remains within the bounds of the respectable while making audible that which is not said. Leduc, focused on her own psychological neediness, breaks those bounds as she writes her pain, her resentment, and fantasies of love and violence. The writing of both

Sarraute and Leduc moves back and forth between precise and luminous observation of minute details of reality and the wanderings of memory and imagination.

If they fit anywhere in the canon of French literature, Violette Leduc's novels belong on the edge of the Nouveau Roman (New Novel) by the way they are written,[8] while her depiction of the isolation, despair, and struggle that mark the human condition would place her with the existentialists.[9]

To come back to my diagram, however, it seems to me that Genet and Leduc are both manifestations of the scandalous.[10] Both are outsiders, both provoke discomfort and create disorder, but because Genet is male, albeit homosexual and criminal, he can use social structures to construct for himself a counter-order. He creates a society of homosexual men with their own codes and hierarchies based on sex and fantasy, within which he finds support, satisfaction, and status.

Association with the scandalous marginalizes women differently. Whereas Genet moves into prison society, Leduc's illegitimate birth, troubled childhood, lack of success, and lesbianism lead her into isolation and periods of insanity. She does not create another order but rather manifests its failure. She writes the failed side of Sarraute's characters. She lives a failed version of Audry's life. She is the shadow side of Beauvoir, without whom she would probably have faded away.

Her works, be they the volumes of autobiography or the novels, explore the process of the act of writing as she re-creates herself in it. In the re-creation of the immediacy of every circumstance from masturbation to mental disorder, presented with no judgment, no context, no boundaries, she forces the reader to observe all her activities. In this way her writing is a constant process of coming out. She comes out as a lover, as illegitimate, as unloved, as ugly, as lesbian, as rejected.

In the process of coming out she oscillates between the risk of the confession and her determination to be noticed and to make her experience known, between her desire for legitimacy, with its assimilation into society, and rebellion, with its defiance of society's strictures. She presents herself as sad clown, and she fantasizes anger and violence. The only control that she appears to have is as an actress in charge of her performance in a play/life over which she has no control.

Leduc became known in 1964 for the first volume of her autobiography *La Bâtarde* (The Bastard). She had previously published two novels *L'Asphyxie* (Asphyxiation, 1946) and *L'Affamée* (The Starving Woman, 1948), the story of an impossible love for a distant woman whom the narrator calls "Madame." This novel is modelled on Leduc's relation with Simone de Beauvoir and her desire for greater intimacy with her. All of Leduc's main themes are present here already: presence and absence; aggression and tenderness; imagination and nothingness; desire for attention and sense of inadequacy; demand for attention and withdrawal into isolation.

Thérèse et Isabelle (1966), together with *Ravages* (Devastation, 1955), is the only other novel with lesbian characters. (She wrote *Thérèse et Isabelle* as the prologue to *Ravages*, but Gallimard cut it, despite vehement protest by Beauvoir. *Thérèse et Isabelle* appeared separately in 1966.) *Thérèse et Isabelle* opens in the toilets of a girl's boarding school, where Thérèse is waiting for Isabelle in one of the stalls. They make love to the accompaniment of comings, goings, and flushing lavatories. This is the first time Isabelle calls Thérèse "mon amour," and the term is a dangerous one. "'My love.' Isabelle was coming from the country of meteors, upheavals, fires and devastation. She threw me a liberated word, a programme [...] She's waiting for me but that isn't security. The word she has said is too strong. We look at each other, we're paralysed. I threw myself into her arms" (8).

Then come the first descriptions of lovemaking, where natural images serve as metaphors to evoke the pleasures of the body, where the power of the image-making and the pleasures of the female body are interrelated to re-create the immediacy and transient nature of passion. "I was looking at her, I was remembering her in the present, I had her beside me from last moment to last moment. When one is in love, one is always on a railway platform" (9).

The novel tells the story of several days of uncontrollable, unbridled adolescent sexual fervour in which the two girls make love all night long and in every possible corner of their days until they are abruptly separated by Thérèse's being called home: "I loved Isabelle without gestures, without outbursts; I offered her my life without showing a sign. Isabelle sat up, she took me in her arms: 'You'll come every evening?' 'Every evening.' 'We won't leave each other?'

'We won't leave.' The next month my mother took me back. I never saw Isabelle again" (120).

The pattern is set. Love is total and doomed. It is forbidden, dangerous, and transitory. The memories are in the body, and the body becomes text. This way of writing prefigures some of the work of Monique Wittig, as we see below. It also reminds me of the novels of the non-lesbian writer Jeanne Hyvrard by its total focus on the author-narrator's self, her relationship with her mother and her lover and by the despair expressed through the same intimate relation between body and text.[11]

Isabelle is the risk-taker, and Thérèse is anxious. The scene in which they rent a room for the afternoon and Thérèse is paralysed by the certainty that they are being observed and overheard foreshadows one in *Ravages* in which Cécile tries to persuade Thérèse to join her in bed and Thérèse resists, sure that Marc is listening under the window.

Ravages continues the telling of Thérèse's life by recounting the failure of two of her relationships – with Cécile and with Marc. The novel is constructed in three parts. First we see the meeting with Marc and the establishment of their connection at a time when Cécile lives away from Paris and Thérèse sees her only at weekends. In part II, Cécile and Thérèse are living together. The relationship is shaky because Thérèse is being kept by Cécile and is bored. Marc arrives one day and upsets the fragile equilibrium of the couple, as he demands Thérèse's attention. He leaves and falls seriously ill. Part III is the failure of Thérèse's marriage to Marc.

Cécile is a teacher, solvent, responsible, patient, and loving. She takes care of Thérèse and strives to eliminate pain and upset from their lives. She is dependable and stable and asks nothing more than to meet Thérèse's needs – the first lesbian whom we have met who maintains a non-anguished and non-dysfunctional way of life as if such were her right in the world. Her care and caring are maternal rather than sexual ,and this would appear to be what Leduc and her female characters desire: a good mother.

Marc is poor, irresponsible, weak, alternately demanding and inadequate, aggressive and tender. He insists on paying for things way beyond his means, for which Thérèse feels she must then pay with emotional care and sexual favours. He is needy in every sense of the word. With Marc, Thérèse is the good mother.

What we see here is not only a barely fictional exploration of Leduc's own experiences but also a classic example of dysfunctional behaviour. Leduc, as we know from her autobiography, adored her mother. Her mother was always emotionally distant but required her daughter's physical presence whenever the current man in her life was not beside her. The full meaning of "my mother took me back" at the end of *Thérèse et Isabelle* becomes clear in this context – and we see the Thérèse of the opening chapters of *Ravages* struggling for some semblance of adult life. Indeed her connection with Marc in the first place – making contact with her neighbour in the cinema in the hope that he would follow up on her advance – was a deliberate gesture towards self-liberation, as well as a risk and provocation of danger. Her mother approves the weekends with Cécile, overtly because the relationship protects her daughter against pregnancy, but implicitly because she does not see another woman as any impediment to her own control over her daughter. After all, she took her away from her love for Isabelle.

Leduc, in all her texts, and Thérèse, her narrator here, are desperate for love, but because of the underlying bond to the unsatisfactory mother the pattern that is established is a destructive one. It is shaped by an oscillation between the need to be accepted and the need to be noticed. Given the mother's behaviour, acceptance necessarily requires assimilation into the life of the beloved to the extent of having no life of one's own. Such annihilation of self produces a sense of loss of identity, which is compensated for by a defiant stand of some kind and a reactive choice to reject the situation of acceptance. This kind of choice tends to create the reciprocal of the original situation, so that the assimilated person accepts someone even needier and less stable than herself in order to be in control.

Ravages is built on this model. In a stand against her mother, Thérèse connects with Marc. Marc is not prepared to let go of her. Thérèse cannot keep a sense of identity when there is no claim on her, and so when she has no work and is living at home, well looked after by Cécile, she loses all sense of self. Cécile is healthy, self-sufficient, and reasonable. She loves Thérèse enough to give her space and freedom. She offers generosity, and Thérèse cannot accept it. Marc is volatile. Thérèse is drawn to his pain. To feel alive she has to feel urgently needed. Her only power over Isabelle, then over Cécile, was to keep each of them waiting when she was at the peak of sexual desire. Failure and separation are essential elements in her life. She has no experience of or model for happiness, autonomy, trust, or the continuation of love. She is always too close to or too far away from the person she desires, withdrawing or demanding attention.

By the patterns of her work, Violette Leduc writes the ongoing reality of many lesbian lives: either closeted (withdrawing) or "in society's face" (demanding attention), moving from relationship to relationship, expecting each to be transitory, and choosing again and again the dysfunctional patterns of childhood, which frequently have their origin in some sense of rejection and inadequacy created by the mother. In the patterns of her own life we see that Leduc also embodied many of the elements of the mythical literary lesbian of the nineteenth century: bad birth (illegitimacy and a philandering father), troubled childhood, discomforting physical appearance (she is reported to have been strikingly ugly or striking and ugly, according to the reaction of the person describing her), elegance, and incipient madness.

Leduc is an important figure in the history of lesbianism in France. She does not theorize her position but poses a challenge both to culture and to literature by her way of being and of writing. There is an urgency, a despair, and a luminous presence in her texts that precipitate the reader into her experience in the moment.

It would be interesting to compare her autobiography with Simone de Beauvoir's in terms of strategies of representation, inclusion, and silences. The one is an exercise in objectivity – a public reflection – the other an eruption of subjectivity, an embodiment of experience. Isabelle de Courtivron suggests that Leduc's whole body of work, read as one text, is a quest to sanctify Beauvoir that actually becomes a mystic pilgrimage leading to Leduc's acknowledgment of herself as writer.[12] Hence she achieved identity and purpose as writing became a place of choices in a life of existential exile.

Leduc holds a significant place as the first self-declared lesbian writer in the history of the French novel. The intertextuality of her autobiography and her fictions makes visible the drama of her lesbian experience within her wider exploration of the pain of marginality in texts such as *La Vieille Fille et la mort* (The Spinster and Death, 1958) and *La Femme au petit renard* (The Woman with the Little Fox Fur, 1965). The last text published in her lifetime, *Le Taxi* (1971), is a statement of the deliciousness of forbidden love-making that can be read as a comment both on Leduc's attitude to her own sexuality and also, once again, on the excitement of taking risks and on the transitory nature of passion. The entire novel is a conversation between a brother and sister as they make love for hours in a taxi that they prepared for this purpose. They have desired each other for years and have no intention of coming together in this way again. The book can and perhaps should be read as a companion piece to *Thérèse et Isabelle*. It is certainly a metaphor of the taboos and silences that marked Leduc's generation and also of the scandalous, of the crossing of forbidden frontiers, of the denial of boundaries in love.

WITTIG AND CIXOUS

Leduc breaks through silences into language even though her images are ones of secrecy. She writes the forbidden moment in all its immediacy. She inscribes the lesbian body into literature, and in doing so she marks and makes the transition between the literature of the traditional perversion, unrealizable love, and despair, which persisted until 1960, and contemporary writing of lesbian experience and the theorizing of female sexuality (homo and bi), which begins in the works of Monique Wittig and Hélène Cixous, born some thirty years after Leduc. Leduc forms the bridge between the old world and the new. She began to publish in 1948, became famous in 1964, and died in 1972. Monique Wittig's *Les Guérillères* (The Guerilla Warrior Women) and Hélène Cixous's *Dedans* (Inside), which begin the speaking out on public and private levels, appeared in 1969.

Between the two generations lie May 1968 and the political events, starting at the Sorbonne and extending into French cultural and economic institutions, that brought second-wave feminism to the fore briefly in France. General social upheaval created a climate that permitted more freedom to writers in general, from which lesbian writers profited, together with their heterosexual peers.

Monique Wittig was the only French theorist of lesbianism to emerge within the field of literature, however. To this day she is the only French lesbian writer of fiction to associate herself with radical politics and to offer an analysis of the social context of lesbianism and social homophobia that breaks down the framework of pathology/monstrosity and private sexuality set up in the nineteenth century. That she now lives in the United States would seem to be a comment on her view of the state of feminism and lesbian awareness in France and on the gap between her writing and that of her contemporaries in France.

Simone de Beauvoir was pulled into second-wave feminism as a result of English and American interest in *The Second Sex*. Her role was mainly one of mentor and figurehead. She did nothing specific to reposition lesbianism in relation to French feminism, although she took part in the setting of its social and political agenda.

Hélène Cixous, together with Luce Irigaray and Julia Kristeva, was involved in the group called "Politique et Psychanalyse" (Politics and Psychoanalysis), which some circles considered synonymous with the French Women's Liberation Movement (MLF). The internal struggles of both "Psych et Po" and "MLF" were many, complicated, and varied, but they had little impact on subjects at issue in this study of lesbians in literature.

Lesbian groups that did form, particularly after the creation in 1971 of the Front Homosexuel d'Action Révolutionnaire (FHAR, the Homosexual Front for Revolutionary Action, a male organization), remained local and have left little trace of their activity. The belief that male power over women was rooted in male control over female sexuality was one of the key issues of French second-wave feminism, but the debate has remained almost exclusively hetero and bisexual and, in the period covered by this chapter, had not noticeably changed the nature of social institutions or the circumstances of lesbian experience.[13] Interrelations, modes of possibility, and networks of reference seem to remain within the very slowly shifting boundaries of literary habit.

Reading and writing chronologically make visible curious and unexpected resemblances and echoes from writer to writer. That Violette Leduc should step forward in literary exploration with Nathalie Sarraute and Marguerite Duras as they move out of strictly rational prose into the evocation of the physical and emotional moment in all its immediacy should not perhaps come as a surprise, given that these women were peers, living in the same intellectual climate, and that difference in sexual choice makes little difference

Contrasting Generations 139

to the way in which these authors evoke emotions in their various writings. That Leduc should prefigure Hyvrard was unexpected, even though the pain of the distanced child as a theme, the emotional intensity of the writing, and the body as text were all known entities. Love and sexuality – heterosexual in Hyvrard's case, homosexual for the most part in Leduc's – overlying the desired love from and for the mother focus the passion of the writing in each case.

That Monique Wittig should write in ways that recall Leduc's prose is perhaps not unexpected, given that Leduc wrote about the lesbian experience at a time when Wittig was herself coming to writing. They share an exquisite awareness of all sensuousness and sensuality and a delight in the rendering of sensations in language that calls all the senses into play. Each of them evokes the natural world in all its variety, both for itself and as metaphor to express feelings of all kinds. Neither uses linear logic consistently, and neither is bound by the traditional patterns for fiction, although Wittig's breaks with the expected are more radical than Leduc's.

Wittig is more political than Leduc or Cixous, and her theorizing is more feminist in the Anglo–American style. None the less, as I think about the writings of Wittig together with those of Cixous, I see similarities that connect them both to Leduc. Both are woman-centred, both are fundamentally poetic writers, fuelled by words, images, and references rather than by ideas, arguments, and rationality. Both challenge the reader and require thought and effort. Both are provocative and subversive of accepted thoughts and attitudes. Both create new forms for fiction. Both challenge male oppression and male occupancy of literary and cultural space. Both see body and text as inseparable. Both begin their writing career with evocations of childhood – Wittig, *L'Opoponax* (1964); Cixous, *Dedans* (1969). Both create a female subject and universalize the feminine in ways that assume a female right to cultural, psychological, and literary space. Their ways of using language, like Leduc's, are deeply female (yet they are different).

The difference between them lies in the direction of their energy. Hélène Cixous, like Leduc, is centred inside herself. Her writing is psychologically based and fundamentally private, despite its quantity. It seems to me that each of her works has its roots in the intuition of some experience in her life that is "unspeakable." In one of her many modes, she circles around the unknown or taboo element until it finally takes form in language and becomes both spoken and speakable. The text then ends, its job accomplished, and Cixous moves on to the next problem and the next psychological and linguistic process, which leads again to herself as centre.

The influence of her early study of the novels of James Joyce is visible in her style[14] – intertextuality, multiplicity, ambiguity, elusiveness – a protean richness particularly for those who recognize her allusions and references. However Joyce's world is homogeneous and knowable to his original public in ways that Cixous's is not, drawing as she does on her Jewish, German, and Algerian experience, as well as her Frenchness.

Cixous's interest is situated mainly in the exploration of desire and sexual difference. She theorizes that patriarchy has repressed the feminine imaginary world and that women should express their sexual nature in writing in order to free themselves from the binary oppositions that structure patriarchal definitions of sexual difference. She posits a bisexuality of gender identity for women and men. Thus "écriture féminine" is the writing of the feminine side of any writer, female or male.

Cixous's search is for a feminine identity in a linguistic world where the male presence is inescapable. In her books she explores the multiplicity of the feminine *per se* in ways that widen any previous inscription of female physical, sexual, and emotional experience. The complexity and extent of her fictional universe put her work beyond the scope of this volume. *Illa* (That One, 1980), *La* (The [feminine], 1976), and *Le Livre de Promethea* (Promethea's Book, 1983) are perhaps the works of most direct interest, treating as they do "the possibility of a relationship of intersubjective identification."[15]

Cixous theorizes the breakdown of binary notions of sexual difference and writing, and in so doing she deconstructs heterosexuality by creating convergence, overlap, and crossover between the feminine and the masculine. Wittig challenges heterosexuality and patriarchal structures differently; she creates more separation by dividing women and lesbians into separate categories, claiming that the term "woman" is so imbued with heterosexual characteristics that it cannot in any way be used to designate lesbian identity.

The result of this divergence is that Cixous universalizes the feminine by bringing both men and women into it in Jungian style. By her use of myth and intertextual references she also deconstructs any notion of a single monolithic entity labelled "the feminine," "woman," or "female [heterosexual] sexuality." However, although her theory and practice challenge some of the clichés and underlying assumptions of patriarchal social structure – and she does call into question the constructed boundaries around gender – she does not address the fundamental issue for lesbians, that of the existence of two categories of sex and gender: woman and man. Be they purely heterosexual or be they bisexual, they are never one without the other, no matter how much the female subject is privileged in order to exist in im/possible equality with the male in an androcentric system, where the presence of the female is immediately overdetermined.

Wittig universalizes the lesbian by making her the only possible subject in circumstances that are in themselves universal. The usually invisible or marginalized gaze thus becomes the only source of information, giving a twist to the reality perceived by and available to the reader.

One of the early examples of narrative control of this kind is Alain Robbe-Grillet's novel *La Jalousie* (1957), whose title means both "jealousy" and slatted (window) blinds, thus indicating the partial nature of the narrator's vision. Robbe-Grillet and his "New Novelist" colleagues explored the nature of perception in fiction in the 1950s. One of the writers, Nathalie Sarraute, whom I mentioned above, is the subject of study in one of Monique Wittig's theoretical essays, "The Site of Action" (1984).[16] Sarraute is interested in the shifts between the particular and the general that take place behind the commonplaces of conversation – the shifts that cause loss of power or marginalization of the "I" subject when faced with an interlocutor (be that another person or an institutional voice). The struggle for subjecthood is central to Wittig's own interest, and she analyses Sarraute's work at some length to reach the conclusion that the movement from the particular to the general works in the opposite direction in human exchange from the direction defined in scientific inquiry:[17] "since each time 'I' is spoken in the singular, it is then, according to Sarraute, that 'I' is the general, an 'infinite,' a 'nebula,' a 'world.' And one interlocutor, only one, is sufficient for the 'I' to pass from the general to a simple particular [...] It is there, in the interval between locution and interlocution, that the conflict emerges: the strange wrenching, the tension in the movement from particular to general, experienced by any human being when from an 'I' – unique in language, shapeless, boundless, infinite – it suddenly becomes nothing or almost nothing, 'you,' 'he,' 'she,' 'a small, rather ugly fellow,' an interlocutor" (98).

As a lesbian whose "I" constantly becomes either subsumed into the "we/they" of women in general ("Lesbians are not women" – the last sentence of "The Straight Mind," 1980) or marginalized into a "she/they" meaning "one of those," Wittig is crucially implicated in such an awareness of the social function of words to liberate or oppress: "through language, 'I' is at once everything, 'I' has every power (as a locutor), and that, suddenly, there is the downfall wherein 'I' loses all power (as an interlocutor) and is endangered by words that can cause madness, kill" (99).

She considers a work of literature as a potential war machine, because "its goal is to pulverize the old forms and formal conventions" ("The Trojan Horse," 1984, 69). This goal is achieved not by the ideas in a work, but by the new use of the words themselves: "As a writer, I would be totally satisfied if every one of my words had on the reader the same effect, the same shock as if they were being read for the first time. It is what I call dealing a blow with words" (72). Success occurs when the reader is "conquered" by the point of view of the text: "But to carry out a literary work one must be modest and know that being gay or anything else is not enough. For reality cannot be directly transferred from the consciousness to the book. The universalization of each point of view demands a particular attention to the formal elements that can be open to history, such as themes, subjects of narratives, as well as the global form of the work. It is the attempted universalization of the point of view that turns or does not turn a literary work into a war machine" (75).

Wittig's political view is that a patriarchal system oppresses women and that having to be something else further or differently oppresses lesbians: "A not-woman, a not-man, a product of society, not a product of nature, for there is no nature in society ("One is not born a woman," 1981, 13). Lesbians refuse not only the role played by women but also its context: "It is the refusal of the economic, ideological, and political power of a man" (13). Thus it is necessary "to always thoroughly dissociate 'women' (the class within which we fight) and 'woman,' the myth. For 'woman' does not exist for us: it is only an imaginary formation, while 'women' is the product of a social relationship" (15).

This political and separatist feminism underlies and informs all of Wittig's fictions but does not direct them. Indeed she wrote the essays later than much of her fiction. Wittig does not write "committed literature," in the sense of political tract or argument. Her creative works (as opposed to her essays) are all generated by the energy between words, by words, and by forms that challenge previous forms and ways of using words. They are exciting, challenging, and difficult in many of the ways in which Cixous's texts are difficult, but the energy in the writing of the two authors moves in opposite directions. Cixous is self-absorbed, drawing into herself all previous texts to create an identity; Wittig makes over and takes over previous literary history and moves out into a newly created subject-in-the world, a differently embodied text.

Her first novel, *L'Opoponax* (1964), is an evocation of childhood written in the language of a child and using "*on*" as the non-gendered, linguistically unmarked subject.[18] Wittig writes about her linguistic choice as the universalization of the point of view of a disempowered class: children. More specifically, however, the narrator is a female child who dearly loves another female child. So, hidden under the indefinite pronoun *on* ("one," or a colloquial form of "we" in English) is a potentially lesbian subject. The inscription of childhood in the novel is extraordinarily vivid. Claude Simon (another New Novelist and Nobel Prize winner) wrote in his review of the main character in the book: "I see, I breathe, I chew, I feel through her eyes, her mouth, her hands, her skin ... I become childhood" (*L'Express*, 30 Nov. 1964).[19] Simon concentrates on the result for the reader; Marguerite Duras, reviewing the book, also focuses on the skill of the writer: It's a book that is both admirable and very important because it is governed by an iron rule, which is never broken, or hardly ever, that of using only one sort of purely descriptive material and one tool, purely objective language. The latter takes its full meaning here. It is the very one – but raised to the level of plainsong by the author – which childhood uses to clear and count its universe" (*France-Observateur*, 5 Nov. 1964).

Wittig has created her universalized subject and revolutionized the representation of childhood. She has also introduced into literature the notion not only of the sexuality of children but of lesbian love as unexceptional in the world as perceived because it is natural to the narrator's point of view and generalized by *on*.

In fact the only "I" in the novel occurs in the final sentence (and is one of the many unattributed but recognizable quotations woven into the text). It is a declaration of love: "On dit, tant je l'aimais qu'en elle encore je vis" (253). Translation: "Catherine Legrand says I loved her [Valerie Borge] so much that I still live in her." The poem quoted is *Délie*, by Maurice Scève (c. 1510–1564), a long poem on sublimated love. Hence we learn that nothing came of the childhood connection that is marked in the text by the constant repetition of their linked names.

Five years later, Wittig published *Les Guérillères* (1969), which has become a classic of feminist and lesbian literature. Her challenge to the traditional ways in which literary subjects are constituted and sustained is much more obvious here, not only because its theme is warfare between women as a class and men.

The novel is written in the feminine plural "elles" (shes) as the stories of a group that sometimes separates into individual women, named or not, each with her own story, only to recombine into the general again in stories of groups.[20] Language and literature are reconfigured in the feminine at every level, from the most powerful: prayer and sacred texts; through myth, history, folklore, and fairy tale; to individual experience. The effect is of a patchwork of women's experience through time and across space. It is a revolutionary text in every sense of the word – circular in structure, punctuated by drawn circles, full of round games and spherical creatures, telling the story of the overthrow of patriarchy, it is the constant movement of a (women's) movement – and a circle in motion *is* a revolution.

The text is revolutionary for the reader also. It lacks the usual literary structures that contextualize narrative and situate it within cultural norms and so, by implication, within a heterosexual androcentric frame. Thus Wittig's words seem new because they are all that the reader has with which to visualize and grasp meaning. Readers find their assumptions challenged by the absence of the expected as much as or even more than by what is present in the writing.

Until the New Novel of the 1950s readers had been used to a separation of subject and object, figure and ground, character and context, description and plot, past, present, and future, author, narrator, and reader. Language was usually rational and linear, stories were usually chronological, with or without flashbacks, and had a beginning, middle, and end. With *Les Guérillères*, Wittig writes a book with no privileged values, no time sequence, no décor, no fixed viewpoint, no climax, no characterization. Sight (the gaze) is only one of the senses called into play, and descriptions imply no point of view or moral tone. Female genitalia, for example, are described in a variety of ways, from the strictly scientific to the evocatively poetic, but there is no objectifying, defining gaze behind the words. Above all, the text is full of women's voices, song, roars of rage, and laughter.

Wittig has created an energy field of networks that the reader is free to follow and organize in many ways. There are multiple paths through the text. Wittig suggests that it is circular, but that too is open to interpretation. She is writing in an Einsteinian universe rather than a Cartesian, Newtonian one. The social taxonomy of earlier writers has turned into a constant dance of interrelated elements and perspectives, apparent contradictions, and unexpected compatibilities, as the richnesses of a female pattern take over.

Not until the female point of view has become the universal does the masculine pronoun enter the text. Isolated in a female linguistic and cultural field, the male is disempowered and marginalized – a fact that Wittig makes evident by the way in which the women tease, humiliate, and torture the un-named males. These humiliations are nothing but gender reversals of ways in which women are routinely treated.

With the female universal in place, Wittig then moves on to establish a developed lesbian subject in *Le Corps lesbien* (1973).[21] *Le Corps lesbien* is written in a fragmented, juxtapositional style similar to that of *Les Guérillères*, full of transformed quotations and references. It is both a lesbianization of myths and metaphors (including female Ulysses, Osiris, and Christ figures) – so a continuation of the work of deconstruction of a centralized, androcentric, heterosexual culture – and an inscription of the female body into literature. This is the female body as experienced by a woman who knows it from the inside (herself) and from the outside (in the body of her lover). This is not the female body as represented in traditional literature. This body is neither objectified, nor sexualized, neither desired nor rejected by the male gaze. This body is present in the moment with its bones and muscles, fluids, orifices, and internal organs.

In this text, pages of body parts, listed in capital letters, serve the function of the lists of names in *Les Guérillères*, which in turn replaced the listing of the children in *L'Opoponax*. The body is loved, tortured, dismembered, and explored on multiple levels at once in a network of interrelated series of paragraphs where "j/e" interacts with "tu." Wittig explains her enterprise this way:

> sometimes I have considered this text a reverie about the beautiful analysis of the pronouns *je* and *tu* by the linguist Emile Benveniste. The bar in the *j/e* of The Lesbian Body is a sign of excess. A sign that helps to imagine an excess of "I," an "I" exalted. "I" has become so powerful in *The Lesbian Body* that it can attack the order of heterosexuality in texts and assault the so-called love, the heroes of love, and lesbianize them, lesbianize the symbols, lesbianize the gods and the goddesses, lesbianize the men and the women. This "I" can be destroyed in the attempt and resuscitated. Nothing resists this "I" (or this *tu*, which is its same, its love), which spreads itself in the whole world of the book, like a lava flow that nothing can stop. ("The Mark of Gender,"87)

Then, to consolidate her reconceptualization of Western culture, and declare universal access to linguistic and cultural authority, Monique Wittig, with Sande Zeig, publishes a lesbian reference book: *Brouillon pour un dictionnaire des amantes* (Roughdraft for a Dictionary of Female Lovers, 1976), ten years before the *Women's Encyclopedia of Myths and Secrets* (1983), Mary Daly's lesbian *Wickedary* (1986), and Jeanne Hyvrard's feminist *La Pensée corps* (Body Thought, 1989) – all "encyclopaedias" reconfiguring the world in a woman-centred way that claims the authority implicit in their chosen format.

Wittig's next novel, *Virgile, non* (Virgil, No, 1985), brings a total shift of style. The text is both a parody of Dante's *Inferno* and an elaborate allegorical criticism of the evils of heterosexual patriarchy's treatment of women. The "lost souls" (*âmes damnées*) are heterosexual women (children are their "annexes") and the angels are dykes – the first ones appearing on (motor)bikes, dykes on bikes of course, because the journey though Hell (sexual slaveries) and Purgatory (marriage and equivalent arrangements) to Paradise (a lesbian open air feast and concert) is set in San Francisco, Wittig's newly adopted home.

I find myself thinking that Wittig constructed this text from the ideas in her essays on materialist feminism: "The Category of Sex" (1976/82), "One is not born a woman" (1981), and "The Straight Mind" (1980).[22] These ideas she translated into brutally visual images, which she then turned back into words. The result is set in San Francisco, complete with parades: cheerleaders and sex workers in one, mutilated and battered women in another.

Wittig, the observing traveller, lesbian aspiring to Paradise, led by Manastabal her guide, gets to pause in a bar once in a while to get out of the fierce winds of Hell or lesser winds of Purgatory. There she can drink, reflect on her experiences, and glimpse the angel for whom she yearns. Told in the first person, this novel appears to be the expression of Wittig's feminism, heavily disguised in order not to fall into the category of "committed literature" condemned by Wittig herself. The ideas, retransformed into rational argument, she then develops further in "On the Social Contract" (1989) and "Homo Sum" (1990).[23]

CONCLUSION

The distance from Violette Leduc's misery and marginalization as a lesbian to Monique Wittig's condemnation of heterosexuality as hell on earth has been covered relatively swiftly. Leduc's fame and her skill as a writer transformed the place of lesbianism in French literature. Monique Wittig was able to move into the public space that Leduc created and open it much further in her fiction while consolidating her position by the publication of her essays. Her theories provide an analysis of lesbian circumstances within patriarchal and heterosexual contexts. Her political attitudes offer a basis for change. Yet no subsequent writer in France has followed in her footsteps; radical response starts and stops with Monique Wittig.

PART THREE

Specifically French Lesbians,
1968–1996

CHAPTER FIVE

Exploring Lesbian Identity

With the 1970s comes a new freedom to name and discuss homosexuality and homophobia. This freedom is apparent throughout
much of the Western world as a result of the social upheavals,
student uprisings, and the like in and around 1968. In Quebec and
in anglophone North America (to write only of the literatures with
which I am familiar) lesbian writing became more and more frequently feminist. Indeed much of the radical social analysis of the
contemporary period (sex and gender studies, gay rights,
theory/fiction ...) is at least partially rooted in the lesbian writing
of early second-wave feminism – Bersianik, Brossard, Causse, and
others in Quebec, Audre Lorde, Adrienne Rich, and others in the
United States. But France was different.

In France, lesbian writers remain uninfluenced by developments
elsewhere. Feminists and social theorists such as Christine Delphy
go in one direction and the writers, except for Monique Wittig and
Françoise d'Eaubonne, go in another. The feminists are political,
the writers are not. Some writers explore the realities or fictions of
lesbian life and take the theme of lesbianism sufficiently for granted
that the writing can occasionally be experimental also; others, as
we have seen throughout the 1960s, use a lesbian character as plot
filler in triangular relationships. As became clear in the previous
chapter, this is a time of overlap. In the 1970s several authors who
were pioneers in the writing of lesbian desire and despair publish
new books: Célia Bertin, Jeanne Galzy, Irène Monési. The Editions
des femmes (Women's Press) publishing house in Paris brings out
not only Hélène Cixous's novels, but texts by other known feminists such as Michèle Causse and Françoise d'Eaubonne. Also, the

152   SPECIFICALLY FRENCH LESBIANS, 1968–1996

1970s see the first novels of Jocelyne François, a writer of poetic intensity and extraordinary lucidity who, in her successive works, focuses on the unfolding of the love and lives of lesbians to the exclusion of all else. Hers is the truest and the most sustained reflection on inner life examined in this book.

In the 1980s more "ancestors" of the lesbian writers' community publish lesbian works: Colette Audry (mentioned above in connection with Violette Leduc), longtime friend and colleague of Simone de Beauvoir, and Rolande Aurivel, who was editor of *Désormais* (From Now On), one of the first lesbian revues in France; and more voices appear – notably that of Mireille Best. The 1990s offer both books that take a real step forward into the depiction of lesbian space and others that fall back into old stereotypes of predatory monsters. Most lesbian novelists or novelists interested in lesbian life and desire, however, either remain one-novel authors (Ferrié, Francillon, Mahyère) or include only a few such texts in their literary output (Galzy, Mallet-Joris, Monési, Rochefort).

The only continuously publishing novelists whose works I have read who maintain lesbians as their central characters and focus are Mireille Best, Jocelyne François, and Hélène de Monferrand, and, as one might expect, they are among the most satisfying to read, as I hope to show in chapter 6.

GALZY'S PROVENÇAL FAMILIES

It was a reference in Monferrand's third novel, *Les Enfants d'Héloïse* (Héloïse's Children, 1997), that sent me back to Jeanne Galzy's work. As I mentioned above in chapter 3, Galzy published three novels between 1929 and 1934 exploring the possibility of lesbian desire; thereafter she seems to have turned into a regular writer of heterosexual novels and literary biography. Then in 1969 she published a volume, the first in a series, entitled *La Surprise de vivre* (Surprise of Life), which was followed swiftly by *Les Sources vives* (Living Springs, 1971), *La Cavalière* (The Female Rider, 1974), and *Le Rossignol aveugle* (The Blind Nightingale, 1976). These novels may well have provided Hélène de Monferrand with inspiration, encouragement, and format – but of that more below.

Galzy's series traces the history of three Provençal families over a period of some forty years, plus flashbacks. This history serves as context for one young married woman's anguished discovery that

Exploring Lesbian Identity 153

she is a lesbian and her daughter's evolution as a lesbian also. Eva, the mother, is nineteen at the beginning of the novels, and Amédée, her daughter, nearly forty at the end of them.

The three families are strongly and distinctly depicted, the characterization is good, the personalities are varied, and the interactions are quite complex. The Deshandrès family – that of Eva's husband, David (who dies in an accident at the time of Amédée's birth) – has urban standing as owner of a bank in Montpellier. The Bastide's, including David's mother, Eva's father, and their rigid, uncompromising sister, Noémi, are the children of a pastor. The Parazol family breeds horses and bulls for Provençal bullfights. Grandfather Parazol breeds racehorses also and is a member of the exclusive and prestigious Paris Jockey Club. All are Protestants. Frédéric Bastide is considered to have married into a strange lot – the Parazols. His wife was unhealthy and died young. Eva is not thought to be entirely desirable for David because she is his cousin and her father has long been estranged from his sisters, who see him as living far from the path of righteousness; she is suspected of having inherited her mother's weak disposition and frivolousness. However, she is rich and the heir to Grandfather Parazol's fortune. Also, unexpected in the atmosphere of uncompromising piety and good works *chez* Deshandrès, she is accepted because David loves and desires her. His mother, Jémina, consciously aware of the sexual nature of her love for David's father, respects and acknowledges the power of desire.

La Surprise de vivre, first novel of Galzy's series, begins with the arrival of Eva and David, returning from their honeymoon to the Deshandrès country mansion. It is soon clear that all is not well, and the reader, party to Eva's reflections, learns how distasteful she finds the abrupt animality of David's lovemaking. On the sexual level at least, she is not sorry that he dies. To the chagrin of the elder Deshandrès women and the surprise of Emmanuelle and Suzanne, her adolescent sisters-in-law, Eva is not delighted to find herself pregnant, nor does she show much maternal warmth towards her baby daughter, although she cares for her attentively enough.

Within the Deshandrès family Eva feels stifled. Nothing but sitting around knitting for the poor seems to be acceptable activity for a married woman and a young widow. Eva, barely twenty and raised to ride freely in the Camargue and swim in the Mediterranean, suffers as much from the physical confinement as from the repressive puritan attitudes and constant biblical references that surround her. She begins to escape into the park in the middle of the night for a breath of freedom. One night she is joined by the English governess, Hilda Steenes.

From the first time Hilda puts her arm around Eva's shoulders, Eva is exquisitely aware of her presence. Hilda's first words to Eva are the same words as David spoke: "I find you attractive" (228–9). Thus is the sexual potential of the contact established. Throughout the rest of the volume Eva wrestles with the conflict between her upbringing and her discovered sexuality. Hilda courts her, seduces her, makes love to her. Physically she responds totally:

A sweetness never felt before made her more sensitive to the smells of the earth, the light of the day, and the suppleness of her own body. She walked a few steps to feel the elasticity of her movements, then came back, straightened the sheets on the crumpled bed, and leaned out of the window.

It was the hour when the noises of house life began – kitchen, stable, the bucket chain in the vegetable garden. And these noises were different, full of lightness and joy.

She touched herself as if in recognition, looked at herself in the mirror, and saw her glowing face. One night had been sufficient to draw another living being out of her. (271)

But, of course, she goes through an identity crisis: "Was she a sort of monstrous exception also? She blushed in the darkness, on this big bed where now, in place of the dead man, she was evoking the memory of the living woman" (278). Her personal reactions are compounded by family pressures of various kinds. Daniel, David's brother, is in love with her, and the parents would like her to marry him next, because then her dowry and all the money on her side of the family would serve as collateral for the ever-shakier bank. Suzanne adores her governess and is jealous of the time Eva spends with Hilda; she watches them obsessively. Also it is not considered appropriate for a member of the family to frequent an employee.

Eva does not have the will to revolt against the family and is astounded by Hilda's ease. Her own emotional disequilibrium and moral unease are compounded by her fear of being discovered. The fear is exacerbated by the way Suzanne inevitably arrives whenever Eva and Hilda are deep in conversation. They are always physically close enough to each other that they jump apart, thus looking (and feeling) guilty.

Galzy is very good at depicting family dynamics as expressed through behaviour, gestures, expressions, and comments. Eva's sense of being constantly watched and judged negatively is evident, as is the weight of the responsibility of living as a member of the Bastide household. The pastor continues to cast a long shadow through the memories, habits, and attitudes of Noémi and Jémina. This shadow falls on the women in particular. The countershadow is that of David's paternal grandfather, Samuel, a known philanderer.

Untouched by all the currents and countercurrents – love, sex, power, money, piety, principles, constraints, repressions, and oppressions – Hilda Steenes keeps herself to herself and lives a double life (as have many governesses in literature). Neither family nor domestic help, neither (French) Catholic nor Protestant, from another culture, and, until the arrival of Eva, in a generation apart – between the children and the adults – she is coded as different from the beginning. Galzy presents her as more free than the other characters in all ways. She is alone, away from country and family, educated, and earning her living. She thinks freely and makes her own choices, encouraging the youngest Deshandrès son, Arnold, in his talent as an artist, for example, against his family's disapproval.

She is morally and sexually free. Symbolically Galzy makes her a creature of the night, living her own life after her charges and her employers are asleep. Her first words to Eva are: "Don't you find it delicious to be free?" (227), and she encourages Eva to meet her, swim naked in the river, and ultimately make love in the darkness – away from the house and all that it represents in terms of upper-class bourgeois appearances, Protestant virtue, and the *status quo*.

And in an interesting statement of Galzy's position in terms of traditional symbolism, Hilda Steenes is fair, her blonde head shining brightly in the darkness. Throughout the novel she is depicted as a light, a force for love, self-development, and freedom, not only for Eva and Amédée, but also for Arnold and to a degree for Suzanne. Hilda is ironic and sometimes sardonic in the face of Eva's troubled indecisiveness, but she has none of the characteristics of the traditional wicked lesbian – except that the readers, Eva, and she herself know that she would so seem to Jémina and Noémi Bastide.

Uncle Otto, half-brother of the dead Samuel, befriends Hilda and lends her his pavilion in the grounds as a place to which she can escape. He offers it also to Eva, who does not accept his offer. (She does meet Hilda there, of course.) Many years later he offers it to Suzanne. The pavilion is a place of escape and love. It is furnished with mementos of Uncle Otto's travels and his lifelong love for his brother's sad, betrayed, and faithful wife, Amédée, after whom Eva's daughter is named. Otto recognizes those around him who do not conform to the Protestant heterosexual model and acknowledges by his action their need for space to themselves – space that they are free to use as they see fit.

La Surprise de vivre, so titled to underline Eva's surprise when her body springs to new life under Hilda's caresses, is a sensitive study of both the sensuality and the anguish of the process of a young woman's realizing her lesbianism and the impossibility of her living a lesbian life within the confines of a family such as the Deshandrès.

Les Sources vives, the second volume, begins at the death of Hilda Steenes. It becomes evident that Eva could and did live as a lesbian under her father's roof. She had returned to the property that Frédéric Bastide managed for his father-in-law, and as soon as Arnold was too old for his governess, Hilda Steenes had joined her, lived as her lover (discreetly and possibly secretly), and raised Amédée. At the beginning of this novel Amédée is twelve, Hilda Steenes has died suddenly of flu, and Eva goes into perpetual mourning.

Positive though Jeanne Galzy is towards lesbianism in her treatment of Hilda in *La Surprise de vivre*, she does not present a happy, ongoing relationship between two women. Either she feels that she cannot portray it in the period she has chosen for her story, or she cannot envision her publisher and public permitting such a situation. Possibly she cannot even imagine it. There had been no literary model to date. It is also possible that Galzy began or wrote the novels long before their dates of publication, by which time she had been publishing for well over fifty years.

Les Sources vives, with its image of water continuing to flow from its source, is essentially the story of Amédée's adolescence. As Eva spends her life at Hilda's grave or in the untouched bedroom where she died, Amédée is sent to boarding school. There, predictably, she has increasingly affectionate friendships with other girls, and these are increasingly visibly lesbian in pattern and tone. In her home life she spends time with her great-grandfather Parazol, who begins to claim her as his direct heir, because he sees himself in her. Amédée is a skilled and fearless rider with an instinct for selecting, training, and tending horses in all circumstances. Parazol would have preferred her to be a boy, but, that once said, he sets the thought aside, raises, appreciates, and loves his great-granddaughter.

Parazol provides the opposite of life with the Deshandrès. Their attitudes and behaviour are confined and repressive, his are open and freeing. Parazol and Amédée live an outdoor life of constant activity. Any challenge is to be taken up, any obstacle overcome, and the old man treats Amédée as he treats himself. She grows in capability and autonomy. Respected for her skills and capacities, she is given the honorary and affectionate name of Parazol II by the jockeys and local people.

As Amédée matures, she is initiated into lesbian sex by a Parisian student some seven years older than she is. When she asks Eva for the key to the beach cabin, where Eva used to go with Hilda, in order to go there to make love with Andrée, Eva hands it over without question. Amédée is then thirteen and already has a steady emotional if not sexual girlfriend, Daisy. Galzy is explicit enough in the descriptions of lovemaking that it is clear that Amédée is uncomplicated in her lesbianism and never questions her sexual orientation. Galzy gives her the traditional masculine look: big, strong, short hair.

The second novel does not have the emotional intensity of the first. There are no struggles here, and very little adolescent angst. The problems that keep the plot moving are heterosexual and financial for the most part. All the concomitant strains are felt by the Deshandrès family as the bank falters and is sold. For the lesbian reader there is an ongoing sense of waiting for Amédée to grow up, together with a suspicion that Suzanne Deshandrès might well become lesbian also, because she remains haunted by her feelings for Hilda Steenes. To bring Suzanne to self-realization from such a confining upbringing would have been more than a little difficult, and Galzy diverts Suzanne into unorthodoxy while maintaining her heterosexuality – she chooses to take as a lover an itinerant writer, gets pregnant, and has an abortion.

Amédée's relationship with the dainty English girl, Daisy, is both the reciprocal and the parallel of the connection between Eva and Hilda. Daisy is jealous but easily dominated. She is indecisive and not able or willing to stand up against her mother's demands, and so she is separated from Amédée. The separation is not supposed to be permanent, but she has not returned by the end of the fourth novel.

Whether Galzy believed that happiness does not make a good novel, or whether the taboo on lesbian satisfaction and contentment, evident in all the novels by women authors presented in this study, remained too strong for her to challenge, clearly it was as yet inconceivable to take lesbianism for granted as the underpinning of the story, for with adulthood Amédée moves into a different world. Sent to Paris by Parazol, who wants her to see other possibilities in order to be able to choose her life from a place of experience, Amédée falls in love with a famous singer, Elina. She is treated with disdain, summoned and discarded at whim by Elina, and becomes a tormented victim of the kind that we have seen all too often – obsessed and powerless. The last scene of La Cavalière leaves her running after the car in which her newly rediscovered beloved is being driven away.

Amédée's exploits in Paris are parallel to those experienced by her great-grandfather when, in his youth, he pursued a Russian dancer. He has told the stories and makes her aware that she must experience such despairs for herself – as indeed she does. However, given the acuity with which Galzy opens the series and writes Eva's awakening to her sexuality, given also the resources given to Amédée: approval, self-assurance, money, family backing – all the things that a lesbian does not usually have – I found it disappointing to see her made to resemble earlier lesbian heroines in her misery.

Once again the undeviating, unisexual lesbian appears to be abandoned by the bisexual woman whom she loves. Thus the implicit message that heterosexuality conquers all is promulgated

Exploring Lesbian Identity   159

yet again. Hilda Steenes is dead, and Eva is perceived by all except her closest family as the sorrowing widow of David. Suzanne is turned aside from her putative lesbianism, put into the arms of a man – a totally unacceptable man, but a man none the less – and when illegitimately pregnant declares: "now I am a woman." Amédée is set aside for a man despite her obvious charms and advantages. Lesbianism would seem to be unproblematic only for adolescents and foreigners, as we have seen.

My impression in reading the first two of these novels was that they were set in the 1920s. The third starts with a genealogy which shows that the first two novels took place between 1895 and about 1910. The 1914–18 war happens during *La Cavalière*. I have great difficulty in believing that before 1914 anyone, however enlightened, would have sent a young woman, under twenty years old, alone to live in Paris and find her own way in society – especially if she were an heiress. The feminist writings of the 1890–1914 period show clearly what a woman in such circumstances would have to deal with. To be set twenty-five years later makes the first three volumes of the series much more probable, and the discrepancy bothers me. This quibble notwithstanding, these are well-written novels in which lesbians not only occupy a significant place in the narrative but are also integrated into an extended family structure and given a social context. Also, Eva and Amédée are to my knowledge the first lesbian mother and daughter in the history of the French novel.

The integration continues in the fourth volume, *Le Rossignol aveugle* (1976). Written in three parts (as are all of Galzy's novels), this last volume is divided into very short chapters and skips from household to household continuously: (1) Jémina, Noémi, and Suzanne; (2) Frédéric and Eva; (3) Parazol, Fabienne, and Daniel; (4) Arnold and his models; (5) Emmanuelle, husband, and children; (6) Amédée, Elina, Frieda, and Jos.

Amédée has reconnected with the singer with whom she fell in love in *La Cavalière*, but Elina is now blind – hence the title of this novel. Frieda is her accompanist and Jos her impresario; together they select her music, teach it to her, organize her concerts, control her musical life. Amédée, despite being Elina's lover, remains marginal. Elina does not remember Amédée in the days of their passion.

She allows Amédée to retell her memories, reteach Elina her body, to make love to her, but she is rarely fully present. As the novel continues she withdraws more and more from Amédée and turns more clearly to religion. When Amédée leaves to go to Jémina's funeral, Elina's withdrawal seems final. The novel ends with a conversation between Parazol and Amédée in which it is obvious that she has not found happiness yet. The old man is sad for her. He, aged nearly one hundred, has recently fallen in love with Fabienne (Daniel's longtime mistress), who returns his love. They are the only really happy people in the story.

Amédée's love for Elina and Eva's love for Hilda are significant parts of the book for the reader. Within the novel, between the characters, the silences subsist. Suzanne, Daniel, and Arnold, ultimately Frédéric Bastide and Parazol, knew about Eva's love for Hilda, although Daniel was the only one who formulated what he suspected and saw. Amédée knew also, and Eva observed and condoned her daughter's increasingly lesbian behaviour, yet between Amédée and Eva there was never a conversation of any consequence. Parazol and Arnold the artist, on separate occasions, come closest to talking directly to Amédée, but they speak allusively, and she replies elusively. Yet by the end everyone except Jémina and Noémi is aware of Amédée's way of life.

The silence accrues around all sexuality outside marriage, in fact, and all the members of the younger generations have secrets. Also, no one of the younger generation, except possibly Emmanuelle, has long-lasting reciprocal loves – so ultimately Amédée is not singled out in her misfortune. In many ways she is freer than those around her because she has the liberty to choose her own life and the money to live it. We know very little of her feelings and attitudes as an adult, however. By making her a devoted, self-sacrificing lover, Galzy situates her in the Protestant ethic of the Deshandrès–Bastide family that she seemed to avoid in childhood, when it appeared likely that she would live with the panache of her great-grandfather. Galzy also avoids representing a developed lesbian relationship yet again, while also avoiding the pitfalls of profligacy. It is true that she also avoids a simplistic repressed = unhappy versus free = happy dichotomy.

Galzy's series of novels is more complex and more accomplished than any of her previous works, and her presentation of lesbianism has vivid details, sensitive nuances of emotion, the expression of secret love, and a real sense of family pressures, but to my disappointment she avoids extended treatment of love and passion, both sexual and psychological. In this way her writing suits the tone of the families of characters with whom she is dealing and their period. It is also perhaps a mark of her own upbringing and generation – she published her first novel in 1912, sixty-four years before *Le Rossignol aveugle* appeared.

To write openly about lesbian relationships, to sketch intimacy, to imply sexual activity, and to depict deep, extended and exclusive love by women for women is already a huge step in the history of lesbians in French novels. To expect the author to focus as well as to cast her net so widely is probably unrealistic on my part. None the less, the symbolic message of the early death of Hilda and Elina's withdrawal into religion is that lesbians will be punished unless they repent. Elina's blindness is slightly more ambiguous and therefore allows for a little irony, but she was passionately sexual before being struck blind and claims to have forgotten her love for Amédée afterwards, suggesting that any other reading than that of punishment is slightly perverse on my part! Galzy empathizes with her lesbians but seems not to condone their behaviour entirely, if we judge by the metaphorical implications of her authorial decisions.

PATTERNS CONTINUE IN THE 1970S

Célia Bertin's *Liens de famille* (Family Ties, 1977) is significantly more interesting than her early novels. (See above, chapter 3.) It is written with energy and drama, and the characters have personality. There is also a powerful sense of family dynamics and of the anguish felt by a woman discovering her lesbian tendencies – in this case late in life. Marie refuses to accept her love for Clarice and is diminished by her decision. Bertin codes the lesbian seductress as exotic, foreign, hysterical, and dark-haired. She is also rich, feminine, and ultimately faithful. Anna, Marie's companion, evolves to a point of recognizing her own homophobia, and there is a retrospective discussion at the end of the novel. So here again patterns are evolving. Although a happy lesbian love is still not permitted, the reasons why this is so are aired, and characters' reactions are eventually looked at clearly.

Irène Monési's novels, in contrast, remain faithful to her theme of the impossibility of a continuing lesbian relationship. As we saw above, *Althia* (1957) was the story of the impossible passion of a married woman for an emotionally, if not always physically, inaccessible dancer. *Une Tragédie superflue* (A Superfluous Tragedy, 1968) was a tragedy brought on herself by a woman who is also unable to create a satisfactory or ongoing love (see chapter 3).

In 1972 Monési published *La Vie d'une bête* (An Animal's Life), subtitled a "récit" (tale), which appears to be at least semi-autobiographical. It has as a frame the story of a girl not like the others who is abused in various ways. Essentially it is a series of reflections on sex and gender, sexuality and the female body, and parental mixed messages of such disturbing force that the child sees herself neither as a feminine daughter nor as a pseudo-son, but as an animal. It is a story of gender confusion in a "mal-aimée."

This text she followed in 1974 with *L'Amour et le dédain* (Love and Disdain) – a lengthy and rather dull chronicle of triangular relationships. Mary and Patricia were a couple joined by Marie-Guillemette. Mary and Marie-Guillemette are a couple at the beginning of the novel, and they are joined by Cécile. The whole novel is a version of history repeating itself. The activities move back and forth from the United States to Paris, but there is no context at all outside Mary's house and Cécile's apartment – no people and no action. There is only daily material detail, talk of personal power relations and complications, and listing of who is visiting whose room. Also, and even more curiously, the novel is devoid of any manifestation of either sex or love. There is no tenderness or sensuality manifest in the writing, conversation, or action, and the characters have no presence, no personality. The entire text rests on the surface of life in the present or in the memory. A complicated text but not a complex one, *L'Amour et le dédain* has a superficially more modern and feminist style than Monési's early novels, but is less satisfactory in its emotional context.

Toutes trois (All Three, 1975), with authors listed as Lisa Liu Gro, is even more superficial than Monési's *L'Amour et le dédain*, full of busy words, with no characters, no plot, no décor, but lots of coming and going. To add to the surface activity it is divided into short sections with headings such as: "Liu, nine-years old, is

Exploring Lesbian Identity 163

building a house of cards." Indeed the whole novel is a house of cards: a bourgeois dash-in-and-out-of-bed novel with neither feeling nor sensuality. Its activity is dressed up with pop philosophy and mundane references. It is a younger version of the previous book.

A third novel of a similar tone and even less interest is Anne Vergue's *La Somnambule* (The Sleepwalker, 1977). It is remarkable only for the fact that both the lesbian characters have yellow eyes and "very few people have yellow eyes, really yellow." The reference to Balzac's *La Fille aux yeux d'or* (The Girl with the Golden Eyes) is clearly not to be passed over unnoticed. The rest of the book is not notable in any way.

In contrast is Nicole-Lise Bernheim and Mireille Cardot's "romance policière" *Personne ne m'aime* (Nobody Loves Me, 1978). This is a racy, slangy murder mystery in the style of Boris Vian.[1] It is full of references to literature, music, and film: the Commissary of Mysteries in the 14th district of Paris is Eugène Sue.[2] Sue is (also) the feminine form of the past participle "knew," thus connecting him with the dead woman Brigitte de Savoir – Brigitte of Knowledge. Her name provides a double reference by both sound and sense, to Simone de Beauvoir as well. Mary Pickford[3] and Renée Vivien[4] are characters in the story, as is Sylvie Delarue-Mardrus[5] and the funeral is held at Avenue de la Grande-Rachilde;[6] the interior minister is Henri Agathe-Christie.

The book is full of new and borrowed plays on words. Rose Sélavy (c'est la vie: that's life!) works for a magazine called *Joyeuses Clitoridiennes* ("Joyful Clitoris Lovers," with an implied pun on "quotidiennes" meaning "daily"),[7] she bears the name of a *personnage* invented by Marcel Duchamp,[8] and one of the characters is called Marie-France Beurque, presumably in criticism of the women's magazine *Marie France*, "beurque" being a slangy evocation of disgust. This text is busy in the right kind of way. It is fun.

In Irène Monési's next novel, *Les Mers profondes* (Deep Seas, 1977), we find the triangular emotional structure repeated. This time the characters are grouped as a married couple and an extra woman. Rouge, a young American woman, has attracted or seduced a French woman. She brings her into the relationship between Rouge and her husband, Murray, and then to all intents and purposes hands her over to him. He uses her and casts her off. The bulk of the novel is not even a reprise of the triangular or bisexual novels of the 1960s, and the suggestion of a lesbian connection between Rouge and Jeanne is ephemeral until the end, where an explanation of events is put into Murray's mouth. Then the lesbian link is affirmed but remains undeveloped.

EXPERIMENTAL NOVELS OF THE 1970S

In contrast to these traditionally constructed novels with all-seeing author or adult narrator, realistic décor, chronological development, psychological characterization, and cause-and-effect plot line, or, as in some of the less successful novels, a sorry lack of same – the experimental novels published by the Editions des femmes follow most obviously in the footsteps of Monique Wittig.

Gisèle Bienne's *Douce amère* (Bittersweet, 1977), the story of an adolescent's loving friendship for a fellow student in her boarding school, reminds me of Wittig's *L'Opoponax*, although it is a simpler story, told more simply also. The occasionally physical nature of the expression of the narrator's affection for Agnès, condemned by her mother as profoundly suspicious, would seem to be the outpouring of a tender heart and hormones destined to become heterosexual in due time. The echo of Wittig's work comes in the school world.

Similarly, Françoise d'Eaubonne's *Le Satellite de l'Amande* (Almond's Satellite, 1975) evokes the world and values of *Les Guérillères* without precisely being part of it. It certainly raises few if any of the challenging issues with which Wittig is dealing. It fits among the pseudo-sci-fi feminist novels of the 1970s which disguise a reinterpretation of the world under some clever conceit. The better books of this kind, such as Quebec novelist Louky Bersianik's *The Euguélionne* (1976),[9] are witty. The others tend to be didactic and somewhat turgid.

Eaubonne's novel is slow to get going and never gets very exciting, which is a pity, because the basic idea is amusing. A spaceship with a female crew – two lesbian couples, one young girl, and two older single women, Conception and Ariane – arrive from planet

Earth to explore the territory called Amande. A new female régime known as Anima has replaced Animus, all men have been eliminated, and to talk about them is taboo. As the women explore the planet the reader gradually realizes that this satellite is actually a huge, living male body curled around so that his feet join the nape of his neck. He breathes, opens and closes his eyes, and has regular erections – one of which knocked a previous spaceship out of the sky!

Conception was in that previous ship. She is set apart from the others because she carries the mark/shame of having been born of biological heterosexual intercourse, which makes a person inferior. She is, however, also the topographer of the expedition, and it is she who first realizes the situation. She provides Ariane with information that makes her realize in her turn the particular nature of the planet and their peculiar circumstances on it.

In the context of this discovery, the title of the novel takes on more equivocal meanings. Eaubonne suggests in the blurb that "Amande" might be a reversal of "demain" (tomorrow) – thus in the future man would be a satellite of woman. "Amande" is also an almond and is a word used to indicate the clitoris in French. Hence the male organ in the novel (a megalith against which Ariane leans to talk to Conception about ways to protect the planet because she has come to love it) becomes the complement of the clitoris and rises when the light of "Amande" shines on it.

The novel is full of feminist references coded into the story. Lesbianism is presented as the norm, and the only men whom these women know are those who were kept prisoner to serve as sex objects and fertilizers at the end of the previous period.

The end of the story suggests a strong attraction between Ariane and the planet. The question is whether this heterosexuality subverts the lesbianism established in the rest of the novel or whether we are supposed to extrapolate from her name that the male planet is the symbolic equivalent of the minotaur. Thus her attraction is monstrous, and no more expeditions should come this way, though neither for the reason that she gives (that there is nothing of interest here) nor for the reason that she holds)her desire to protect the living man).

Conception subversively suggests that they – she and Ariane – could none the less return. Every space traveller has the right to a return trip to a planet visited for official purposes. However, it is not clear how they might do so.

I find myself thinking of this novel in the context of Wittig's *Les Guérillères* because the society that serves as backdrop to the story is a slightly sketched-in version of the society of amazons evoked by Wittig. Likewise the systematic exploration of the male planet-body suggests Wittig's representation of the female body in *Le Corps lesbien*. But again, Wittig represents the body in all its physiological complexity for exploratory theoretical reasons, whereas Eaubonne creates a mildly intriguing puzzle. Published in 1969 and 1973, Wittig's texts ante-date *Le Satellite de l'Amande*, and it would be reasonable to suppose that Eaubonne had read them. She adds nothing to Wittig's analysis, however. If anything, her novel is an amusing idea grossly over-extended. As a short story it would have been fun.

Michèle Causse published mostly in Quebec. Her early poetic text *L'Encontre* (Contrary, 1975) has the evocative flow of some of Cixous's writing, but it seems to me that it fits more neatly into the patterns, styles, and theories of Quebec than of France. (I have included none of her Quebec publications in this volume.) I am thinking too of the writing of other Québécoises in this period: Monique Bosco, Nicole Brossard, Madeleine Gagnon, and France Théoret, where their focus was on the female body, gender, and sexuality, explored in a mixture of poetry and theory.[10] Their purpose was at least in part political, which gave the writing an edge not present in Hélène Cixous's more psycho-analytic and self-focused texts, but which takes up Wittig's radical challenge with regard to both political lesbianism and the structures and content of fiction. Theory-fiction as it developed in Quebec is different from Wittig's version, but the subversive intentions are the same.

As I mentioned above, lesbian writing of this period in North America and elsewhere is overtly feminist. This is not the case in France, where Michèle Causse, Françoise d'Eaubonne, Christiane Rochefort, and Wittig challenge the *status quo* head on. Best and Monferrand, and in a philosophical way Jocelyne François also, create women who are the product of a more feminist environment than do earlier writers, but Best and François affirm individual and personal strength, and Monferrand makes it the result of class privilege claimed by women (as well as men). None is political *per se*.

Exploring Lesbian Identity 167

DEEPER EXPLORATIONS IN THE 1970S

Except for Jeanne Galzy's three novels, all the texts of the 1970s discussed above are to some degree facile. Four other novels – by Rigal, Labarraque-Reyssac, Beck, and Ferrié – seem to me to probe somewhat further, while making clear the taboo that continues to subsist around the prospect of lesbian relationships and the concept of lesbian love as a full and complete form of human interconnection. The depiction of adolescent love has been by far the most frequent throughout this study, and these four novels fit into that pattern in various ways.

Muriel Rigal's *L'Envers des choses* (The Wrong Side of Things, 1977) is reminiscent of Mallet-Joris's *Le Rempart des Béguines* in the situation of the narrator, who is a lonely, motherless child with a distant and silent father, and of Monési's *Althia* in the context of the dancing class and love for the ballet teacher. Tatiana and the narrator, whom she calls Douchka, share a passion for dance. Douchka is mothered as a dancer and loved through her dance. Tatiana nurtures her spirit, meanwhile consoling herself perhaps for the loss of the daughter of Douchka's age left in Russia with Tatiana's husband and son.

After a dance improvisation one day, Douchka is kissed by Tatiana and desperately kisses back. Rigal has her narrator comment: "Long after, there had been men, normalcy. I had never found again that total pleasure that laid pain to rest ... You [father], you would have called that homosexuality and you would have tried to treat it. I simply called it love" (31). While Douchka seeks love, Tatiana thinks in terms of dance: "One doesn't dance with one's sex organs, one dances with one's soul" (35). The father thinks in terms of homosexuality. The three agendas are not compatible.

After finishing school the daughter is forbidden to dance any more and is sent to medical school. When she returns for a holiday, Tatiana has disappeared. It appears that someone saw her kissing the narrator, and the father chased her out of town. The narrator in fury tells her father that he has stolen her life because he is afraid that people will call her lesbian and he cannot understand the purity of their love. The issue here is homophobia, and it is identified as a small-town response, as in *La Bonifas* and in *Douce amère*.

From then on the narrator searches for Tatiana. No one else will do: "At certain times, I asked myself if I wasn't in fact 'lesbian.' But no girl attracted me. I didn't love others. I didn't love anyone" (74). Some years later she meets Tatiana again in Paris, and they go to a restaurant. Of the encounter the narrator writes: "Her eyes caress my body, I shiver under this caress, I make love completely for the first time without being raped. My face moves through an infernal ballet. I want to shout. I howl with happiness" (136). But that non-physical encounter is all there is. Tatiana leaves a note saying "Too late" and disappears again. However, the reaction of the narrator and the fact that she makes love to Tatiana in fantasy, thinking of her every night, certainly calls into question her earlier affirmation of purity. It does not necessarily negate the need to be mothered that is evident in the text, however.

Tatiana fosters the spark of passion in Douchka, who, when she has lost Tatiana, can no longer dance with passion either. The dancing is a symbol of making love; the love a manifestation of shared passion; the dance a manifestation of mother–daughter love. The strands are tightly woven, and their implication would seem to be that a motherless child, deprived of love, seeks that love above all other. This love will take the place of other love or may itself become sexualized. The other implication is that homophobia may inadvertently be the cause of homosexuality – the loss of Tatiana cut Douchka off not only from that love but from her father and future male lovers.

Homosexuality/lesbianism discussed openly by name in novels is a product of the 1970s. Claude Labarraque-Reyssac's *Lesbos à Poitiers* (Lesbos in Poitiers, 1978) has a title that brings expectations of pornography or sociology rather than literature, and it is indeed a novel that has subtle components of both. The story, told in flashback from memories triggered rather elegantly by the sight of a portrait in a gallery, is one of both homophobia and seduction.

The author (male or female? I ask myself, given that Claude could be either) sets a tone of titillation and discreet outrage by declaring that there is a fashionable epidemic of lesbianism in the normal school at Poitiers, where "love between girls was displayed shamelessly and, curiously enough, without fear of any consequences (13).

The narrator, Hélène Duvalier, nineteen years old, joins the other students in the evening to dance for exercise and to keep warm. She likes dancing with Gladys best "because she leads well," to which remark she receives the suggestive (in this context) reply: "And you are easy to lead. Light, you understand at once what is wanted (36). Slowly, throughout the three years of her course Hélène is courted and initiated by Gladys. Hélène complies, listens, is kissed and caressed, protesting faintly from time to time: "Those caresses between girls disgust me" (98). "It's that her love seemed unnatural to me, I pushed it away with all my rationality and perhaps against my instinct" (131). "It is following a fashion created by the influence of Gide, Proust, and certain women poets or novelists who were fashionable at the turn of the century. It is also a sensuality that needs to be satisfied and which makes do with what it can find, like those poor wives in a harem who cannot all be satisfied by their one master" (138). All justifications are good, even the argument that at least she won't get pregnant!

Finally, the last night arrives, together with the ultimate in hypocritical and homophobic pleasure: "and this time I don't struggle any more. I'm tired, curious too, tempted perhaps. She slides an arm under my neck. Her kisses, soft and light, caress my eyelids, my cheeks, my neck, while her left hand lightly strokes my breasts, lingers on their hardening points. Shivers run through me and a strange warmth makes my sex tingle, which is waiting, calling perhaps. And I find her mouth on my mouth pleasant, her soft living tongue, which is exploring and to which I respond [...] And she again begins the conquest of my body, spread, awakened, curious. How many times I have dreamed of abandoning myself so to John" (216–17).

She then starts thinking about fear of pregnancy: "But with Gladys there is no fear of an accident. It is possible to abandon myself to the voluptuousness she can give. Expert, she reveals me to myself. But when, changing position, she wants the same caresses from me, a sudden nausea comes over me and I push her away violently (217). Hélène comments: "I felt grotesque ... I saw us as grotesque" (218). Her recoil and refusal to make love to Gladys transform her gentle, patient, and finally successful lover into the vengeful monstrous lesbian of the nineteenth-century tradition. Gladys leaves threatening revenge. She takes her revenge by stealing Hélène's fiancé and finally gets her comeuppance by being murdered by another lesbian who had accused her of seducing her husband. All the old clichés come rolling back.

Béatrix Beck's *Noli* (1978) does not quite fall into the clichés but has the same double attitude of homophobia and attraction. The novel opens with the narrator's statement that her purpose is to kill her feelings for Camille, and to that end she proposes to write her memories of the connection between them and also her recollections of psychoanalysis that she was undertaking at the same time, all during a prolonged visit to a town in Quebec. Both the obsessive friendship and the analysis turned out badly. The text purports to be a cathartic letting go of the experience; I find that it reads like a vengeful settling of accounts. Its rather coy pretence at confidentiality allows the narrator freedom to be spiteful in her criticism and analysis. Beck makes her narrator both homophobic in general and jealous of Camille's close friendship with Elizabeth, which she vilifies as lesbian. She also categorizes Camille as androgynous: "Male homophilia did not displease me – whereas, paradoxically, sapphism horrified me. And even though in principle 'homosexuality' and 'homophilia' are synonymous, the second term seemed to suit my feelings much better because it didn't contain the word 'sex' which, applied to two women, disgusted me. Especially relative to Camille. I even had difficulty with the idea, the image that she had natural functions, internal organs, nudity" (28).

The novel draws to a close with a reversal of the original situation. This time the narrator herself is the person refusing the love offered to her. Supposedly included to allow her to understand Camille's irritation with her, this story actually permits a reaffirmation of the homophobia: "Sapphism disgusts me. Can you give me a child? Then you don't interest me" (117). This is followed by the hypocrisy: "She proposed that we should each have a child by the same man. The idea, which seems awful, might have seduced me if Pilar had attracted me. But no" (117). And the novel ends with the narrator unchanged in her double standard, confusion, and anger that she has been put into such an uncomfortable state.

Beck's narrator is certainly obsessed with Camille. Equally obviously she refuses all physicality and the very concept of lesbian sex. In her memories I find no evidence of affection or friendship in the

Exploring Lesbian Identity 171

proximity between the two women. There is certainly no love. The feelings depicted and evoked are those of irritation, anger, resentment, denial of desire, and homophobia.

It is interesting to see how difficult it is for most of the authors in this study to combine real feeling and loving sex. So far the novels that transmit tenderness, love, sincerity of feeling, even when that feeling is one of acute desire, do not combine the emotions with sexual practice. The works that provide descriptions of sensuality and sexual activity tend to combine the lovemaking with some moral judgment, attribution of blame or guilt, and final punishment or suffering. To date the only authors who might claim to bring both love and sex into their texts do so by remaining on the surface to such an extent that neither is really present.

The only novel of the 1970s to combine the two (except for the works of Jocelyne François, to whom I return below) is Françoise Ferrié's *L'Accident d'amour* (Accident of Love, 1975). As I have been reading for this project I have occasionally been touched by the depth of sincerity and sense of truth of a novel. This is one of them.

L'Accident d'amour actually juxtaposes love with calculated sexual virtuosity, innocent women in love, and a version of the (old traditional) cold and predatory lesbian whose actions project the lovers out of their state of innocent bliss into one of acknowledged sexual love and discretion. The substructure is very Garden of Edenish, but, even though there are rupture and suffering for a while, there is no guilt.

As in Rigal's *L'Envers*, one of the important issues made visible here is the relationship between mothering and lesbian love. *L'Accident d'amour* is the story of a sixteen- and a forty-six-year-old. Catherine is in hospital, having been in a coma for two weeks after being hit by the car of Dominique Dolls, a Swiss woman passing through town. Madame Dolls, feeling responsible, stays to visit and (symbolically) feed Catherine. Then she takes her back to Switzerland for convalescence, more to be sure that Catherine has not sustained any permanent damage than for any other reason. The image none the less is of rebirth and rebonding.

Madame Dolls introduces Catherine to painting and then, as Tatiana did for Douchka, fosters her passion and immediately visible talent. For the first part of the novel Madame Dolls is solicitous, affectionate, and somewhat nervous that Catherine might come to love her too fiercely. She also responds to Catherine because she is the childless second wife of a man who pays much more attention to his own daughter, Caroline, than he does to her. He has refused to have more children with Dominique in order to protect Caroline's uniqueness and her inheritance.

The family dynamic is charged. Monsieur Dolls is charmingly courteous to his wife but gives her little support or affection. However Caroline has not yet succeeded in breaking the marriage. She, Caroline, is ironic, sardonic, and insolent towards her step-mother but does not visit very often. Into this tense but superficially civilized triangle comes Catherine. She is young and impulsive and defends Dominique Dolls against Caroline, thus creating recurrence of the head pain caused by the accident.

Her passion creates a dilemma: "Madame Dolls was sitting on the edge of the bed and Catherine kneeling on the covers, her hands tight between her thighs to prevent her arms from wrapping them-selves around Madame Dolls and in Catherine's heart a huge flame of love which could light up the world. Madame Dolls didn't dare move. Catherine's passion terrified her because she didn't know what to call it. A burst of enthusiasm ... a pure affection ... or a more violent love joining the catastrophe of the accident ... [...] Because Catherine loved her in this way, Madame Dolls could not keep her there. And Catherine would not tolerate any separation" (64). Catherine is wondering the same thing, but first reassures her: "You are my joy in life, she said gravely. Do not think that I love you too much or badly" (65).

They both get progressively more passionate about each other, but each shows her feelings only by constrained or impulsive responses that the other understands only too well. The richness and luminosity of this book come from the loving insights and the insights into the workings of love that the author has a gift for seeing and translating into words and gestures. A moment at Catherine's first art show is one of my favourites: "'To be there, near you, when you show the best of yourself to the outside world.' Madame Dolls' last sentence. The most beautiful. The one that put all the others out of mind. Catherine suddenly understood its meaning. Truth was in that sentence and was called love" (85).

Catherine has times of serious depression triggered by the thought that at the end of six months she has to go home. One night she begs Madame Dolls to sleep in her bed with her. Madame Dolls lies awake and thinks her way through her physical and emotional response to Catherine. There is no false denial here, no moral judgment, no hiding from self: "And then suddenly, she thought of nothing but this body snuggled against her own [...] her arms closed around the sleeping Catherine. And with a terrified happiness, she listened to the rise of this voluptuous tenderness coming to her from this young body attached to hers" (97). The next morning, watching Catherine sleeping: "Contemplating Catherine's happiness outside time and reality. Such sweet joy where was mingled such abundance that it became intolerable pain" (100). As she reflects she realizes the truth of their situation: "The reflex of a lover who falls asleep after lovemaking and, in sleep, still seeks the presence of his [sic] happiness [...] A whole body, heavy with unconsciousness and that was speaking none the less. [...] And she had loved this weight of flesh that had made of her a woman rich in tenderness, a woman satisfied and more"(100).

Madame Dolls does not react negatively to her new understanding. Their closeness and awareness evolve in complex ways until finally Catherine demands a kiss. She says that it is to rid herself of her obsession; the result is of course quite the opposite:

She kissed Catherine as she would smell a flower. With too much tenderness. With too much love. Almost with respect. Because Catherine offered, eyes closed, a face so imprinted with purity and joy that Madame Dolls thought of the face of a child taking communion for the first time.

Then she thought of nothing but the coolness of these lips under hers [...] the heat flowing through her with such violence that she closed her eyes.

A great void was in her. It was in Catherine too.

They looked at each other for a few moments without speaking, as if frightened by what they had just discovered through that shared emotion, that joy they had received. (120)

They are clearly in love, but as they have no knowledge of lesbian sexuality, Caroline's role is necessary to move the action along. She seduces and initiates Catherine in order to upset her stepmother's happiness. Catherine is left feeling besmirched and guilty, joyless but knowledgeable. After a week of silence, tension, and pain,

174   SPECIFICALLY FRENCH LESBIANS, 1968–1996

Catherine and Madame Dolls fall into each other's arms: "Two yards away there was the divan with its exotic cover. Arms conveyed her gently towards these colours from another world, and she let herself be led, ears humming, eyes closed, forehead damp like a being deprived of consciousness and given over to instinct. There was no other solution. There had never been another [...] Then came a torrent of passion, of transport, suffering, a tearing apart of happiness, which produced two groaning, tortured beings, thrown onto this bed in the eye of a hurricane of deliverance and sincerity" (172–3).

Interrupted by nothing less than a telephone call from Monsieur Dolls, they continue that night: "That night nothing kept them apart. Catherine knew the triumph of love, the marvel of holding a vanquished being in her arms, a shared devouring hunger to discover each other, to find each other again, to go beyond their limits without any weariness. Just before dawn, they finally fell asleep, arms and legs intertwined, like an animal with eight limbs" (177).

The love is consummated. Madame Dolls realizes that Caroline may well have achieved her aim, though not in the manner anticipated: Monsieur Dolls would return home and destroy this happiness. This is of course true. After a week of passion they have to live, restrained and discreet, in the house with him. Neither can stand it, and Catherine leaves. Five years later Monsieur Dolls is dead, and Madame Dolls joins Catherine in Paris.

At last a joyful love and a happy ending! The book is written with great awareness and sensitivity of language and an incredible sureness of feeling. It is a real find, touching, sensuous, delightful, and honest – a treasure of a book and one of the most effective (in the sense of both ringing true and being a pleasure to read) of the period.

THE 1980S: NEW AUTHORS

The 1980s brings more of the same admixture as the 1970s. It would seem that the field is now separating clearly into four recognizable types. First, there are the frantic and overstuffed badgirl novels, represented in this decade by Sophie Chauveau's *Débandade* (Rout, 1982), which has one short chapter on lesbian sex in a book totally stuffed with sexual activity and potted feminism. Second, there are the "clever" novels with a gimmick: Anne Garréta's *Sphinx* (1986) is a grammatical *tour de force*, which may or may not have its place in this study, as it is not possible to tell in any way whether the disc-jockey protagonist is male or female. The girlfriend is indeed female – but I cannot know whether or not she might be lesbian! Such linguistic ambiguity is certainly a clever way of remaining in a literary closet, if this is the case. If it is not, there is no reason to look at the novel further.

Third, there are the triangulated sex plots. France Huser follows in the footsteps of Irène Monési with *La Maison du désir* (The House of Desire, 1982) and *La Chambre ouverte* (The Open Bedroom, 1986). *La Maison du désir* is a text of juxtaposed fragments, structured around three keys, three apartments, and three lovers. In one of the series of sections the "tu" addressed by the narrator is female. The novel feels young and hard, with the intention of being outrageous. It is a novel apparently exploring desire but is more gymnastic than sensual. The writing does not evoke any physical feeling of sexuality, any sense of woman, or of desire. Ultimately I found it arid.

By the time of *La Chambre ouverte* Huser is writing more effective prose. Her theme is still sexual desire – that desire is being used and the person feeling it exploited. Again a triangular story – Sabine begins by being attracted to Louise, who is in a relationship with Antoine. Louise agrees to make love to Sabine only if Sabine makes love to Antoine. Sabine gradually falls in love with Antoine (we are told by Louise) and loses all the lightness that made Louise think at first that she must be a dancer. It is a rather unpleasant novel of ensnarement and destruction.

Reine Bud-Printems's *Lil* (1985) has a similar dark streak. This time the story is not one of sexuality between the women characters although they both have sex with their own and the other's partner, as we learn ultimately). It is a novel of fascination and abandonment, which reminds me of Béatrix Beck's *Noli*.

Representing the final group is Martine Roffinella's *Elle* (She, 1988), also a novel of fascination and adolescent love. It joins a tradition of introspective novels written in the first person, and it has all the intensity of the tormented novels of the 1950s. However, in a twist, that satisfied me as an act of revenge for all the previous suffering heroines and perhaps also as a step towards lesbian

176   SPECIFICALLY FRENCH LESBIANS, 1968–1996

murder mysteries, this narrator kills the beloved who scorns her. A step out of suicidal despair into a crime of passion strikes me as a move into visibility and the claiming of the right of this lesbian passion to exist and be acknowledged. I hail *Elle* as a step towards lesbian liberation.

ANCESTORS: AUDRY AND AURIVEL

Liberation takes another major form in the 1980s. As a result of the more open attitude towards women's experience created by feminist activity – perhaps an aftermath of the fame of Violette Leduc's autobiography or the publication of Jeanne Galzy's series *La Surprise de vivre*, perhaps as a response to their need to claim their lives fully while they still could and take advantage of the new climate in which there was a respectful context for such work – Colette Audry and Rolande Aurivel, two more authors born in the early years of the century, published autobiographical and fictional writings. Audry is a contemporary of Beauvoir, Galzy, Leduc, and Yourcenar. Aurival is perhaps a little younger.

Colette Audry's *La Statue* (The Statue, 1983) is described in its blurb as "a romantic novel which is not fictionalized. The adventure happened." It is the tale of the author's adolescence. Audry writes beautifully, evocatively, and thoughtfully. She depicts the intellectual exploration of Colette, her protagonist-self, as well as the emotional and behavioural upheavals of adolescence, the realities of school and family life. Above all she re-creates Colette's love for Mathilde, her teacher. This love begins as a secret crush and develops into devotion and frequent visits in which Colette sits tongue-tied, absorbing influences that shape her thoughts and attitudes. But parallel to this awkward surface reality is the inner relationship that the girl creates with her beloved – all the conversations that she has in her head, all the events and connections that she imagines. These continue long after she has left Britanny for Paris, when the connection between Colette and Mathilde is sustained only by the odd postcard from Mathilde in response to Colette's constant correspondence and by brief meetings at the end or beginning of term, as Mathilde passes through Paris.

When finally Colette believes herself free of her love for

Mathilde, she writes a non-constrained letter, which is answered immediately by an invitation to visit Mathilde for a while. She pours out the story of the love that she has felt in order (she believes) to bring that phase of her life to completion. Instead it provokes the beginning of a love affair that lasts two years and from which she moves away without ever really ceasing to be haunted by Mathilde. The volume, published (and apparently written) some fifty years after the end of their relationship, bears witness to the importance of the love and the experience.

Rolande Aurivel's story of her long lesbian relationship – forty-three years with the same partner – is valuable because of the statement made by such a life, the first in this whole history. It is not legitimately part of this study, however, in that it is pure auto-biography, and despite its promising title, *Dans l'ombre et au soleil de Lesbos* (In the Shade and the Sun of Lesbos, 1988), it is dull.

L'Oiseau de Sapho (Sappho's Bird, 1989), Aurivel's novel, which was actually written by 1978, displays a nice sense of irony that is absent from the autobiography. It could be seen as an alternative to the life that Jeanne Galzy gives to Amédée in *La Cavalière*, if Amédée were to live in ways more reminiscent of her great-grand-father. And in synopsis it certainly sounds like a novel from the "Naughty (Eighteen) Nineties." Elizabeth de Mageroy, bastard daughter of a duke, full of pride and panache, is expelled from school because of lesbian activity. Aurivel pulls no punches: "Braids hanging down her back, on her knees, Liliane had her face buried in the opening of a pair of lowered jodhpurs" (13). Then she adds laconically: "The discretion surrounding the scandal was equivalent to its outrageousness" (13).

Elizabeth marries a very rich papal baron in his forties,[11] and by her attitude discourages him almost entirely from making sexual advances to her. He gradually realizes that she is picking up women. She discovers Eliane, who is an orphan (conveniently) who works for Elizabeth's horse trainer. Elizabeth wastes no time in making love to her: "She undressed Eliane [...] She immediately went for what was to her the greatest pleasure: active contact between the points of two excited sex organs. It didn't take long before she fell into that black and ruby hole where love gets lost for a few moments [...] then, still quivering, she came to herself and finished the caress with her tongue while her fingers entered deep into a welcoming belly" (36–7). "And, of course, they made love with passion because their desires met in a veritable communion of the flesh. The reciprocal knowledge of their bodies was almost perfect. They were young, voracious, burning, somewhat restrained in the daytime" (39).

The description is obviously written by an author with lesbian imagination, but it reads like a constructed description rather than an experience. Also, the context is literary: Eliane is beautiful; Elizabeth is superb in the larger-than-life way that lesbians have often been presented in French novels, since Balzac and Gautier established the precedents – imperative, somewhat masculine, and usually a little cruel.

Elizabeth's husband watches over them, arranging their travels, in a manner reminiscent of Colette's Claudine, Rézi, and Renaud. Eventually he brings into the house another lesbian, Marguerite Downes, who is an Egyptologist. (This is another touch that makes this novel feel as though it belongs much earlier. Archaeology and sociology are the avant-garde professions in novels written around 1900.) Eliane, who has been studying and wants to make something of herself, is intrigued, takes the bait, goes to Egypt. By this time Elizabeth and Eliane have been together nine years, and the reader knows almost nothing about either of them. Eliane returns to Egypt and inevitably makes love with Marguerite. Elizabeth collapses at Eliane's departure and then gradually recovers, rediscovers desire, and finds new lovers within her social circle and outside. Eliane reappears, disfigured, having had a dreadful accident. They make their peace but do not reconnect. Robert, the husband, dies of a stroke and is buried in Venice. The book ends as it began, with Elizabeth in Venice.

There she meets a lovely young woman whose family is very dubious. Elizabeth knows that Ingrid's father is not what he seems to be but is so captivated by the girl that she believes in her. On discovering that Ingrid is part of his plot to steal her famous ring, Elizabeth impales herself on Ingrid's brother's knife and dies – to be buried with her husband.

The plot is more than somewhat melodramatic. Elizabeth has the feeling of a character from another age, perhaps even from as far back as Balzac's *La Fille aux yeux d'or*. It is curious that, in a book written by a lesbian to celebrate women, the only moment of feeling and sense of dignity and love that I found was connected to a man. Robert's last letter to Elizabeth was that of a truly gracious human being.

I assert that the novel was written to celebrate women because in her preface Aurival wrote: "Love between women is lived in tenderness, in the moment, in the face of death, opposite the other, the third, in the face of habit, and in that it is like any other love story." It is a pity that her skill as a novelist was not adequate for her to translate her thought into literature – at least for me. However her novel acts as a bridge here between earlier times (those evoked by Jeanne Galzy) and the immediate future, to be found in the novels of Hélène de Monferrand, where Elizabeth de Mageroy would not be entirely out of place.

One novel that does fit Aurivel's definition of love is Régine Deforges's *Pour l'amour de Marie Salat* (1986) – comprised of letters exchanged between two women in a village. It is a tale of gentle, daily love. The book was adapted into a delightful play, which ran successfully at the Théâtre de Poche in Montparnasse for a while.

Aurivel's autobiography also points forward to the novels published by the Editions Geneviève Pastre,[12] because to date all the books in the collection Les Octaviennes/romans read as though the authors are telling their own stories and cannot quite get far enough away from them to transform them into satisfactory novels. My criticism of the works is not meant to denigrate the existence of a lesbian publishing house in Paris. The very possibility of bearing witness to lesbian experience without having to disguise or diminish its importance in the text is crucial to the development of fine and undistorted lesbian literature, of which there is as yet very little.

BEARING WITNESS

By 1996 Les Editions Geneviève Pastre had published four novels: Catherine Hubert's *Jessica ou l'île* (Jessica or the Island, 1993) and *Vers l'ouest* (Towards the West, 1996), Odette Menteau's *Un*

Chemin semé de graviers mauves (A Path Sprinkled with Mauve Gravel, 1994), and Lucie Rivière's *La Soupe aux fruits* (Fruit Soup, 1994).

The first one, *Jessica ou l'île*, is subtitled "drame," and so it is – a drama that lasts twenty-four hours, in the tradition of classical theatre. It is a curious little text written in the conditional mode, in brief sentences set out on the page as notes might be. It reads like description for a scenario made for one of the actresses. The characters are "elle" (she) and "toi" (you). A brief love story with an ambiguous ending, it works well.

In contrast Hubert's other book, *Vers l'ouest*, does not read well at all. Apparently the third in a series of four volumes covering the period from the heroine's childhood in the 1960s to adulthood and 1995, this particular section is set mostly in the United States in the 1970s and 1980s. *Vers l'ouest* is the only volume published, which in my view is just as well. The brief, flat sentences of *Jessica ou l'île* worked because of the slight unreality of the context, the ambiguities and absences, the conditional narration, and the unresolved nature of the piece. A similar declarative style, used to trace a life chronologically action by action, without décor, characterization, or plot, is dull to the ear and the mind. The author provides no colour and leaves no space for the reader to provide her own.

Menteau's *Un chemin semé de graviers mauves* is also a chronological life story. It follows Pauline, the narrator, from the early age of two to twenty, during which time both she and her older sister, Louise, discover their own and ultimately each other's lesbianism. The author spends too much time, to my taste, on Pauline's early childhood. Also Pauline has essentially the same vocabulary and style no matter what her age may be – a fault that bothered me at the beginning of the novel and again at the very end. However, the writing is lively. Pauline has spunk and a sharp eye for what is going on around her. Her friends and her family come alive for the reader, making the novel fun to read. *Un chemin semé de graviers mauves*, though not as sophisticated in literary terms, fits well with Wittig's *L'Opoponax*, Gisèle Bienne's *Douce amère*, and Mireille Best's *Hymne aux murènes* (Hymn to Moray Eels).

Menteau takes on the issue of homophobia directly and is the first French novelist to do so without ambiguity. Her characters discuss the effects of social and cultural silences concerning lesbianism and their state of ignorance and isolation as working-class girls. They also see and comment on the pressures put on girls to be heterosexual, to be decorative and desirable. Menteau's characters are all from a poor background and have little schooling and less access to serious knowledge, but they are aware of the oppressions under which they suffer and talk about them lucidly. Only one of the young women has some notions of feminism. She also speaks English and has a grandmother who is comfortably off and so, we must suppose, comes from a higher economic class than Louise and Pauline. (Pauline always describes her family as "nombreuse et nécessiteuse" [big and poor] in terms that make me think immediately of official reports.) Her feminism is much appreciated and endorsed by the other young women, who act on what they learn. Menteau's novel is energetic, optimistic, humorous, and socially astute. That it lacks polish is only a minor disadvantage.

Lucie Rivière's text is the most successful of the four, perhaps because it has focus. *La Soupe aux fruits* is the story of Armelle, a woman of thirty-five, who meets and falls in love with a young lesbian. The novel traces their meetings, their upsets, and their increasing recognition of the importance of their connection. The story covers a period of some six months, from the moment when they first meet in a train until they find each other again (and forever ...).

Lucie Rivière writes with sensitivity in *La Soupe aux fruits*. She does include what seem to have become during the 1980s obligatory journeys to Greece and to the United States, which many authors use to fill out thin plots, but she uses her geographical contexts with some individuality and a certain credibility.

The pleasant thing about these novels is that they allow the heroine to get her girl and expect a modicum of normality and happiness. I ask myself whether this is a function of having a lesbian publisher. Other publishing houses sometimes deal with lesbian texts, as we saw above, but these books never end well, and I wonder whether the almost inevitable suffering of the protagonist is a conscious or subconscious response to cultural homophobia.

And if so, is this prejudice actually exhibited by publishers and their readers and editors, or is it proof of internalized homophobia on the part of the writers themselves? Be that as it may, except for the novels produced by Pastre, those of the 1990s offer little in the way of satisfaction to their lesbian progagonists.

THE 1990S: LOST LOVES

The theme of unattainable love – the major theme of the 1950s – returns with a twist in several novels. Cécile Wajsbrot's *Le Désir d'Equateur* (Desire for Ecuador, 1995), told by a protagonist who soothes her grief by the symbolic action of swimming laps in a pool, is, as one may imagine, a stream of consciousness. There unfold the memories of two lovers, one male, one female, one overt, one clandestine. Neither is named; they have no depth and no context. There is the mention of various contemporary events in the non-fictional world and, within the fiction, a possible job in Ecuador. The work is structured around a series of meetings between the lovers. It focuses on the desire that the narrator feels for the other woman, the way in which this grows and then turns sour. The novel ends, as it begins, with a reflection on loss.

An earlier novel of Wajsbrot's, *Une vie à soi* (A Life of One's Own, 1982), is much more traditional in presentation and more open in its flirting with lesbianism. In it, Wajsbrot uses the cliché of the foreign lesbian temptress – a pop singer ironically named Jane Handy – who intrigues and finally makes love once to each of two married French women reporters, Véronique and Anne, who then return to their husbands and safe lives, albeit with a little regret and nostalgia. At another level the author uses a foreign lesbian temptress again as one of the reporters, Anne, is fascinated by Virginia Woolf to the point of getting almost totally absorbed into a re-creation of Woolf's state of mind and interest in madness – a project out of which she intends to write a book that Woolf had mentioned as a preoccupation in her journal. Hence the triangular situations in the present of the novel (of which there are six) find echoes in the relations of Virginia Woolf, Vita Sackville-West, and Ethel Smyth[13] and in the balance between heterosexuality and lesbianism and between sanity and madness.

This novel is clearly a predecessor of *Désir d'Equateur*. It has similar fluidity and love of complexity. In some ways it is more ambitious, and as a result of the inter-textual expansion made possible through the reference to works of Woolf included, it is more interesting to readers of women's literature. Both the novels are stories of unsatisfactory, unfulfilled potential.

La Pluie sur la mer (Rain on the Sea, 1996), by Nita Rousseau, is also a remembering of love and loss, but this time the love is not sexual and the loss is definitive because Sonia is dead. This book continues the tradition of outrageous actress (singer/dancer) who is adored and who removes herself from the life of the (young) woman who adores her, so that each of them suffers in some way. It reminds me of Monési's *Althia* and Rigal's *L'Envers des choses* for these reasons. The difference here is that Sonia kills herself, not because of Alexandra, who is required to approve the death and attend to the disposal of the body of her beloved, but because of the behaviour of Alexandra's good-for-nothing brother, who had become Sonia's lover. Alexandra is left alone, burdened with the secret of Sonia's death and of her love for her.

L'Insectueuse [sic] (Insectuous Woman, 1991), by Evelyne Hugues, offers an even less attainable love. The novel is made up of forty letters from the narrator/lover who purports to tell the story of their love affair back to her beloved. The letters read like an obsessive journal written to "vous" (you) about events from nine months earlier. The text ranges from observation, through descriptions of lovemaking, expressions of hatred and contempt, and attempts to shock, to erotic fantasies. Gradually the opening description of the narrator watching a reversed dung beetle struggling to turn back on its feet joins with the continual reference to the image of the beloved in the street below reflected in the glass of a picture and with the fact that the picture is a print of cranes. In French the word for crane – "grue" – is slang for a prostitute, and the reader comes to realize that the entire text is the product of fantasies that the narrator has projected onto a passerby. The love invoked and profaned has never existed. The woman observed has been as unaware of her observer and of the danger that the observer represents to her as was the beetle whom the narrator could have chosen to crush as easily as to set on its feet.

184   SPECIFICALLY FRENCH LESBIANS, 1968–1996

Just as bizarre in its attitudes and story line is Anne Michel's *La Dame noire* (The Black Lady, 1992). Claude, a thirty-five-year-old French woman, is fascinated by Angèle, a rich, talented, exuberant, and very often very drunk young woman from the Ivory Coast. Their relationship is ambiguously affectionate but not sexual. Claude describes herself as a friend, a governess, and a captive. Angèle takes Claude to Africa. The first half of the novel concerns Angèle and her tumultuous relationship with her mother, who is imperious, rich, and as big as she is powerful. Angèle then disappears – into a clinic for detoxification, as she frequently does, the reader learns. Claude is left to deal with Ameh Lakkar, the mother, who terrifies her, violates her, and then seduces her. Finally when Claude is totally captivated by Ameh and ready to stay with her forever, she is unceremoniously shipped back to France.

The novel appears emancipated while actually playing on a gamut of old prejudices and stereotypes. Ameh Lakkar is both the figure of the wild, overly sexual, exotic black woman of racist imagination and a new form of the calculating lesbian predator popular in the nineteenth century.

Noëlle Loriot's *Les Méchantes Dames* (Naughty Ladies, 1995) is built on similar premises. In tone it is an extraordinarily old-fashioned book, reminding me of the male-authored novels of the 1890s. In structure it has the complicated plot line and lack of characterization of the average murder mystery. "Les méchantes dames" is said to be the term used by some Hollywood star to refer to lesbians, and the phrase recurs *ad nauseam*. There are two narrators – a male, married doctor who is curious about lesbians and a middle-aged practising lesbian. The plot turns around a famous lawyer and his lesbian wife who is equally renowned, though for her sexual exploits and not her professional competence, and around the women who are involved with each of them. The context is bourgeois middle-aged lesbian society in Paris. The lesbians seem to me to be included simply to add spice and a sense of social wickedness to an otherwise superficial story of multiple adultery. All the stereotypes are there: masculine clothes, short hair, brusqueness, predatory behaviour, and complaisant husbands. In a quiet way, this tale plays with the latent homophobia and prejudice of its readers as well as on the revival

Exploring Lesbian Identity   185

of the behaviour of the "Naughty Nineties." It is held together by the element of mystery, which whets our curiosity sufficiently to hold us to the end.

Lesbian murder mysteries in the North American style, or rather in the particular style of the French "Série noire," also arrive in the 1990s. Dorothé Jaguar published *Un Linceul de peinture bleue* (A Painted Blue Shroud) in 1994, and Emma Christa's *Elles sont pas croyables!* (They're Unbelievable!) appeared in 1996. What to say? They are what they are – racy, slangy, violent, fast moving, laced with graphic sex and equally graphic blood and gore. Jaguar's writing is less abrasive than Christa's, but each is successful in its own way. Their very existence would suggest greater tolerance for lesbian visibility on the literary scene than ever before.

There is perhaps also some sense of *déjà vu*. French male authors, Boris Vian for one, followed American authors into crime and gangster novels in the 1930s, quickly creating a style that has a cultural flavour particular to France. Similarly French lesbian writers seem to have been influenced by successful American lesbian authors such as Katherine V. Forrest, Barbara Wilson, and Mary Wings in their choice of genre, meanwhile adding a distinctive twist towards the works of their male compatriot precedessors.

CONCLUSION

Despite the burgeoning of lesbian literature and theory in Europe and North America during the period covered by this chapter, the French tradition remains curiously resistant to influence from outside. Such isolation is even more curious when one considers that the (bad) translation of Beauvoir's *The Second Sex* serves as the root text for many white second-wave feminists, that Wittig's *Les Guérillères* was a cult novel for lesbians, and that Wittig was a major name in early lesbian theory. Similarly Foucault, via Judith Butler's *Gender Trouble* (1990), is crucial to North American sex and gender studies, where his *Histoire de la sexualité* (1980–86) is an authoritative source, as are works by Cixous and Luce Irigaray.

Once again, as at the end of the nineteenth century, French authors are translated and influence Anglo–American culture (and perhaps others) in ways that have no impact in France. French lesbian writers remain uninfluenced by the "exported theories," and no "imported theory" seems to touch them either. An increasing number of lesbian classics – Barnes, Stein, Woolf (to name the most familiar to me) – have been translated into French during this period. However, they remain relatively difficult to obtain outside Paris, and they leave no visible trace in French writing.

CHAPTER SIX

Contrasting Perspectives:
François, Best, and Monferrand

Three writers stand out currently, for their sustained attention to
the depiction of lesbians in the world and for the quality of that
attention. Their lesbian characters are first and always complex,
interesting human beings, living out their joys and pain in a real
world. Here are no stereotypes, no traditional monsters, but no
revolutionary feminists and not much social analysis either. The
characters are clear-sighted, and their circumstances are drawn with
explicit or implicit awareness of social and cultural homophobia
and its consequences. There the similarities between the novels of
Jocelyne François, Mireille Best, and Hélène de Monferrand come
to an end.

Jocelyne François explores the depths and richness of the human
condition from within the experiences of her own life. Her focus is
on the absolute nature of love in the human heart and spirit. She is
a poet and a philosopher with a Racinian eye.[1] Mireille Best has
more of a sociologist's eye and a strong sense of the absurd. Her
centre of interest is damaged children in working-class families in
particular. She looks at how daughters survive. Hélène de Monferrand's characters live in a world of ambassadors and industrialists.
Aristocratic or rich, right-wing in their politics, her lesbians do not
hesitate to stride out into what is customarily considered male
space and occupy it without qualm or problem.

Monferrand, like Galzy before her, writes novels of epic propor-
tions, with multitudes of characters travelling continuously across
the geography of northern Europe. Best focuses on a group in a
communal space or neighbourhood. François chooses only her narrator's immediate circle and one room per person at most.

JOCELYNE FRANÇOIS: THE MOVEMENTS OF LOVE

François's interest is in inner space, for which outer activity serves only as context and reflection, much as alchemists occupied themselves with laboratory experiments as physical parallels to their spiritual growth. It is not fortuitous that the narrator and her partner make pots, working with clay, glazes, and fire to sustain themselves materially, while as an avocation one writes, the other sings and paints. The activity accepted in its reality shows the practical creativity that informs their lives; as a metaphor it speaks to their connection to the earth and the elements, the integrity of their effort, and the fragility of their wholeness.

Jocelyne François has written five novels which she herself claims as autobiographical. The first four cover periods of great importance in her own life. The last – *La Femme sans tombe* (1995) – fills in the family background of her partner and so equalizes the picture of their lives, if it does not complete it. All the novels can also be situated in the silences in and around François's journal *Le Cahier vert: Journal 1961–1989 (The Green Notebook: Journal 1961–1989)*, published in 1990.[2]

The first novel, *Les Bonheurs* (Happinesses, 1970), by its very title raises the question of the nature of happiness, on what plane humans should look for it, and whose happiness is at issue at any given time, because that title is at apparent odds with much of the content of the novel. Indeed the book begins with the establishment of an atmosphere of utter anguish. Sarah, the narrator, in love with Anne, a woman who loved her as totally, has been devastated by the sudden, incomprehensible engagement and marriage of her beloved. Anne, obviously broken-hearted too, stated her decision and offered no explanation. The rest of the book covers the ten years that it takes before they come to live together again, during which time they, the author, and – unlikely as it may seem – the reader never seriously doubt the love that they feel for each other. Nor is this novel all pink clouds, sugar, and unrealistic idealism. It is a study of pain, patience, trust, and fortitude, in all their complexity. It is a study of love in a hostile context, of lesbian love in a heterosexual world, trying to survive alongside religious belief dictated by a homophobic church.

An observation in the preface to the new edition of 1982 presents the author's sense of the problem that she had faced: "Vegetation, so blurred by water, resembles life, which cannot be approached easily even though it always gives the illusion of proximity" (12). All of Jocelyn François's novels are attempts to make clear circumstances of great human complexity. What is amazing is the acuity of her vision as she peers into the deep and often murky waters of shifting feelings, as is her ability to appreciate at the same time the sun sparkles on the surface and varieties of vegetation and fish that she happens on in passing. Because of the lucid philosophical nature of her gaze and the poetic nature of her sensibility, the focus that she brings to bear on the particular circumstances around her really does transform the personal into the universal – and to bring about such an illumination of the general from the perspective of a much-disparaged minority is no small feat. Jocelyne François is an important writer who deserves much more recognition than she has received.

Les Bonheurs is narrated in a variety of ways: in part Sarah is the narrator; some information comes from Anne's journal, which Sarah acquires; parts of the novel are in the third person. The language is complicated by the ambiguous nature of "tu" (you) in the various voices. "Tu" for Sarah can be either Anne or Jean, a man with whom she has an affair. Likewise "tu" for Anne is sometimes Sarah, sometimes Michel, her husband. The complexity of the patterns of intimacy follow the "tu" for each of the women. They are the major voices surrounded by four men and ultimately three children. Two of the men are priests, two are sexual partners of the women.

We learn that in the innocence of her joyful love for Sarah, Anne went to Ulrich, an apparently friendly, open priest who worked with students, and asked him directly and simply to help Sarah and herself live together. His response was equally direct, but much less simple and certainly not innocent. He told Anne that as the elder of the two and the instigator of their sexual relations she must take responsibility for saving Sarah despite herself from the sin of lesbianism. Their relations must be broken off, and Sarah must not know why. Anne obeyed. She accepted Michel's proposal of marriage *because* he said that he would never love her, and Sarah faced a *fait accompli*. She was abandoned with no consultation, no explanation, no possible appeal, yet supposedly for the right reason. Ulrich disposed of both of them in a way that suited his conscience and the rules of his employer, the Roman Catholic church. He showed no compassion, no humanity, and only he profited from the secrecy that he imposed.

It was not until after I had read François's third novel, *Joue-nous "España," roman de mémoire* (Play Us "España," Memory Novel, 1980), that I came to understand how Anne could have obeyed Ulrich so uncompromisingly and without question in *Les Bonheurs*. In the later novel, based on the author's childhood and adolescence, François shows, consciously or not, how she learned from the nuns at her boarding school a purity of focus, lucid clarity of perception, and desire for the absolute, which shaped her understanding, her relation with the world and with the divine, and her concept of love. She also learned patience and fortitude. Once it was clear in *Les Bonheurs* that Sarah would continue to love Anne, then the central questions for them and thus for readers become whether, how, and when they will come together again.

Gradually it becomes apparent that Michel, Anne's husband, is a lay version of Ulrich. Both men deny the reality of the love between Sarah and Anne; both believe in a "cure." Ulrich believes that a cure by separation brings salvation. Michel sees the cure as coming by reason and bringing normality. Both men are sure of their power within the institution of the church and of marriage; each is controlling and insensitive. Michel is possessive and unloving, treating Anne as an object that belongs to him – his wife, the mother of his children.

Anne's sexual relations with Michel are the best part of their life together. Sarah has sexual relations with a man also. Jean is married already; towards Sarah he is loving and understanding but ultimately demanding in his need for her, and she breaks off their affair. Neither woman is averse to heterosexual relations. The point that Jocelyne François makes clear is that Sarah and Anne's love for each other is total and absolute. It has a rightness that is inexorable. François's novels are all studies of the rare moments when their trust in each other is put to the test because the attention of one or the other is diverted for a while.

Les Bonheurs is about love and non-love and about sexual expression. The range extends from sensual pleasure, through love-making in tenderness and its opposite – sex as the taking possession of another – to absolute love and union. François explores despair and joy, separation and union. Love is heterosexual, homosexual, and maternal. Anne stays with Michel until their separation can be

Contrasting Perspectives 191

accomplished with gentleness. The last page, separated as a sort of epilogue, suggests that the love between Anne and Sarah might well be the stronger for the test of time.

Jocelyne François's way of focusing on the essential, which for her is the innermost feelings of her characters, tends to leave these characters suspended in a luminosity ungrounded in measurable time and space. The separation of Sarah and Anne would have taken place about 1952. Similar kinds of separation were the subject of most of the lesbian novels of the 1950s. Ulrich's counsel would not have been unusual; Anne would have had nowhere else to turn for advice, nor would her choice of a loveless marriage have been unusual in the conservative climate of postwar France or within the heterosexual and intensely coupled culture of France, which has never offered social space for women to live without men.

What is amazing, and what might lead a reader to assume that the novel takes place later, given its autobiographical nature, is the total acceptance of the rightness of the love between Anne and Sarah that imbues the book. Anne might obey Ulrich, but she does not condemn her own behaviour or her feelings. We see no guilt, no homophobia, no self-castigation, no doubt even, in this and François's other novels. Their love is. The mistakes examined are those that prevent the love from being lived to the full, not, as in most writing, those that prevent love.

Les Amantes (The Women Lovers, 1978), the second novel, takes place some years after *Les Bonheurs,* when Sarah and the unnamed narrator have been living for some time in a tiny village in Provence. They make pots; Sarah is a painter, the narrator a poet. One child (referred to as "the child who lives in the house") lives with them, and two others (unnamed also) arrive in school holidays. This is the context of the story, and it is almost as briefly invoked in the novel. Despite the narrator's comment – "In a woman's life, too many hours are swallowed up by the irritating need of things" (15) – the reader learns very little of the daily life of the household. There are descriptions of moments: a change of light, a meal by the fire, a poem, a feeling, a conversation, but these are not connected to form a total context. Again the focus is on the deep story. not on the surface of events.

This time Jocelyne François is examining friendship juxtaposed to love and sexuality. The narrator has a new friend – male and a famous poet. With him she hopes to live an adventure of loving friendship, shared ideas, and writing – pushing beyond the normal bounds of friendship into deeper trust and understanding.

It goes without saying, for her, that her love for Sarah remains the core of her life and that with that love comes absolute sexual fidelity. Apparently unaware of excluding Sarah, she focuses her gaze totally on the new friend. In fact, Sarah is as absent from the narrative as she is from the narrator's gaze. Not included, she withdraws further, until her anguish is palpable and the narrator pays attention and reassures her in convincing ways.

The book is punctuated by the summer and winter visits of the children, by the arrival of spring and autumn, so that there is a sense of the unrolling of time and an implication that there is an undescribed, ongoing life that binds Sarah, the child, and the narrator together. Sarah and the child inhabit the book and create an emotional contact, however evanescent their presence. But the intensity of the text lies in the narrator's involvement with him, the (unnamed) poet: "*This* is the friend she wants. He is her twin whom she recognizes" (32). She wants him because of her involvement in writing. She knows him through the intimacy of poetry. As she says much later, he knows what she is saying. The connection is immediate, passionate, and fascinating to her. She soon realizes, however, that he is in love with her and that for him love implies sexuality.

The scene where she refuses to make love with him because of her love for Sarah is the most gentle and elegant handling of a refusal that I have ever read. She loves him and tells him so, but that love will have no physical expression because she loves Sarah also and she chose Sarah first. A love once given is absolute, and she will not compromise. Her feelings are complicated by the fact that he has been diagnosed with some apparently incurable illness. She is drawn in to his pain as well as to his poetry, and however bad his behaviour she finds it difficult to disentangle herself.

In a number of ways this man reminds me of Michel, the husband in *Les Bonheurs*. He manipulates her through his pain and his need for her, but his declared understanding of her, through poetry, has no effect on his behaviour. Increasingly we see that his intentions are sexual and that, despite his apparent acceptance of her position and her love for Sarah, he in no way abandons his desire. His maleness destroys his human sensitivity, and he is ruthless, though indirect, in pursuit of his ends.

His way of being is almost certainly the cause of Sarah's initial anguish – after all, the narrator left her for a man once before.[3] He is not short of women. Whenever there is tension between him and the narrator, a woman turns up to live with him as a visible threat of ultimate exclusion and an impediment to immediate contact for the narrator. This particular game does not have much effect, because she does not want to sleep with him. It does, however, make clear his attitude with regard to rivalry and supremacy. His attitude to Sarah is one of disregard. He desires the narrator, and Sarah is an obstacle. There is no indication in the novel that he is homophobic, just that he will brook no rival. And by his emphasis on sexual satisfaction, he destroys his relationship with the narrator altogether.

François explores a parallel situation in the fourth novel, *Histoire de Volubilis* (Story of Volubilis,[4] 1986), with the point of view reversed. This time the painter, now called Elisabeth, becomes attracted by Agatha, a psychologist who leads her on for the apparent purpose of destroying the relationship between Elisabeth and Cécile, the writer. Agatha's husband, Julio, works simultaneously to demoralize and insult Cécile. The implications here are much more homophobic and deliberately destructive than those in *Les Amantes*.

The novel starts with catastrophe – attempted suicides and illness of Cécile's (now adult) children and their partners, and Cécile's awareness that she "is living on not very stable ground" (19). Then Cécile experiences what Sarah lived through in *Les Amantes* – namely, the sense of being invisible to the beloved's gaze. Elisabeth may be living alongside Cécile, but she is not there and, after Agatha breaks off all connection with her, she is in shock and grieving, as was the narrator in *Les Amantes*.

The metaphor for the relationship in *Les Amantes* was that of two roses, side by side, killed overnight by frost but still upright on their stems. The metaphor in *Histoire de Volubilis* is that of Cécile's scoliosis. She has not grown straight, and now things are less and less right. The explanation that she gives is this: "Everything that has deviated seems to her like a living metaphor of herself because she tore the straight thread of her life, she knows that, and nothing is without consequences" (23). In *Les Amantes* the external world came in the form of a nuclear power station to be built nearby – just as the poet's house and others had been built near the village. The intrusions are dangerous.

This time the danger comes in the guise of friends who buy a house in the village. Thus it becomes obvious that the village itself is a metaphor for the withdrawal of Cécile and Elisabeth (the narrator and Sarah, Jocelyne François and her partner) as far from family, their past, and even contemporary French life as possible. They have a studio and a study in a house that looks out into the countryside from a village with two streets and, at first, neither electricity nor running water. That village is both hidden and protected by ramparts of natural rock. Their contact with anyone is minimal, their need to hide enormous – and with cause, for, as we see, as soon as they open to the outside someone sets out to destroy their love and their life. This whole novel is about the discomfort of things, about a sense of a loss of rightness and focus, and also about awareness of the need for non-intervention together with an intensity of presence.

As well as being concerned for herself and for Elisabeth, neither of whom is healthy, Cécile reflects constantly on the state of her children and on the nature of motherhood. In that way *Histoire de Volubilis* connects with *Les Bonheurs* and the early years of the children. She sees her life as full of dangers, risks, and worries, all caused by the disruption of the straight thread of her life, when she destroyed the absolute rightness of her first love (for Elisabeth) and with it her own integrity. It is true that the children are a source of happiness as well as worry and that Cécile herself is increasingly open to moments of joy provoked by details of the natural world, but her sense of safety has gone. Cécile needs to take what is precious to her to another place for another start: "when she looks at Elisabeth and is looked at in her turn, that exchange where the past is buried but the present too, there, suddenly in its instant brilliance and, always contained, the hope* of the future" (179; *esperance*: religious hope).

Thus even though their love, their lesbian love, is the clear and undisputed centre of their world, so much so that its existence is the basis rather than the subject of François's novels, it has had to be somewhat hidden and always protected from direct attack. The parents of the writer (narrator/Anne) are always described as

Contrasting Perspectives

being hostile to their daughter's orientation, as is also her ex-husband.

The novel that gives the most insight into the author's family situation and personal attitudes, therefore providing a basis of understanding for the other, is *Joue-nous "España", roman de mémoire* (Play Us "España," Memory Novel, 1980). In it she tells the story of her childhood and adolescence, the birth of her love for the woman who becomes her life partner, and again the initial tearing separation from her, which was the basis of *Les Bonheurs*.

In all her writing, Jocelyne François observes and reflects on the delights and complexities of being human from her specific and precise point of observation: woman, lesbian, mother, poet. At the centre of her being is love – for her partner, her children, nature, God, special friends – in all its different manifestations and complex interactions, including the pain of loss. *Les Bonheurs* had as a major theme the pain of separation; *Les Amantes,* that of rupture and death. In *Joue-nous "España"* we can see how the author became her adult self, how her way of being, and therefore her style, is rooted in her origins and education. And through the structure of the text, we feel the direct connections between the child described, the woman thinking back in the text and framing it, and the author making the book.

The three quotations at the beginning of the volume point the direction: "I write in order to see (Bernard Noël)." "The universal is not a law, which for being the same everywhere has no real value anywhere. The universal has its place. The universal is in each place in the gaze one takes from it, the use one can make of it (Yves Bonnefoy)." "A novel is a life in book-form (Novalis)." The life that she traces is that of a perceptive little girl who is set apart from the beginning – "Wherever did we go to get her?" (12) is the opening sentence of the retrospective story. Her father wanted a boy, although she seems sure of his "bonté" (good will and kindness), as of that of her grandfather. (Note that she does not choose the word "love.") Whether her mother ever loved her is one of the recurring questions. Her elder brother Pierre is already dead, so she is familiar with visits to the cemetery. The next brother (born after her and also called Pierre) and the little sister receive tender treatment from their mother. The distance between mother and elder daughter has the benefit that Jocelyne is sent away to school, but not just to any school. She goes to a Catholic boarding school in the country, where the simplicity, austerity, purity of intention, and silence suit and shape her in important ways.

Before that, however, comes her life in Nancy and her discovery of music. There is also the war. She happens on a deportation of a group of Jewish families, and at the same time her friend from music class disappears. There is also her discovery of the joy of writing, the comforts of her grandmother, and her compassion for the woman next door, who becomes slowly ever more paralysed throughout the book. Jocelyne visits her regularly, talks to her, reads to her, and takes her flowers.

This little girl already sees right into the essential nature of things. She delights in moments, in perceptions, and language. (The author transmits the idea of a child's speech in her use of simple words and rhythms, without attempting to imitate directly, as Monique Wittig does in *L'Opoponax*.) She also grasps horror and injustice, transmits the intensity that she feels, and then moves on. She has a gift of lucidity, of seeing the magic in things, and taking of joy in it even in the midst of pain: smells, tastes, and changes of light catch her attention already. She is precisely aware of her surroundings, and in this novel they take more prominence than in the others. I gave the book to a friend from Nancy, and he was delighted by the coincidence between his memories and the town that François evoked, the sureness and rightness of her touch.

Life in boarding school provides space and order, order that she increasingly contrasts with the disorder at home, as her father's adulterous behaviour disrupts the family. In the atmosphere of the convent Jocelyne thrives. From the nuns she learns purity of focus, desire for clarity, and the habit of thought and reflection. She admires and acquires their taste for the absolute, and she becomes sufficient to herself.

Throughout the book, we see the narrator looking for her place in the world, becoming aware of complications and complexities at the same time as she grows in wisdom and understanding. She writes: "Very early I acquired a visceral need of silence, and solitude, counterpoint to love, is indispensable to me" (149). She sees the nuns as living a life of focused love, and it is while watching the ceremony of a nun taking the veil that she thinks: "The order of love is unknown to me but it is by it that I want to live. Can one make a choice before one knows? Yes one can" (158). She reflects at length on the nature of love, particularly after Marie-Claire has become her beloved friend (not yet recognized as lesbian love) and she, Jocelyne, is about to leave the school. She realizes that she can direct love towards God either directly and exclusively – directly, as in an enclosed order of nuns, or by usefulness to others, as in a working order, or indirectly through her love for Marie-Claire.

Marie-Claire, a student younger than Jocelyne, had sung with her in the choir. Gradually she becomes more special until one day Jocelyne asks her to be her friend – even though in ordinary terms they already were friends. And everything changes. This is love, although it is not so named:

Inside me everything accelerates, I have the feeling that I have gained a treasure beyond price. The air, which was light before, has become a thousand times lighter. I take her hand, I hold it.

From that moment on nothing is the same. The next day it is I who get up and it's not me. This void with burning edges which has installed itself in my chest and which breathes instead of me, this alertness in my whole body, I have to adjust to it and don't know how. There's wavering, air intake, slippage. An energy keeps bringing me back to a centre where I escape myself again, not that I want to, but this overfull centre can't be opened. I find myself in a totally unknown state. What happened the day before seemed like a primal scene, already far away in time, a scene so perfectly simple and complete that I have no thought about it.

Afterwards whenever I am with Marie-Claire, engaged with her in the most ordinary daily actions, I say to myself "She's here." That feeling goes beyond all other feelings. (163–4).

From then on they talk and talk. We see that each has suffered from her mother's own affective deprivation, which was in some way visited on the daughter. Gradually, after Jocelyne leaves the school, their friendship deepens, and they realize that what they feel is love. But the realization takes a long time. At first they do not even have words for the missing of each other. They write, and their feelings show, so much so that Jocelyne is summoned by Marie-Claire's mother, but all goes well. Not until Marie-Claire is at university also do they have any space and privacy.

Even so it is not until Jocelyne reads Claudel's *Le Partage de Midi*[5] that she realizes that she is in love. She writes to Marie-Claire that she loves her, and they then learn how to make love. "An immense territory is ours until the morning, when weariness puts us to sleep, naked in the heat of the bed that the cold of the room surrounds. My ignorance is equalled only by yours, the same passion devours us, drying up our saliva, knowledge not known in advance, slowness to stop the heart" (188).

For three months they are happy, then in her total innocence and confidence Jocelyne asks the priest-adviser for help, and he forbids her to have any contact beyond friendship with Marie-Claire. She obeys – and the result is the pain of *Les Bonheurs*. Here, at the end of this book, Jocelyne François writes: "Jean Streiff is Bishop of Nevers today. Perhaps this very old story comes up in his memory occasionally. He did his duty, he dispensed dogma, and whether he dispensed it with compassion only he can tell. But he committed a crime in all tranquility. That of having used secrecy as a weapon of separation, as a lever of dislocation and of having watched the body of love crack asunder unendurably, for I obeyed him" (190).

This is the only bitterness or blame to be found in the novels, and it is a measure of the suffering caused. The author goes on to reflect how she deliberately shut herself into marriage and how she continued to suffer: "Marriage is indissoluble, say the priests. Marriage but not love. Love can be torn out like couch-grass, especially between two women. It is doing a service for the body of society. The perfect joy that would not be able to take root in the mire, the perfect joy of renunciation freely chosen, did not come. Sometimes I met you, you were nothing but an open wound. And always, upon us, that mortal silence" (192). Others had to suffer also in order for her to heal: "To reestablish the old unity and repair the injustice, to reincorporate love" (193). And she pays tribute to the light that Marie-Claire has brought to her life. The priest denied that light and caused her to break the clear and direct thread of her life, as we have seen.

François's last novel is not as powerful as the previous ones, although it fills gaps in the collective story of her and Marie-Claire. *La Femme sans tombe* (The Tombless Woman, 1995) starts from the death of Mathilde (Marie-Claire's mother) and tells the story of Marie-Claire's family. This novel, though interesting and certainly well written, does not have the luminosity of the others. Whether this is because the author is telling a story told to her, rather than one that she has experienced, or because she suffered a long illness, thus delaying the book for many years, I do not know.[6] It does serve to provide balance, insight, and background for the earlier novels, and it brings the author's fictionalized autobiography up to date.

Jocelyne François is a striking and insightful writer. I found myself noting many of her thoughts as starting points for my own reflections. Her gift of language is precious and rare. She is intelligent and positive; she is also true to herself and true to others – a writer of integrity.

MIREILLE BEST: ANGUISH AND HUMOUR

Mireille Best also has the gift of translating observation, perception, and insight into strikingly effective language, but hers is language of a very different kind. Whereas François's is measured and has a translucent quality, Best's is emphatic, unexpected, disruptive of order, and frequently funny. I found myself laughing aloud from time to time at the apt juxtapositions that throw circumstances into relief. The author has a sharp and critical eye and a cynical line in black humour.

Best's heroines, like François's narrators, migrate from northern France to Provence, but there the similarity ends. François's world is that of the Catholic middle class in Lorraine. Best's characters are poor, coastal, urban, and working class. (The town named is Le Havre.) The author has written several volumes of short stories, which I am not including here, and three novels: *Hymne aux murènes* (Hymn to Moray Eels, 1986); *Camille en octobre* (Camille in October, 1988), and *Il n'y a pas d'hommes au Paradis* (There Are No Men in Paradise, 1995).

Hymne aux murènes is a story of childhood and adolescence in which, like Jocelyne, Mila of the unpronounceable surname spends her childhood at home and her adolescence away. This time the girls are in some kind of sanatorium that has a director, monitors, and regular medical control, but they all do correspondence courses, and there are no teachers. The most salient feature of the institution is that the girls are made to change rooms and roommates every month or so, so that they won't get "habits." These constant upheavals keep the story moving and provoke much of the humour.

Mila's family is more or less dysfunctional. She has two younger brothers, Jan, who is dyslexic, and Tristan, who does not seem to learn to talk. All the children have different fathers. Tristan's father is in residence at the beginning of the novel. Jan and Mila refer to him as the "pater définitif" (the final pater/father), and as Jan is Mila's half-brother, they consider Tristan their quarter-brother. Mila does well in school, talks very little, and slides through the world without much trouble, until the family discovers her illness. We learn all this in flashback from her adolescence.

Adolescence, under a surface of cynicism, laughter, tears, and mutual support of the gang of friends, is for Mila a story of confusion, desire, love, betrayal, revenge, and escape, all described with laconic humour. Indeed the "love story" is not very different in its essence from those in the adolescent novels of the 1950s. Mila is attracted to Paule and believes Paule to feel something similar, but Paule is a game player and maintains a maximum of ambiguity around her words and actions. Their first meeting sets the tone clearly:

The first day, Paule smiled at me. Mila? Mila what? [...] She put her hands on my shoulders. Hard hands. Yet she spoke to me with gentleness, in a voice that came from her chest and hollowed a strange little coldness in the middle of mine. It will hurt.

Indeed, it did hurt. [...]

Again her hard hands. But her dark eyes were laughing – were hesitating between laughter and the will not to laugh – [...] she had a little line in the left corner of her mouth – hardly a line: a shadow, effaced immediately – whose gentleness contrasted with the brutality of her hands. Deliberate brutality. I'm sure of it. But why deliberate? [...] Again we found ourselves face to face, and our gaze fell into the same holes. It was a bit as though we'd got our tools entangled: we didn't really know how to get them apart. (18–19)

None the less Paule invites Mila to come to her room whenever she likes, although her behaviour remains unpredictable. The night before she (Paule) is to go to hospital for surgery – the girls talk about "having their wings clipped" – she and Mila kiss: "Her hands in my hair again. [...] Then a sharp exhalation of the whole body – like flowers have, in jerks – come from who knows where, from who knows who (perhaps from both of us at once) includes us

Contrasting Perspectives

slowly in the same swirl, joins us to the same vibrations, as if the air between us the clothes and even our very skin had disappeared, wiping out even the clear awareness of being oneself facing the other one ... It's only when she pushes me away that I understand that we have just kissed. Completely dispossessed of myself, emptied on the spot of my senses my guts my breath" (143).

Then they spend the night together in Paule's bed, though wrapped in covers in such a way that their bodies do not touch. Paule falls asleep and Mila watches. When Paule wakes up, she's brusque. Only by tiny signs can Mila find affirmation of the connection between them: "Infinitessimal disorder of eyelashes, of little lines around the eyes where the arrogance that is in the process of settling in again suddenly skids and goes away ... Paule's gaze suddenly misses me, as one might miss a step, while all her features go rigid in that maintained indefinitely, fixed smile that one sees on people on railway station platforms" (158).

Paule is away for a long time and writes only rarely to Mila, who broods, waits, and tends Paule's plants. Then Paule brings back a young helpless blonde girl, Odile, about whom she feels maternal. Mila's revenge is to stage a version of "The Little Mermaid," with Petitodile as the mermaid and herself as the prince, which makes the betrayal absolutely clear. She then runs away home, taking with her Slim, the dog who is her alter ego in the the novel.

As I said above, the novel is very funny. The characters are drawn well, and some are very engaging; they are all disturbed, however. Some are totally closed in on themselves and emotionally unapproachable like Paule or like Josette, accordion player and singer of Brecht and Kurt Weill, who possibly loves Mila but will not operate in any mode but the ironic. Others are totally vulnerable like Nicoli and Lili, who weep like fountains and are constantly being mopped up.

It is clear that their undefined illness is a metaphor for something wrong with each of them. It is never made clear what this wrongness is, but it is implied that the fault may lie in their sexual tendencies. The illness can be cured, we are told. In some cases it can be operated on, leaving two small scars and a loss of energy. Josette says: "Enough to make (us) believe they've had their steam cut off" (14). Josette and Mila are considered inoperable. When they leave the institution they make no direct promises to each other but leave open the possibility of their meeting in the future.

Hymne aux murènes is about the pain of a lesbian adolescence made even more difficult by the hurt defensiveness of many young women. Already they do not know how to give and receive love. The experience here is very different from the opening to love described by Jocelyne François. These young women live in physical and emotional disorder.

Camille en octobre explores similar terrain from a different angle. This time the community to which Camille returns, the group where all the discussion takes place, is a group not of adolescents but of working-class mothers who drink coffee together in the afternoon. Hence, where the adolescents fantasized about their future in *Hymne aux murènes*, the mothers in *Camille en octobre* gossip about and criticize each other's past.

Camille's family is not unlike Mila's. She too is the oldest of three. Her brother Abel is strange and somewhat feared; no one really wants to be near him. He has blackout fits. Ariane, the little one, sings defiance at the world, she is observant, perceptive, blunt, and funny. Camille is somewhat vague in the attention she pays to her surroundings.

Camille falls in love with the dentist's wife, Clara, who leads her on in ambiguous ways, cuts her hair (as Paule always wanted to cut Mila's), and makes love to her on her seventeenth birthday, only to tell her immediately afterwards that she, Clara, is pregnant. Ariane, at fourteen, changes completely, from a cynical, aware, self-confident human being to one obsessed with clothes, romances, and being a girl. At fifteen she is pregnant and leaves home with a man twice her age because he has an expensive car. He marries her, and they live far away, on the other side of France.

The circumstances here are as dysfunctional as those in the first novel; everyone has been hurt and is defensive, no dreams are or have ever been realized. The ones who sing loudly and defiantly – Ariane, Josette, and ultimately Josèphe's father – are those who best understand the complexity of the horror surrounding them. Josette withstands it in silence. Ariane runs away. Josèphe's father renounces any life for himself and dies too young.

The major metaphors recur also. Clara cuts Camille's hair and buys her jeans so that she takes on an ambiguously masculine or potentially lesbian look. Likewise, for the play, Mila has Josette cut her hair and strides out in tights as the handsome prince. Just as

Paule feels maternal about Petitodile after she has been to bed with Mila, so Clara actually is pregnant when she makes love to Camille.

Most significant perhaps is the dog. Each novel has a dog who is beaten. In *Hymne aux murènes* Slim belongs to Miss April, the director. He is loving, uncontrolled, always in trouble, and afraid to leap over walls. When she is in despair, Mila beats him, then crawls into his kennel and stays with him. She takes him with her when she leaves. Camille prevents a drunken man from continuing to hit his dog but leaves it beside its master, who has collapsed in a stupor. Both scenes are most unsettling. They are finally resolved in *Il n'y a pas d'hommes au Paradis*. A female boxer (dog) escapes her abusive master twice to come to Josèphe. The first time Josèphe returns the dog, sees it beaten, and is so upset that she changes her route through town in order not to see the dog who loves her. The second time, when urged by a friend, she negotiates to keep the dog, buys her from the drunken owner, and takes her along when she returns to her hometown, perhaps to her beloved. The parallels between the young women trapped in their upbringing like the dogs with unpredictable and harmful owners are self-evident. At least Mila and Josèphe claim their alter egos and move off with them.

Il n'y a pas d'hommes au Paradis is by far the most complex of Best's novels. The issues touched on in the first two reappear much more fully and in interwoven patterns. The premises are, however, the same: children brought up amid family silences and parental anguish, no matter how well hidden or disguised, grow up emotionally defensive and unable to give or receive love, although they will feel it.

This time the dysfunction is on a continental scale: the silences are the untold memories and losses of the Spanish Civil War and the 1939–45 war; the central families are Spanish, French, and Jewish. Enrique, Josèphe's best friend from childhood, discovers after his father is dead that he had been a hero and that all his family had been killed. Judith, Rachel, and Raphaël do not hear until they are teenagers that everyone in the family of their mother, Rosa, died in the war – her brothers in the Resistance, her father in concentration camp, and her mother as a result of the camp. Josèphe finally reaches the unpalatable conclusion that her mother had written anonymous letters to betray Jews to the authorities. What is not clear is whether she did this because she was anti-Semitic or because she was jealous of her husband's childhood and ongoing friendship with Simone, a Jewish woman.

The lives of the characters are set in context by the emotional turmoil caused by the various war experiences in their upbringing and that of the Algerian War (1958–62) and May 1968 in their present. Enrique falls in love with Judith, has two boys (named after Rosa's dead brothers), marries, and divorces her twice. Josèphe falls in love with Rachel and, at the time she is narrating the novel, has been separated from her for a couple of years. Each is still yearning for the other, and both are incapable (Josèphe) or unwilling (Rachel) to take the first step towards reconciliation. Raphaël is homosexual, anguished, an incessant and brilliant talker, and a sensational mime.

The split in Raphaël – words as a cover, silence and body language as truth – is the metaphor for them all. Josèphe's mother reads constantly about the Holocaust, only to deny the truth of every book. Enrique dances flamenco to compensate for his inarticulate rage. Rachel plays the violin, and Josèphe's father the accordion, to express the silenced parts of themselves. The cat, whom Josèphe wants to call "Animula vagula" (the little lost soul), becomes instead "Animus," with all that that implies in the way of cover-up. Josèphe remarks at one point that perhaps even her mother "was also screaming inside while searching everywhere for a way out" (197). The description fits everyone in the novel; some scream more visibly or audibly than others. The story begins with a nightmare, and in many ways it is a nightmare.

This time, however, the narrator, Josèphe, loves and is loved by Rachel. She is apart from her none the less, and suspects that she (Josèphe) had actually been trying from the beginning to drive her away. Jocelyne François wrote of the horror of becoming invisible to the beloved's gaze; Josèphe as a child watched herself become invisible to her mother as her mother turned to drink and apathy or to anger as a means to fight her own demons. At such times, Josèphe would howl in terror, and her father would arrive and take care of her. It is not until the death of Maria, the neighbour who used to spit on Germans and on the doorsteps of collaborators during the war, that Josèphe realizes how much her mother had been afraid; only when Maria's funeral procession went by could she at last relax.

As an adult Josèphe, feeling unlovable, would make her love invisible to Rachel and then not know how to extricate herself from the resulting void. In part it is the love that the boxer shows for her and its persistence in breaking free and coming to her no matter how much it hurt itself in the process that shows her the way out. The novel closes with a story that Rosa had told: "one day a lover went far away from her lover, who called to her, 'Come back!' She replied 'I can't !' So the other one said to her, 'Listen, come as close as you can, and I will come the rest of the way ... '" (284). Josèphe packs her bag, takes her dog, and goes. By that action she has stepped out of the patterns set up by her parents, each of whom in his or her own way directly or indirectly betrayed her father's friend Simone and let her go to her death, not realizing how much of their own life would be lost with her.

In her novels, Mireille Best has traced and named causes of dysfunction, social and personal, and the struggle necessary to emerge from it. Her characters are disadvantaged at every level, and survival for them is hard, although she does not present lesbianism as much more problematic in itself than heterosexuality. The difficulties lie in the cultural expectations of parents and the emotional blocks of the lovers.

HÉLÈNE DE MONFERRAND: PRIVILEGE AND TOLERANCE

It would be hard to create a bigger shift than the one from Best's world of material poverty and emotional impoverishment to that described by Hélène de Monferrand in *Les Amies d'Héloïse* (Heloïse's Friends, 1990), *Journal de Suzanne* (Suzanne's Journal, 1991), and recently *Les Enfants d'Héloïse* (Héloïse's Children, 1997), for hers is a world of total privilege, devoid of anguish, doubt, or fear for all characters but one: Erika. Erika had an unloving mother and grew up with a tragic attitude to love, and all-encompassing possessiveness, and jealousy. She is also beautiful, charming, intelligent, extremely competent, and heiress to an industrial pharmaceutical empire that she runs with ease.

The other characters move in similarly elite circles. Héloïse de Marèges is the daughter of an ambassador, as is her Spanish friend Pilar. Marie-Thérèse is the daughter of a duke. Manuela is the younger sister of Erika, each with the same German father and different French mothers. Claire, Héloïse's closest friend, and soon her sister-in-law, had poor grandparents, but her mother married into a fortune. Both parents are French colonials repatriated from Algeria. Suzanne, lover in turn of Erika and of Héloïse, is headmistress of a Paris high school and co-owner, with her brother, of a very prosperous and highly rated vineyard near Bordeaux. Members of the younger generation are effortlessly intelligent and talented from birth or turn out to be so as soon as their sorrows come to an end. All in the older generation are war heroes. They spend their time collecting or dispensing with lovers, male or female according to taste, giving birth to an astonishing number of children, and travelling back and forth from Paris to Vienna, Stockholm, Copenhagen, or Tauberg (Erika and Manuela's family home in northern Germany), with the occasional trip to London or Switzerland.

The Marèges family is very old, is very illustrious, and belongs to the Protestant aristocracy. Hector, Héloïse's father, is a count. The Lacombe family (Suzanne's) is equally renowned in the dynasties of wine growing. The Taubergs hold a similar position in financial circles. The lesbian dramas of Héloïse, Erika, and Suzanne play out against a background of reference to historical upheaval in various periods – the Crusades (the Marèges), 1939–45 war (Taubergs, Anne de Marèges, Héloïse's mother, and Suzanne), Algeria (Claire Rochaz), and May 1968 (Suzanne). Three of the characters have a serious interest in history, and it is clear that the author must have one also. Who else would have a seduction scene centre on a discussion of the Treaty of Utrecht, which united the Catholic and Protestant provinces of the Low Countries in 1579? The politics here are right wing throughout.

Les Amies d'Héloïse, which won the Goncourt Prize in the category best first novel in 1990, is certainly very different from anything else I have discussed in this volume. Written in the form of an exchange of letters between Héloïse and Claire, with occasional excursions into the journals of Erika and Manuela and the odd note from Suzanne, its form requires that I make at least a passing reference to Laclos's *Les Liaisons dangereuses* (Dangerous Liaisons, 1782), even though there is no mention of it in *Les Amies d'Héloïse*.[7] Héloïse's friends and lovers may not be as villainous and wicked as Valmont and Madame de Merteuil, but they do move in equivalent circles and have equally libidinous aims. Neither Erika nor Héloïse is killed in a duel, like Valmont, but Erika does shoot Héloïse and wound her. Suzanne is not externally disfigured by smallpox like Madame de Merteuil; she is internally disfigured by a brain tumour and commits suicide. They all observe, scheme, and gossip about their love lives, and their liaisons are certainly dangerous, given that Héloïse is barely fifteen when Erika seduces her and is still a minor during her relationship with Suzanne, her mother's friend from concentration camp.

Perhaps the most striking link with *Les Liaisons dangereuses* is that Hélène de Monferrand gives all her characters the kinds of attitudes to love and life that are usually associated with men. And they all have or choose male-dominated professions in which they make their way successfully and without obstacle. They are an unblemished race of superwomen.

That Héloïse should be loved so passionately also conjures up the image of Héloïse and Abelard – and it is an ironic reflection on the original story that the lovers of Monferrand's Héloïse are certainly non-men like their castrated predecessor. There is no direct reference to any medieval antecedents in the text, however, other than general scholarly attitudes and the writing of letters to tell the story. The novel covers some sixteen years, during which time Claire and Héloïse discover their respective sexual orientations. Claire marries Héloïse's elder brother, Hugo, and they produce five children, while each parent passes competitive examinations and establishes a career in high administration. Héloïse learns lesbian lovemaking from Erika (thirty years old) and has an affair with her. She then falls for Suzanne (fifty or so), her great love. Suzanne dies, and Héloïse in despair marries Marie-Thérèse's twin brother François (the duc d'Ennecour, his mother's pet – weak, feminine, and addicted to prescription drugs). She starts divorce proceedings, he commits suicide, and she discovers that she is pregnant again and has twin girls. Finally she and Erika, who has languished through some ten years of brief flings, get back together again.

The book is brisk and full of action. The characters are intellectuals and intellectually created, moving with decision, full of ideas and information. They chose love rather than fall into it, and no one has more than token anguish about being loved. Erika is the exception, we are told, but we never actually see any of her scenes. All is recounted and thereby removed from the realm of the directly physical or emotional. The women are well brought up and therefore proud of being reserved.

This is not a novel of steamy sex, although the author intimates that a lot of it occurs. Because of a sort of cultural prudishness (or perhaps a publisher's prudence), all the sex that does not take place in the context of an ongoing love partnership takes place either in Vienna or in Scandinavia. In this the author plays into the old tradition of lesbians as lecherous foreigners and also into the stereotypical view of Freud's Vienna and the sexual freedom of Sweden and Denmark.

Lesbianism in France, it seems, is practised freely but disguised with care. All the distinguished families are apparently absolutely free of homophobia. Anne de Marèges does not even falter when she discovers that her underaged daughter is the lover of her oldest female friend. The only clearly homophobic reaction is that of Suzanne's childhood friend and sister-in-law, Jacqueline. However, it should be noted that Héloïse's father is carefully not told about his daughter's proclivities, even though we are constantly reassured that when he does come to know he will not be upset.

The implicit suggestions in the novel are that lesbianism has at least some genetic component and that it can be the result of an unloving mother. Héloïse has a lesbian aunt and in *Les Enfants d'Héloïse* will have a lesbian daughter. Suzanne's brother Pierre and his homophobic wife have a daughter suspected of lesbian tendencies. Erika is offered as the example of bad mothering.

The typically male attitudes of the women in the novel are not attributed to the lesbians only. All the women treat their lovers in a cavalier fashion. The lesbians choose to use the word "mistress" (rather than "lover") with all that it implies of mastery (mistressry?) and of economic imbalance. Héloïse is certainly generously subsidized, if not kept, by Suzanne in particular. Suzanne likes to buy her mistresses gifts of clothing – so that she can take it off, as she says directly and does forthwith.

The professional context is rigorously intellectual. Héloïse and Claire open and close their letters with Latin salutations and quote Greek in the original to each other. (We poor readers are supplied with translation in footnotes.) Literary and historic references abound throughout. In terms of career, everyone is either in pharmaceuticals and medicine, or diplomacy and the equivalent bureau-cracy, or wine – i.e., status and money.

Suprisingly – or perhaps not, given that I am an intellectual and my field is French literature – I found this novel good to read. I was amused by my own previously unrecognized assumption that a lesbian author would be *ipso facto* left wing, and I was irritated by the characters' complaint that it can be difficult to be treated as a human being when one has a title and money, even though I am sure that that is probably so. But in the main, it was cheering to read for once about a collection of delightful, positive, active, un-complex-ridden women who give each other tremendous support in all circumstances. The support between the lesbian and heterosex-ual women in this novel is amazing. It crosses generational lines, religion, nationality, and relative wealth. What it is true to is class – the notion of an elite. Superwomen they may all be, but I found them interesting, engaging, and for the most part attractive. This was also true for the most part of their fathers, brothers, and sons. It is certainly unrealistic to depict such a totally pleasant lot of people, but I enjoyed the read.

Gaps in the first story are filled in by the *Journal de Suzanne*, and the saga continues in *Les Enfants d'Héloïse* – which could, in my view, have benefited from a good editor. There are too many huge chunks of history badly integrated into the text. In this one, all the babies born to Héloïse and her friends grow to young adulthood. Héloïse lives more or less calmly with Erika and has occasional secret flings on the side.

Hélène de Monferrand seems to be following in the footsteps of Jeanne Galzy (whose titles she quotes in her texts) in the creation of a family saga. Monferrand's method of letters and journal does not permit the development of much depth in character or even of cir-cumstances and allows no complexity of novel structure. Engaging as some of her characters were at first, there is not much that she can do with them, so she adds more. Good novels are not made in this way, so if she is to continue I think that she has to change her style. Unfortunately, from reading the three novels already pub-lished I have the feeling that she does not have much taste for psy-chological complexity or philosophical reflection. We shall see in due time, no doubt.

CONCLUSION

The three authors presented in this chapter are the most interesting of the period since 1968 in terms of accessible lesbian stories and a good read. (Wittig and Cixous are important because of their exploration and theorizing, not their storytelling.) They form a fitting end to this journey through two centuries of lesbians in French novels. Between them they cover a wide spectrum of issues and offer a variety of characters and of writing styles. Monferrand's saga of the elite normalizes lesbianism in ways that show the possibilities opened by a tolerant family structure, but at the same time her jet-setting women, out and outrageous in Copenhagen, Vienna, or London, remain tightly closeted in Paris. Best depicts with considerable black humour the anguish of young lower-class lesbians, struggling with their feelings in a context of family dysfunction. François goes into herself, using her philosophical mind and her poetic heart to chart the movements of love. Hers is the most intimate and most profound presentation of lesbian living and loving that I have read in French. All three deserve a place in the history of the contemporary novel.

CHAPTER SEVEN

Conclusion

Two hundred years of lesbians in French novels, yet the path that they have traced has remained almost invisible. To this day the ones who do exist in the cultural imagination are "la fille aux yeux d'or" of Balzac and Gautier's Madelaine de Maupin, both from the mid-1830s, made memorable not by their stories, which remain unread by most people, but by Baudelaire's 1857 categorization of lesbians as women damned. There are a number of reasons for this situation, I think, all of them woven into the fabric of French culture and society.

As I have written above, French society is extremely heterosexual and through time has been more coupled than many others. It has never had any acknowledged, public, and visible space for single women or women in groups such as the English tradition, for example, provided.[1] Women accompany men in France, and they accompany them always. In domestic space and proper, acceptable social space, an upper- or middle-class man is to be seen with his wife; in places of dubious propriety – theatres, cafés, cabarets – he is with his mistress. The result is that for much of the period covered here it was well-nigh impossible for a woman to move in society without having a male companion. Hence all the male writers and many of the women conceptualized lesbianism within or at least overlapping the boundaries of heterosexuality (as they did male homosexuality[2]), and within that context it can survive on the edges of society.

French culture actually prides itself on being *sexual*. Heterosexuality is central to social expectations and behaviour, but any variant is permissible as long as it is done with discretion, preferably under the cover of an outwardly respectable marriage. The problems described by Balzac, Belot, and Maupassant are those of excess. The morality here is the same as in the seventeenth century (even if the philosophical attitudes have shifted) – namely, that excess, obsessive behaviour, and passion disrupt social stability and harmony. From this perspective we can sort all the male authors in this study into Racinian and Molièresque piles: those who deal in passion and tragedy, and those who deal in social behaviour, economics, bigotry, and ridicule.

Male authors make "true" lesbians as predatory as the male protagonists of their novels. The two groups are therefore rivals in conquest. The unspoken assumption underlying these stories therefore is that many if not all women are potentially bisexual. This thread of problematic or unproblematic bisexuality or of lesbianism surviving within respectable heterosexuality runs through many of the novels by female authors from Colette to Jocelyne François and Hélène de Monferrand.

If the lesbian characters are given a physical, material, and social context in these texts, the context is heterosexual. There is no sense of lesbian community in any of the novels discussed in this book, nor indeed is there a female community – and certainly not a feminist one – in the wide social sense. Only in the theoretically based novels of Cixous, Eaubonne, and Wittig can such potentially subversive groups be suggested. There are novels set in the transitory female community created by boarding school or women's college, such as those by Best, François, Galzy, and Leduc, but the authors give no suggestion that such connections and friendships will continue. Only in very recent novels, frequently working class in circumstance and situation, by Mireille Best and authors published by Geneviève Pastre – Odette Menteau and Lucie Rivière – do we see networks of lesbians coming into being and feminist questions being asked.

The history of the lesbian in the French novel is the story of serial isolation, to such an extent that I had the feeling as I read that many of these writers did not even know that the others existed. Not until Hélène de Monferrand mentions Jeanne Galzy does one author refer to another.

The styles in which the women write are the traditional ones of male authors. There are first-person narratives of self-absorbed, self-reflecting anguish and unassuaged passion. There are triangu-

Conclusion 213

lar love affairs. The French propensity for abstract and rational language is prevalent, which, given the focus on personal sexuality, tends frequently to produce curiously insubstantial characters and events. Little is grounded in material surroundings, and so the books often remain unsatisfying and unengaging because not connected with any tangible reality.

On reflection, I have come to the conclusion that the intensely personal, uncontextualized nature of many of the texts – no décor, no social context, no developed characters – indeed no characters outside narrator and beloved sometimes – and the barest of chronologies are the result of the ungroundedness of lesbian life in France. (I am talking not about modern, postmodern, or otherwise avant-garde writing, where these traditional characteristics of novel writing have been dispensed with for a purpose, but about stories where the lack of traditional building materials shows in the shaky product.) Most lesbians in France live if not closeted at least discreet public lives. As a group they have been virtually invisible. The lack of material and social context in the novels is a reflection of the same lack in lesbian life. Novels with presence would have to address the double or split life that most lesbians appear to lead.

The heart of the issue lies probably in the permissiveness of French culture – or perhaps, more precisely, in Parisian culture – because as long as they stay on the margins lesbians are and have been tolerated. Tacitly ignored, but not oppressed directly, they have chosen visible clandestinity as a mode of survival. The culture endorses the habit of sex as personal and widely variable, and so the permission that it accords to men to do whatever they can get away with without causing scandal spills over, and lesbians profit from it too.

The absence of overwhelming oppression and of community has resulted in ongoing individuality and isolation. It has also impeded analysis (except in academic circles) and political activity. Contemporary theory of the North American and English sort (perhaps others too, but I don't know them well enough to say) – queer theory, gender analysis, and so on – cannot usefully serve to examine this body of writing because the lines of sight that they offer are too different to provide either perspective or understanding. Politics and sexuality are separate in France, and the literary creation of lesbians is proof, for it is absolutely a-political.

It is perhaps disengagement from society – a sense of not being wholly visible or visibly whole, a choosing to be absent from the public gaze – that has produced so many novels in this overview that are somewhat unsatisfactory. For the most part the texts are either about emotion or about physical sex; they either have a social context and a lot of superficial characters or a couple floating in a bubble of obsessiveness.

Then there are the gems, the novels that show the connections between feelings and lovemaking, in which the protagonists have family, friends, personal territory and history, and a personality with which the reader can engage. My list of novels that touched and delighted me is made up of Adrienne Saint-Agen, *Charmeuse de femmes* (1906); Jacques de Lacretelle, *La Bonifas* (1925); Clarisse Francillon, *La Lettre* (1958); Christiane Rochefort, *Les Stances à Sophie* (1963); Françoise Ferrié, *Accident d'amour* (1975); and Colette Audry, *La Statue* (1983), together with the works of Violette Leduc, Jocelyne François, and Mireille Best.

All the authors considered in this study, be they good or mediocre, create by their very existence a lesbian, literary sensibility and a narrative space marked by asymmetrical gender structures and disruption, however slight, of expected social hierarchies and power balances. A lesbian subject provokes a repositioning of the narrative role, bringing a non-male gaze and a consequent shift in perspective. It also demands a change in relational identity, because lesbians shift with regard to other women as their experience emerges into a developing discourse that drives the narrative in non-standard ways, no matter how subdued their voice may be.

There is a realignment of desire involved as well. Right from the novels of Balzac and Gautier, lesbians disrupt the patterns of desiring subject and desired object, and that disruption makes visible the male fear of uncontrolled female sexuality. Hence the depiction of the lesbian as monster, unnatural, vicious, and deadly, because unregulated by men or by reproduction. By her very nature she is a transgressive body, subversive of patriarchal order.

The female creators of lesbian protagonists sometimes reflect the shame and guilt associated with the male tradition. But as yet they do not exploit the latent energy for challenge and change implicit in the archetypal fear that lesbians generate and in the potential for subversive action that they embody. Except for Wittig and Cixous,

Conclusion 215

the female authors studied in this book all write within male-defined parameters, and their purpose is not to make waves. None the less they have inscribed lesbian experience into literature, and my intention is to make sure that their inscriptions are not erased but rather included in the compilation that comprises the written history of the modern French novel.

Notes

INTRODUCTION

1 See Andermatt Conley, *Hélène Cixous*; Shiach, *Hélène Cixous*; and Whitford, *Luce Irigaray* for further information.

CHAPTER ONE

1 *La Religieuse* was written in 1760 but not published until 1796.
2 May, *Diderot et "La Religieuse."*
3 Charles de Secondat, baron de Montesquieu (1689–1755) was a political philosopher best known for his *Esprit des Lois* (The Spirit of the Law, 1748). *Les Lettres Persanes* (The Persian Letters, 1721) is a volume of social criticism disguised as innocent observations made by travellers from the "Orient."
4 Voltaire (François-Marie Arouet, 1694–1778) was a poet, historian, philosopher, and social critic. *Candide ou l'optimisme* (Candide, or Optimism, 1759), a philosophical tale with social criticisms similar to those proffered by Montesquieu, is his best-known work.
5 Mylne, *Diderot, La Religieuse* and "What Suzanne Knew: Lesbianism and *La Religieuse.*"
6 Bartky, *Femininity and Domination.*
7 *L'Encyclopédie*, an encyclopaedic dictionary, 17 volumes of text and 11 volumes of plates published between 1751 and 1772 (seven more volumes published later). It embodied the philosophic spirit of the eighteenth century and attempted to give a rational explanation of the universe. Diderot was the principal director of the project, assisted at various times by d'Alembert, Jaucourt, Marmontel, and

NOTES TO PAGES 17–48

Voltaire. Most of the eminent French thinkers of the period con-
tributed to the work.

8 Diderot, *La Religieuse,* in *Oeuvres Complètes* Vol. IV (Paris: Le Club
français du livre, 1969). All quotations are from this edition. All
translations are my own.

9 See chapter 4 of this book. Lilian Faderman has a different response
again; see her *Surpassing the Love of Men.*

10 Balzac, *La Fille aux yeux d'or,* in *Oeuvres Complètes,* vol. IX (Paris:
Furne, J.J. Dubochet et Cie et J. Hetzel, 1842): *The Girl with the
Golden Eyes,* trans. Ernest Dowson (London: Leonard Smithers,
1896). All quotations are from these editions.

11 *La Comédie humaine* (1842–48) is a collection of seventeen volumes
of novels and short stories that offer an overall picture of French
society from the time of the Consulate (1799–1804) to the July
Monarchy (1830). Balzac covers public and private, Parisian and
provincial lifestyles in his vast canvas.

12 Theorists reading the term "Orientalism" will probably think of
recent work linking sexuality and race in work by Edward Said *et al.*
The direction and content of the contemporary work are such that it
casts no light on the issues that I am discussing here.

13 Dijkstra, *Idols of Perversity.*

14 Gautier, *Mademoiselle de Maupin* (1835), Introduction and notes by
Adolphe Boschot. All quotations are from this edition.

15 Paglia, *Sexual Personae.*

16 I realize that the usual title of the poem in translation is "doomed
women," but there is an important difference between being doomed
in this world and damned in the next. Baudelaire chose "damned
women" for his title, and I do likewise throughout this volume.

17 I am grateful to my colleague Deborah Yaffe for this observation.

18 Again thanks to Deborah Yaffe for her thoughtful awareness.

19 Bonnet, *Les Relations amoureuses,*216–23.

20 Maupassant, "La Femme de Paul," in *Contes et nouvelles* (Paris:
Gallimard, 1979). "Paul's Mistress," in *The Complete Short Stories
of Guy de Maupassant,* Intro. Artine Artinian (Garden City, NY:
Hanover House, 1955). All quotations are from these editions.

21 Mathilde de Marny, duchesse de Belbeuf, called Missy, was a known
lesbian who had an affair with Colette. For more information see
Sarde, *Colette libre.*

22 Faderman *Surpassing the Love of Men,* and Benstock, *Women of the
Left Bank.*

Notes to pages 49–94

CHAPTER TWO

1 Jean Martin Charcot (1825–1893) was a doctor, researcher, and teacher at the Salpetrière Hospital in Paris. Freud was one of his students. Richard von Krafft-Ebing (1840–1902) was a doctor and teacher in Strasbourg, Graz, and Vienna. His book *Psychopathia Sexualis* (1886) on sexual aberrations was translated into French in 1892 and became very influential.

2 Castle, *The Apparitional Lesbian*; Faderman, *Surpassing the Love of Men*.

3 Martin-Fugier, *La Bourgeoise*.

4 Waelti-Walters and Hause, eds., *Feminisms*.

5 See ibid. for further documentation.

6 Waelti-Walters, *Feminist Novelists*.

7 Beauvoir, *Le Deuxième Sexe*.

8 Wittig, *The Straight Mind and Other Essays*.

9 Bonnet, *Les Relations amoureuses*, chap. 2.

10 Laqueur, *Making Sex*.

11 Waelti-Walters, *Feminist Novelists*, 139–55.

12 French publishers are legally required to deposit a copy of all books that they publish in the Bibiothèque de France (Bibliothèque Nationale), but in the period around 1900 some did not comply with the law. However, quite frequently the library holds all the books by a given author *except* the one(s) purported to have lesbian content. Such is the case with Henriette Willette.

13 Jay, *The Amazon and the Page*.

14 Proust, *Un Amour de Swann* (Swann's Love) in *Du Coté de chez Swann* (Swann's Way), the first volume of *A la recherche du temps perdu* (Remembrance of Time Past).

15 Gide, *La Porte étroite* (Strait is the Gate).

16 This act can be interpreted symbolically as a violently sexual one: a pussy impaled on a deadly spike. Lacretelle does not have Marie Bonifas see the action in that light, nor does he specify what is on the poster. There are no other metaphors of that kind in the novel, and I do not know at what period the slang association came into French. The cat in the novel is male, whereas the usual terminology for female genitalia is female: "la chatte."

NOTES TO PAGES 97–132

CHAPTER THREE

1 See Courtivron, *Violette Leduc*, and Baird, *Simone de Beauvoir*.
2 A "cheroub" is an Assyrian sphinx-type androgynous creature.

CHAPTER FOUR

1 Marguerite Yourcenar (1902–1987), actually Marguerite Antoinette Jeanne Marie Ghislaine de Crayencour, was born in Brussels. After 1938 she lived in the United States with Grace Frick. She was the first woman elected to the French Academy. Throughout her life she denied that her relationship with Frick was lesbian, and her private papers will not be available until 2037. She wrote about male homosexuality in a number of her novels.

2 Simone de Beauvoir (1908–1986) never discussed lesbianism except in *The Second Sex*. For those who read of her passion for Zaza in *Mémoires d'une jeune fille rangée* (1958, pub. as *Memoirs of a Dutiful Daughter*, trans. J. Kirkup (Harmondsworth: Penguin, 1963) and who look carefully at the triangle in *L'Invitée* (1943) pub. as *She Came to Stay*, trans. Y. Moyse and R. Stenhouse (London: Flamingo, 1984), Beauvoir's interest in women is clear. During the last years of her life she was constantly in the company of Sylvie LeBon, whom she adopted as her daughter in 1980.

3 Lamblin, *Mémoires d'une jeune fille dérangée*.

4 Beauvoir, *Le Deuxième Sexe*: *The Second Sex*, trans. H.M. Parshley. Parshley's translation has serious flaws. Not only does it obliterate all the language of existentialist philosophy, which shapes Beauvoir's view of women's condition, but it eliminates sentences, quotations, and whole paragraphs without any indication.

5 All page references in the quotations are to the two editions – Paris: Gallimard, 1949, and New York: Vintage Books, 1974.

6 See chapter 5 below.

7 Nathalie Sarraute (b.1902) was one of the group of writers called "New Novelists" who in the 1950s challenged the parameters of the traditional (nineteenth-century) novel. They espoused the work on perception done by Maurice Merleau-Ponty. Sarraute's essays *L'Ere du soupçon* (Era of Suspicion, 1956) and *L'Usage de la parole* (The Use of Words, 1980) explain her point of view.

8 The original "New Novelists" were Samuel Beckett, Michel Butor, Marguerite Duras, Claude Pinget, Alain Robbe-Grillet, Nathalie Sar-

Notes to pages 132–45 221

raute, and Claude Simon. All their early novels were published in Paris by Editions de Minuit.

9 Especially Simone de Beauvoir, Albert Camus, and Jean-Paul Sartre.

10 Jean Genet (1910–1986), a homosexual and criminal, was famous for his semi-autobiographical novels *Notre Dame des fleurs* (Our Lady of the Flowers, 1946) and *Miracle de la rose* (The Rose Miracle, 1947) and plays such as *Les Bonnes* (The Maids, 1947), *Les Nègres* (The Blacks, 1958), *Le Balcon* (The Balcony, 1960), and *Les Paravants* (The Screens, 1966).

11 Waelti-Walters, *Jeanne Hyvrard*.

12 Courtivron, *Violette Leduc*.

13 For a concise history of second-wave feminism in France see Kaplan, *Contemporary Western European Feminism*.

14 Cixous, *L'Exil de James Joyce ou l'art de remplacement*.

15 Shiach, *Hélène Cixous*, 96.

16 Wittig, "The Site of Action," in *The Straight Mind*. All other essays referred to in this chapter are also published in *The Straight Mind*. Wittig wrote them in English.

17 See note 7 above.

18 Monique Wittig's novels create enormous problems for translators because of the way in which she uses pronouns to create her particular world. "On" in French is only occasionally the equivalent of "one" in English. The tone and usage of the two are quite different. "On" is not marked by class, as "one" now tends to be. It is sometimes the equivalent of "they" or when used slangily or by children is frequently an alternative to "we" – though remaining general.

19 Quoted in English by Wittig in "The Mark of Gender" (1985), in *The Straight Mind*, 84.

20 Again Wittig's choice of narrative form causes problems for translators into English. "Elles" is a standard feminine plural in French; there is no feminine form of "they" in English. David LeVay, translator of the Beacon Press edition (Boston, 1969) chose to use "the women," thus obliterating all possibility of stories from female children in the text and, in my view, distorting the reader's perception of Wittig's world. A more creative choice might have been "shes" or "shey." LeVay did not attempt to translate the title either.

21 *Le Corps lesbien* (The Lesbian Body, 1973) is narrated by a divided self "j/e" in French, which the translator has transcribed as "I" cut in half with a slash. The effect of each is very different.

22 To be found in *The Straight Mind*, as indicated above.
23 Ibid.

CHAPTER FIVE

1 Boris Vian (1920–1959) was a jazz trumpeter and writer. In all his novels he played with the visual potential of words. Under the pseudonym Vernon Sullivan he wrote American-style murder mysteries. He was something of a cult figure in the 1960s and 1970s.

2 Eugène Sue (1804–1857) wrote the first serial novels in French literature. His best-known book is *Les Mystères de Paris* (Paris Mysteries, 1842–43).

3 Mary Pickford (1893–1979), née Gladys Smith, was a Toronto-born star of silent films, who made the transition to sound, winning an Academy Award for best actress for 1928–29 for her role in *Coquette*. She and her husband Douglas Fairbanks were two of the founders of United Artists studios.

4 Renée Vivien, pseudonymn for Pauline Mary Tarn (1877–1909), was a lesbian poet and novelist; see chapter 3 above.

5 Lucie Delarue-Mardrus (1875–1945) was a bisexual poet and novelist; see chapter 3 above

6 Rachilde, pseudonym for Marguerite Eymery (1862–1953), was a writer and journalist, co-founder (with her husband, Alfred Valette) of the *Mercure de France*, and author of scandalous novels concerning many and varied sexual deviances and perversions, all of which are heterosexual.

7 My thanks to Deborah Yaffe for the pun.

8 Marcel Duchamp (1887–1968) was a painter who turned to experimental writing after 1923. "Rose Sélavy" is one of his verbal inventions; she can be found in *Marchand du sel* (Paris: Flammarion, 1975), 153–4.

9 Bersianik, *L'Euguélionne* (Montreal: La Presse, 1976): *The Euguélionne*, trans. G. Denis, A. Hewitt, D. Murray, and M. O'Brien (Victoria: Press Porcépic, 1981).

10 See the journal *Room of One's Own* 4 nos. 1 and 2 (1978) for examples of their writing. I have not included here any of Michèle Causse's work published in Quebec.

11 The pope has historic authority to give titles to secular persons as well as to the religious hierarchy within the Roman Catholic church.

Notes to pages 178–211   223

12 Geneviève Pastre herself writes poetry, prose poems and essays, but not novels so far.

13 Ethel Smyth (1858–1944), composer, and lesbian, was a friend of Virginia Woolf.

CHAPTER SIX

1 Jean Racine (1639–1669) was a dramatist known for the depth and poetic finesse of his psychological analysis.

2 François, *Les Bonheurs*; *Les Amantes*; *Joue-nous "España", roman de mémoire*; *Histoire de Volubilis*; *Le Cahier vert: Journal 1961–1989*; and *La Femme sans tombe*.

3 The connection between *Les Amantes* and *Les Bonheurs* is not made explicitly in the novel, but Sarah has the same name, the narrator has the same number of children ...

4 Volubilis is a Roman site in Morocco. Jocelyne François draws parallels between it and Glanum, near her home in Provence. The excavation would seem to be a metaphor for the writing of her life and that of her partner.

5 Paul Claudel (1868–1955) was a lyric Catholic dramatist. *Partage de Midi* (1906) is the story of an absolute and perfect love that could not be – the lovers die rather than separate. Wallace Fowlie translated it as *Break of Noon*.

6 See François, *Le Cahier vert*.

7 Pierre Choderlos de Laclos (1741–1803) was a novelist. *Les Liaisons dangereuses* (1782) is an epistolary novel depicting deliberately destructive seduction of aristocratic women by a cynical and unscrupulous man, Valmont, who is aided by an evil accomplice, Madame de Merteuil. As Laclos claimed to be a moralist, both these characters come to a bad end.

CHAPTER SEVEN

1 The only exception to this generalization that I have found in French literature is *La Rebelle* (1905) by Marcelle Tinayre, in which elderly single women are depicted by the author and treated by the characters with respect.

2 Marcel Proust and André Gide are prime examples.

Appendix:
French Quotations

CHAPTER ONE

Diderot, *La Religieuse*, 629–30. ... enfin il vint un moment, je ne sais si ce fut de plaisir ou de peine, où elle devint pâle comme la mort; ses yeux se fermèrent, tout son corps s'étendit avec violence, ses lèvres se fermèrent d'abord, elles étaient humectées comme d'une mousse légère; puis sa bouche s'entrouvrit, et elle me parut mourir en poussant un grand soupir.

Ibid, 630. Je ne sais ce qui se passait en moi; je craignais, je tremblais, le coeur me palpitait, j'avais de la peine à respirer, je me sentais troublée, oppressée, agitée, j'avais peur, il me semblait que les forces m'abondonnient et que j'allais défaillir; cependant je ne saurais dire que ce fût de la peine que je ressentisse. J'allais près d'elle; elle me fit signe encore de la main de m'asseoir sur ses genoux; je m'assis. Elle était comme morte, et moi comme si j'allais mourir.

Ibid, 613. C'est une petite femme toute ronde, cependent prompte et vive dans ses mouvements; sa tête n'est jamais rassise sur ses épaules; il y a toujours quelque chose qui cloche dans son vêtement; sa figure est plutôt bien que mal; ses yeux, dont l'un, c'est le droit, est plus haut et plus grand que l'autre, sont pleins de feu et distraits; quand elle marche, elle jette ses bras en avant et en arrière. Veut-elle parler, elle ouvre la bouche avant que d'avoir arrangé ses idées; aussi bégaye-t-elle un peu. Est-elle assise, elle s'agite sur son fauteuil, comme si quelque chose l'incommodait; elle oublie toute bienséance, elle lève sa guimpe pour se frotter la peau, elle croise ses jambes. Elle vous interroge, vous lui répondez, et elle ne vous écoute pas; elle vous parle, et elle se perd, s'arrête tout court, ne sait plus où elle en est,

se fâche, et vous appelle grosse bête, stupide, imbécile, si vous ne la remet-
tez sur la voie. Elle est tantôt familière jusqu'à tutoyer, tantôt impérieuse
et fière jusqu'au dédain; ses moments de dignité sont courts; elle est alter-
nativement compatissante et dure. Sa figure décomposée marque tout le
décousu de son esprit et toute l'inégalité de son caractère; aussi l'ordre et
le désordre se succédaient-ils dans la maison.

Balzac, *La Fille aux yeux d'or*, 299–300. La marquise avait les cheveux
arrachés, elle était couverte de morsures, dont plusieurs saignaient, et sa
robe déchirée la laissait voir à demi nue, les seins égratignés. Elle était
sublime ainsi. Sa tête avide et furieuse respirait l'odeur du sang. Sa bouche
haletante restait entr'ouverte, et ses narines ne suffisaient pas à ses aspi-
rations. Certains animaux, mis en fureur, fondent sur leur ennemi, le
mettent à mort, et, tranquilles dans leur victoire, semblent avoir tout
oublié. Il en est d'autres qui tournent autour de leur victime [...] elle était
trop enivrée de sang chaud, trop animée par la lutte, trop exaltée pour
apercevoir Paris entier, si Paris avait formé un cirque autour d'elle. Elle
n'aurait pas senti la foudre. Elle n'avait même pas entendu le dernier
soupir de Paquita.

Ibid., 249. ce mouvement excessif des fabrications, des intérêts, des arts et
de l'or.

Ibid., 252–3. Vers la fin de 1814, Henri de Marsay n'avait donc sur terre
aucun sentiment obligatoire et se trouvait libre autant que l'oiseau sans
compagne. Quoiqu'il eût vingt-deux ans accomplis, il paraissait en avoir à
peine dix-sept. Généralement, les plus difficiles de ses rivaux le regardaient
comme le plus joli garçon de Paris [...].
   Sous cette fraîcheur de vie, et malgré l'eau limpide de ses yeux, Henri
avait un courage de lion, une adresse de singe. Il coupait une balle à dix
pas dans la lame d'un couteau; montait à cheval de manière à réaliser la
fable du centaure; conduisait avec grâce une voiture à grandes guides; était
leste comme Chérubin et tranquille comme un mouton; mais il savait
battre un homme du faubourg au terrible jeu de la savate ou du bâton; [...]
Hélas toutes ces belles qualités, ces jolis défauts étaient ternis par un épou-
vantable vice: il ne croyait ni aux hommes ni aux femmes, ni à Dieu ni au
diable. La capricieuse nature avait commencé à le douer; un prêtre l'avait
achevé.

Ibid., 253. pour rendre compréhensible cette aventure

Ibid., 249. Néanmoins, il est à Paris une portion d'êtres privilégiés auxquels profite ce mouvement excessif des fabrications, des intérêts, des affaires, des arts et de l'or. Ces êtres sont les femmes. Quoiqu'elles aient aussi mille causes secrètes qui là, plus qu'ailleurs, détruisent leur physionomie, il se rencontre, dans le monde féminin, de petites peuplades heureuses qui vivent à l'orientale, et peuvent conserver leur beauté; mais ces femmes se montrent rarement à pied dans les rues, elles demeurent cachées, comme des plantes rares qui ne déploient leurs pétales qu'à certaines heures, et qui constituent de véritables exceptions exotiques.

Ibid., 253. afin d'éviter les poursuites de la justice anglaise qui, de l'Orient, ne protège que la marchandise.

Ibid., 253. Ah! c'est mon fils. Quel malheur!

Ibid., 259. – Enfin, mon cher, que me fait celle que je n'ai point vue!

Ibid., 259. Depuis que j'étudie les femmes, mon inconnue est la seule dont le sein vierge, les formes ardentes et voluptueuses m'aient réalisé la seule femme que j'aie rêvée, moi!

Ibid., 296. Henri garda l'attitude flegmatique de l'homme fort qui se sent vaincu; contenance froide, silencieuse, tout anglaise, qui annonçait la conscience de sa dignité par une résignation momentanée. D'ailleurs il avait déjà pensé, malgré l'emportement de sa colère, qu'il était peu prudent de se commettre avec la justice en tuant cette fille à l'improviste et sans en avoir préparé le meurtre de manière à s'assurer l'impunité.

Ibid., 297. inébranlable dans ses bons comme dans ses mauvais sentiments.

Ibid., 299. La Marquise était femme: elle avait calculé sa vengeance avec cette perfection de perfidie qui distingue les animaux faibles.

Ibid., 302. ce qui nous a paru être l'infini

Gautier, *Mademoiselle de Maupin*, 296. cette réflexion me vint que les hommes étaient plus favorisés que nous dans leurs amours, que nous leur donnions à posséder les plus charmants trésors, et qu'ils n'avaient rien de pareil à nous offrir. – Quel plaisir ce doit être de parcourir de ses lèvres cette peau si fine et si polie, et ces contours si bien arrondis, qui semblent aller au-devant du baiser et le provoquer! ces chairs satinées [...] quels motifs inépuisables de délicates voluptés que nous n'avons pas avec les hommes!

Ibid., 299. Ma situation devenait fort embarrassante et passablement ridicule; [...] – Les façons entreprenantes m'étaient interdites, et c'étaient les seules qui eussent été convenables. J'étais trop sûre de ne pas éprouver de résistance pour m'y risquer, [...] Dire des galanteries et débiter des madrigaux, cela eût été bon dans le commencement, mais rien n'eût paru plus fade au point où nous en étions arrivées; – me lever et sortir eût été de la dernière grossièreté; [...] et puis, je l'avouerai à ma honte, cette scène, tout équivoque que le caractère en fût pour moi, ne manquait pas d'un certain charme qui me retenait plus qu'il n'eût fallu; cet ardent désir m'échauffait de sa flamme, et j'étais réellement fâchée de ne le pouvoir satisfaire: je souhaitai même d'être un homme, comme effectivement je le paraissais, afin de couronner cet amour, et je regrettai fort que Rosette se trompât.

Ibid., 326–7. J'étais émue, et je fis à Rosette quelques caresses plus tendres qu'à l'ordinaire; de ses cheveux ma main était descendue à son cou velouté, et de là à son épaule ronde et polie que je flattais doucement et dont je suivais la ligne frémissante. L'enfant vibrait sous mon toucher comme un clavier sous les doigts d'un musicien; sa chair tressaillait et sautait brusquement, et d'amoureux frissons couraient le long de son corps.

Moi-même j'éprouvais une espèce de désir vague et confus dont je ne pouvais démêler le but, et je sentais une grande volupté à parcourir ces formes pures et délicates. – Je quittai son épaule, et, profitant de l'hiatus d'un pli, j'enfermai subitement dans ma main sa petite gorge effarée, qui palpitait éperdument comme une tourterelle surprise au nid; – de l'extrême contour de sa joue, que j'effleurais d'un baiser à peine sensible, j'arrivai à sa bouche mi-ouverte: nous restâmes ainsi quelque temps. [...] Rosette me nouait de plus en plus avec ses bras et m'enveloppait de son corps; – elle se penchait sur moi convulsivement et me pressait sur sa poitrine nue et haletante; à chaque baiser, sa vie semblait accourir tout entière à la place touchée, et abandonner le reste de sa personne. – Des idées singulières me passaient par la tête; j'aurais, si je n'avais craint de trahir mon incognito, laissé un champ libre aux élans passionnés de Rosette, [...] et ces vives attaques, ces caresses réitérées, le contact de ce beau corps, ces doux noms perdus dans des baisers me troublaient au dernier point, – quoiqu'ils fussent d'une femme; – et puis cette visite nocturne, cette passion romanesque, ce clair de lune, tout cela avait pour moi une fraîcheur et un charme de nouveauté qui me faisaient oublier qu'au bout du compte je n'étais pas un homme.

Ibid., 368–9. Au lieu de retourner dans sa chambre, elle entra chez Rosette. – Ce qu'elle y dit, ce qu'elle y fit, je n'ai jamais pu le savoir, quoique j'aie fait les plus consciencieuses recherches. [...] Seulement une femme de chambre de Rosette m'apprit cette circonstance singulière: bien que sa maîtresse n'eût pas couché cette nuit-là avec son amant, le lit était rompu et défait, et portait l'empreinte de deux corps. – De plus, elle me montra deux perles, parfaitement semblables à celles que Théodore portait dans ses cheveux en jouant le rôle de Rosalinde. Elle les avait trouvées dans le lit en le faisant. Je livre cette remarque à la sagacité du lecteur, [...] quant à moi, j'ai fait là-dessus mille conjectures, toutes plus déraisonnables les unes que les autres, et si saugrenues que je n'ose véritablement les écrire, même dans le style le plus honnêtement périphrasé.

Baudelaire, "Femmes damnées." L'âpre stérilité de votre jouissance / Altère votre soif et roidit votre peau, / Et le vent furibond de la concupiscence / Fait claquer votre chair ainsi qu'un vieux drapeau.

Ibid. Et fuyez l'infini que vous portez en vous.

Balzac, *La Fille*, 302. Rien ne console d'avoir perdu ce qui nous a paru être l'infini.

Belot, *Mademoiselle Giraud*, 19. indolente et souple, voluptueuse dans ses moindres mouvements [...] Avant qu'elle ait parlé j'ai déjà entendu sa voix vibrante, accentuée, presque masculine. Que de volupté dans ses grands yeux noirs à moitié voilés par de longs cils et entourés d'un cercle bleuâtre! Que de sensualité sur ses lèvres rouges un peu épaisses, pour ainsi dire roulées sur elles-mêmes et recouvertes d'un irritant duvet!

Ibid., 242. Le plus souvent, j'en suis persuadée, ce ne sont pas les hommes qui perdent les femmes; ce sont les femmes qui se perdent entre elles.

Chevalier, *De L'Inversion de l'instant sexuel*, 71. Quant à la cause de la perversion, les auteurs s'accordent à incriminer la sensibilité amative [sic] naturelle de la femme, la recherche des sensations nouvelles, la rage des plaisirs étranges, l'attrait des voluptés aiguës, l'excès de civilisation affinant les sens, enfin et surtout les conditions sociales, réunissant un grand nombre d'individus du même sexe à l'exclusion de l'autre, dans de grandes agglomérations telles que les armées, les prisons, les couvents, les pensions, les internats, etc., etc.

Ibid., 72–4. Ces amours contre nature, les romanciers nous les peignent comme violentes, jalouses, terribles, implacables, avec tous les emportements, toutes les ivresses et toutes les douleurs du véritable amour; elles absorbent l'individu qu'elles possèdent et ne lui laissent que de l'aversion pour l'autre sexe. Dans le tableau de ces passions féminines ils donnent toujours à une de leurs héroïnes le rôle de l'homme, celui du commandement, de la direction, de l'attaque et à l'autre la soumission et l'obéissance. La première est souvent une femme aux formes accusées, presque masculines, une nature violente et indomptable, pliant sa compagne sous sa domination, exerçant sur elle une sorte de fascination et un despotisme absolu, ayant conscience de sa perversion et au besoin s'en faisant gloire. L'autre, malléable, se laisse, sans résistance conduire où l'on veut, inconsciente et résignée.

Dans quelle classe de la société se montre le plus souvent cette corruption? L'accord des romanciers est unanime: dans les hautes classes, dans la bourgeoisie où l'absence d'occupations prédispose admirablement; jamais chez les paysans ou les ouvriers dont les rudes travaux constituent pour eux une protection efficace.

Sont-ce des débauchés ou des malades, les héros et les héroïnes de leurs études? Croyant surtout au vice, mais entrevoyant vaguement chez eux une faiblesse maladive d'organisation, ils ont adopté une opinion mixte, tenant le milieu entre la pédérastie ou la tribadisme et l'inversion proprement dite de l'instinct sexuel; c'est de la *névrose*, expression ambiguë et commode qui pour eux explique tout, et dont ils abusent; leurs héros sont des névropathes, des déséquilibrés, des *détraqués*. Ils arrivent à la dépravation comme d'autres deviennent gourmands par suite du manque d'appétit. Ils raffinent l'amour pour pouvoir aimer, comme d'autres ont recours à de nouvelles épices pour pouvoir manger; c'est la *faiblesse irritable* des médecins.

On doit connaître ce côté des défectuosités de la nature humaine: averti, on pourra prévenir le danger. Quant au remède, il s'indique de lui-même: fortifier les organisations particulières et supprimer l'internat, cette cause puissante des promiscuités honteuses dans l'âge périlleux de la puberté.

Telles sont, brièvement résumées, les conclusions principales auxquelles sont arrivés des romanciers sur un point de pathologie mentale.

Maupassant, "La Femme de Paul," 1218. Ce lieu sue la bêtise, pue la canaillerie et la galanterie de bazar. Mâles et femelles s'y valent. Il y flotte une odeur d'amour, et l'on s'y bat pour un oui ou pour un non, afin de soutenir des réputations vermoulues que les coups d'épée et les balles de pistolet ne font que crever davantage.

Ibid., 1219. Un canot couvert d'une tente et monté par quatre femmes descendait lentement le courant. Celle qui ramait était petite, maigre, fanée, vêtue d'un costume de mousse avec ses cheveux relevés sous un chapeau ciré. En face d'elle, une grosse blondasse habillée en homme, avec un veston de flanelle blanche, se tenait couchée sur le dos au fond du bateau, les jambes en l'air sur le banc des deux côtés de la rameuse, et elle fumait une cigarette, tandis qu'à chaque effort des avirons sa poitrine et son ventre frémissaient, ballottés par la secousse. Tout à l'arrière, sous la tente, deux belles filles grandes et minces, l'une brune et l'autre blonde, se tenaient par la taille en regardant sans cesse leurs compagnes.

Ibid., 1219. Voici Lesbos

Ibid., 1219. clameur furieuse: une bousculade effrayante

Ibid., 1219. hurlement effroyable

Ibid., 1219. La rameuse, devant cette ovation, s'était arrêtée tranquillement. La grosse blonde étendue au fond du canot tourna la tête d'un air nonchalant, se soulevant sur les coudes; et les deux belles filles, à l'arrière, se mirent à rire en saluant la foule.

Ibid., 1220. On eût dit que ce peuple, ce ramassis de corrompus, saluait un chef, comme ces escadres qui tirent le canon quand un amiral passe sur leur front.

Ibid., 1220. C'est honteux! On devrait les noyer comme des chiennes avec une pierre au cou.

Ibid., 1220. Mais lui, semblait exaspéré, comme soulevé par une jalousie d'homme, par une fureur profonde, instinctive, désordonnée.

Ibid., 1222. C'est qu'il aimait éperdument, sans savoir pourquoi, malgré ses instincts délicats, malgré sa raison, malgré sa volonté même. Il était

232   QUOTATIONS ON PAGES 42-4

tombé dans cet amour comme on tombe dans un trou bourbeux. D'une nature attendrie et fine, il avait rêvé des liaisons exquises, idéales et passionnées; et voilà que ce petit criquet de femme, bête, comme toutes les filles, d'une bêtise exaspérante, pas jolie même, maigre et rageuse, l'avait pris, captivé, possédé des pieds à la tête, corps et âme. Il subissait cet ensorcellement féminin, mystérieux et tout-puissant, cette force inconnue, cette domination prodigieuse, venue on ne sait d'où, du démon de la chair, et qui jette l'homme le plus sensé aux pieds d'une fille quelconque sans que rien en elle explique son pouvoir fatal et souverain.

Ibid., 1225 (my emphasis). Mais elle avait compris la ruse, et elle lui lança ce regard énigmatique, *ce regard à perfidies qui apparaît si vite au fond de l'oeil de la femme*. Puis, après avoir réfléchi, elle répondit: "Tu te coucheras si tu veux, moi j'ai promis d'aller au bal de la Grenouillère."

Ibid., 1228 (my emphasis). La grisante poésie de cette soirée d'été entrait dans Paul malgré lui, traversait son angoisse affolée, remuait son coeur avec une ironie féroce, développant jusqu'à la rage en son âme douce et contemplative des besoins d'idéale tendresse, d'épanchements passionnés dans le sein *d'une femme adorée et fidèle*.

Ibid., 1229. On parlait de nouveau; et il s'approcha, courbé en deux. Puis un léger cri courut sous les branches tout près de lui. Un cri! Un de ces cris d'amour qu'il avait appris à connaître aux heures éperdues de leur tendresse. Il avançait encore, toujours, comme malgré lui, attiré invinciblement, sans avoir conscience de rien ... et il les vit.

Oh! Si c'eût été un homme, l'autre! mais cela! cela! Il se sentait enchaîné par leur infamie même. Et il restait là, anéanti, bouleversé comme s'il eût découvert tout à coup un cadavre cher et mutilé, un crime contre nature, monstrueux, une immonde profanation.

Ibid., 1232 (my emphasis). Alors Pauline prit dans ses bras la pauvre Madeleine éplorée, la câlina, l'embrassa longtemps, la consola:

"Que veux-tu, ce n'est point ta faute, n'est-ce pas? On ne peut pourtant pas empêcher les hommes de faire des bêtises. Il l'a voulu, tant pis pour lui, après tout!"

Puis, la relevant:

"Allons, ma chérie, viens-t'en coucher à la maison; tu ne peux pas rentrer chez Grillon ce soir."

Elle l'embrassa de nouveau: "Va, nous te guérirons," dit-elle.

Madeleine se releva, et, pleurant toujours, mais avec des sanglots affaiblis, la tête sur l'épaule de Pauline, *comme réfugiée dans une tendresse plus intime et plus sûre, plus familière et plus confiante,* elle partit à tout petits pas.

Ibid., 1220. pluie d'injures fangeuses: il lui semblait que les mots sortant de cette bouche et tombant sur lui le salissaient comme des ordures.

Ibid., 1231. Une espèce d'enduit noirâtre liquide couvrait tout son corps. La figure paraissait enflée, et de ses cheveux collés par le limon une eau sale coulait sans cesse.

Ibid., 1223. il lui sembla que cet hameçon c'était son amour et que, s'il fallait l'arracher, tout ce qu'il avait dans la poitrine sortirait ainsi au bout d'un fer recourbé, accroché au fond de lui, et dont Madeleine tenait le fil.

CHAPTER TWO

Peladan,. *La Gynandre,* n.p. *La Gynandre* prétend valoir même devant le savant et le confesseur, comme la seule monographie de la sodomie féminine.
L'aberration y est étudiée, à hauteur d'art, et si inférieure à *La Fille aux yeux d'or,* combien plus morale!

Ibid., 26. Lesbos peut se classer parmi les sortes de jouir, non pas au nombre des façons d'aimer; Lesbos peut se rubriquer à l'article Luxure, non pas à celui Amour.

Ibid., 83. L'infériorité de Lesbos, c'est son besoin de galerie mâle. Si un homme n'est pas témoin de nos menues caresses, nous les éprouvons moins vivement.

Ibid., 97. La sodomie féminine n'existe pas en tant que passion; c'est une forme dépravée du dandysme; c'est le travesti porté au moral et joué dans la vie.

Ibid., 105. Les natives, garçonnières dès l'enfance jouent le rôle positif en aberration, obéissant à un idéal faussé et, aussi insensuelles qu'insexuelles, des garçons avortés en femmes, des âmes de lycéens en des corps féminins; [...]

Les devenues, normales pendant l'enfance, jouant encore par la suite le rôle passif et féminin en aberration, obéissant, celles-là, à une fausse innervation et simplement ennemies de l'homme par inaccommodation de la vibrabilité voluptueuse, âmes féminines en des corps également féminins, mais rebelles à l'orgasme sexuel et dont la chair, pour prendre une image à la musique, souffre hors d'un contrepoint définissable mais demandant chez le mari ou l'amoureux une intelligence raisonnée du clavier féminin et son contrepoint; [...] Et cette catégorie reste guérissable par une simple vibration heureusement donnée!

Ibid., 340. Lesbos, imposture du corps et déception de l'âme, cauchemar des nuits décadentes, Lesbos, tu n'existeras jamais!

Et vous, femmes lamentables, déçues et révoltées, ne prétendez qu'à la pitié qu'appelle toute douleur; devant l'intelligence attentive, vous n'avez jamais eu lieu, vains fantômes d'un amour impossible, actrices de la vie, actrices de l'amour, gamins et malades, Gynandres!

D'Argis, *Gomorrhe*, 312. Si Mme Sonnet voulait qu'il lui amenât Marthe, ce ne pouvait être que pour... aussitôt il referma violemment et pour toujours la porte de sa conscience qui avait tenté de s'entr'ouvrir.

Mendès, *Méphistophéla*, 20. Jamais aucun visage humain n'a exprimé avec une plus parfaite hideur le découragement d'avoir vécu, l'aveu d'une irrémédiable agonie. Oh! Quel dégoût de soi [...].

Ibid., 33. Baiser de deux bouches de fillettes qui ne se baisent pas exprès! battement, seins contre seins, presque pas seins encore, de deux poitrines de qui la sexualité s'ignore, en un enlacement si pur, par que [sic] pourtant sera moins doux et moins réalisateur des songes le rude corps-à-corps de la nuit nuptiale!

Ibid., 138. elle convoitait, voilà tout, cette chose vivante, elle la convoitait avec une folie de bête qui a faim. Le monstre qui, de tout temps, fut en elle, en voulait sortir et se satisfaire.

Ibid., 567. exemplaire lamentable de la Névrose ou de la Possession, elle bavera [...]. Elle croira voir grouiller, et grimper sur elle, comme un assaut de vermine, la fourmilière de ses anciens péchés.

La Vaudère, *Les Demi-sexes*, 15–16. Au fond, elle était une de ces détraquées contemporaines qui ont trop de nerfs pour suivre les sentiers battus de la médiocrité humaine.

Ibid., 147. La séduction corruptrice et froide, la complication morbide de toutes ces névrosées les troublaient réciproquement de passions et d'agitations violentes.

Monfort, *Le Journal d'une Saphiste*, 212. agitée par quelque Satan jaloux de nos amours passés.

Ibid., 215–16. Femmes, ne recherchez comme Amour, que l'Unique et le Fort, celui qui régit toute l'humanité: l'Amour Sain et Honnête, Réconfortant et Sublime parce que Procréateur, celui de l'Homme.

Willy, *La Môme Picrate*, 309. Nue elle aussi [Picrate], elle se jette dans les bras de son amie [Tortille/vrai nom Gilberte] qui la reçoit avec un plaisir non dissimulé. Un instant, toutes deux s'étreignent fougueusement (si fougueusement qu'elles en sont chastes), comme deux soeurs qui vont se quitter, l'une restant au pays latin et l'autre partant pour la Grèce, mais pas pour Lesbos, j'espère. Mais (faux départ), après s'être voluptueusement contemplées, elles s'enlacent de nouveau. Leurs cheveux dénoués se mêlent. Leurs lèvres se joignent. D'autres caresses sont imminentes.

Claudine s'en va, 126. Elle penche son visage et m'éblouit de ses yeux fauves, si dominateurs soudain que je ferme les miens accablée...

Claudine en ménage, 113. Elle *est* pour femmes.

Ibid., 113. Si je n'aime pas les hommes, je *dois* rechercher les femmes, ô simplicité de l'esprit masculin.

Ibid., 122. Une amie plus que tendre.

Ibid., 122–3. – Non, ce n'est pas la même chose! Vous pouvez tout faire, vous autres. C'est charmant, et c'est sans importance...
  – Sans importance... je ne suis pas de votre avis.
  – Si, je dis bien! C'est entre vous, petites bêtes jolies, une... comment dire? ... une consolation de nous, une diversion qui vous repose...
  – Oh?
  – ...ou du moins qui vous dédommage, la recherche logique d'un parte-

naire plus parfait, d'une beauté plus pareille à la vôtre, où se mirent et se reconnaissent votre sensibilité et vos défaillances... Si j'osais (mais je n'oserai pas), je dirais qu'à certaines femmes il faut la femme pour leur conserver le goût de l'homme.

Claudine à Paris, 157–8. Tout son corps souple suit mon jeu, avec une complaisance traîtresse[...]
- Oui, Claudine, nous arriverons!
- Où?
- Penchez-vous, je vais vous le dire tout bas.
J'obéis, crédule. Et c'est sa bouche que je rencontre. J'écoute, longtemps, ce que sa bouche dit à la mienne... Elle n'a pas menti, nous arrivons... Ma hâte égale la sienne, la domine et la soumet. Révélée à moi-même, j'écarte les mains caressantes de Rézi qui comprend, frémit, lutte un court instant, puis demeure, les bras tombés...
Le coup sourd d'une lointaine porte cochère me met debout. Vaguement, je distingue la tache pâle de Rézi assise devant moi, et qui colle à mon poignet ses lèvres chaudes. D'un bras à sa taille, je la dresse, je la serre à moi toute, je la ploie et la baise au hasard sur ses yeux, dans ses cheveux en buisson, sur sa nuque moite...
- Demain!
- Demain... je t'aime...

Saint-Agen, *Charmeuse de femmes*, 17. O toi que j'ai divinisée, souveraine idole qui règnes sur mon âme [...] dis-moi d'être infâme et je serai infâme!...

Ibid., 101. qui sont fatales, qui détraquent et qui tuent!

Ibid., 255. irresistibles tentatrices [...] la débauche [...] le vice [...] les compromissions immondes.

Ibid., 264. – Oh! mon Dieu! sanglota-t-elle, puisque vous m'avez permis d'aimer Reine... permettez-moi de le lui dire, donnez m'en le droit en m'en donnant le courage!

Ibid., 71. Elle s'oubliait pour moi, toi tu m'oubliais pour toi.

Ibid., 251–2. si j'avais accompli, sans le vouloir, une chose irréparable [...] certains initiations pénètrent jusqu'au sang.

Ibid., 235. Embrasse-moi de toute ton âme, ton baiser sera le dernier que je recevrai d'un être humain.

Ibid., 236. Un instinct secret venait de les avertir qu'une sensation extra-ordinaire et coupable les faisait complices dans une volupté défendue, nou-velle et d'une saveur si intense qu'elles en étaient encore frémissantes.

Ibid., 240. Reine! [...] La bougie consumée s'éteignit sur la dernière syllabe de ce nom doublement cher à Hélène, et les ténèbres – complices de toutes les hontes, incitatrices de toutes les voluptés, gardiennes fidèles des secrets ignominieux, des pures extases, protectrices de toutes les pudeurs – enveloppèrent de leurs voiles tentateurs, la couche où deux chevelures brunes s'emmêlaient leurs longues soies souples.

Rivière, *Sous le manteau de Fourvière*, 43–4. Aidée d'une compagne chérie, elle avait étudié, déjouant toutes les surveillances, les mesures appropriées à susciter d'abord l'éveil des sens, puis à leur donner les satis-factions approximatives en son pouvoir.

Ibid., 57. Les frôlements sont rapides..., furtifs..., tout naturels.
Mais quand la voiture s'arrête [...] Irène est toute drôle, toute rouge... d'avoir tant ri sans doute... Jupes et corsages sont tout froissés, chiffonnés.

Ibid., 69–70. [...] Ses [Irène] lèvres entr'ouvertes sont closes sous celles de Marguerite. En même temps, un émoi inconnu saisit toute sa chair aux caresses de son amie [...]
Insensiblement, progressivement, au plus profond d'elle-même une corde a vibré.
Une sensation nouvelle envahit ...[...]
Bientôt, elle halète, se crispe, se contracte toute..., puis..., tout à coup..., se détend, angoissée, gémissante et vibrante, toute secouée à ondes courtes par un mal délicieux dont elle sent brusquement les griffes la saisir.

Ibid., 88. Et, le soir où Irène, blessée, étouffant sa plainte, gémit de douleur et de plaisir, il fallut l'intensité nouvelle et complète, cette fois, de la crise voluptueuse, pour lui révéler qu'elle avait passé, presque sans s'en douter, des mains de Marguerite dans les bras de son frère.

Proust, *À la recherche*, II, 842. Elles ne se gênèrent pas plus que si elles avaient été dans leur lit.

Ibid., II, 852. La cousine de Bloch alla s'asseoir à une table où elle regarda un magazine. Bientôt la jeune femme vint s'asseoir d'un air distrait à côté d'elle. Mais sous la table on aurait pu voir bientôt se tourmenter leurs pieds, puis leurs jambes et leurs mains qui étaient confondues. Les paroles suivirent, la conversation s'engagea, et le naïf mari de la jeune femme, qui la cherchait partout, fut étonné de la trouver faisant des projets pour le soir même avec une jeune fille qu'il ne connaissait pas. Sa femme lui présenta comme une amie d'enfance la cousine de Bloch, sous un nom inintelligible, car elle avait oublié de lui demander comment elle s'appelait.

Ibid., II, 795–6. Une des jeunes filles que je ne connaissais pas se mit au piano, et Andrée demanda à Albertine de valser avec elle. [...] je fis remarquer à Cottard comme elles dansaient bien. Mais lui, du point de vue spécial du médecin, et avec une mauvaise éducation qui ne tenait pas compte de ce que je connaissais ces jeunes filles, à qui il avait pourtant dû me voir dire bonjour, me répondit: "Oui, mais les parents sont bien imprudents qui laissent leurs filles prendre de pareilles habitudes. Je ne permettrais certainement pas aux miennes de venir ici. Sont-elles jolies au moins? Je ne distingue pas leurs traits. Tenez, regardez, ajouta-t-il en me montrant Albertine et Andrée qui valsaient lentement, serrées l'une contre l'autre, j'ai oublié mon lorgnon et je ne vois pas bien, mais elles sont certainement au comble de la jouissance. On ne sait pas assez que c'est surtout par les seins que les femmes l'éprouvent. Et, voyez, les leurs se touchent complèment." En effet, le contact n'avait pas cessé entre ceux d'Andrée et ceux d'Albertine. Je ne sais si elles entendirent ou devinèrent la réflexion de Cottard, mais elles se détachèrent légèrement l'une de l'autre tout en continuant à valser. [...] Albertine avait l'air d'y montrer, de faire constater à Andrée quelque frémissement voluptueux et secret.

Lacretelle, *La Bonifas*, 12. On apercevait au milieu de la partie rose et charnue un trait qui dessinait le contour extérieur des lèvres. Bizarrerie plutôt que difformité, mais qui ajoutait à l'impression disgracieuse.

Ibid., 12. une pensée droite et sauvage

Ibid., 57. –C'est parce qu'elle a des lèvres plus grosses que les miennes que tu te laisses embrasser plus souvent par Marie Bonifas?

Ibid., 56. C'est que l'amour de Marie passait par tous les détours et toutes les défaites d'un grand amour. Il n'y a point de différence entre les sentiments qui se font jour dans notre coeur lorsque nous sommes enfants et ceux que nous éprouvons plus tard. La somme de nos joies est la même, nous endurons les mêmes peines, nous tentons les mêmes remèdes. On en juge autrement, on rapetisse les premiers, parce que les réactions immédiates qu'ils provoquent sont le plus souvent sans importance. Mais, voit-on immédiatement tous les effets d'une passion? Sait-on quels germes, lents à se développer, elle laisse dans l'organisme? Le psychologue qui dédaigne l'âme des enfants est comparable au médecin qui observerait ses sujets sans s'occuper de leurs antécédents; et un romancier qui veut peindre un caractère et ne prend pas son personnage dans l'oeuf m'a toujours paru omettre la tâche primordiale. Enfin, à mesure qu'on avancera dans ce récit, on décidera si l'innocent amour de Marie Bonifas pour son amie de pension aurait dû être négligé.

Ibid., 297. Oui c'est une femme, une simple femme qui vous chasse, misérable!

CHAPTER THREE

Cahun, *Aveux mon avenus*, 176. Brouiller les cartes.
  Masculin? féminin? mais ça dépend des cas. Neutre est le seul genre qui me convienne [sic] toujours. S'il existait dans notre langue on n'observerait pas ce flottement de ma pensée. Je serais pour de bon l'abeille ouvrière.

Galzy, *Jeunes Filles en serre chaude*, 274. [elle] se remémora Baudelaire et ses paradis artificiels et aussitôt le divin dialogue de tristesse qu'échangent les femmes damnées. Et d'un coup un tranchant de fer perça son coeur.

Ibid., 286. découvrait ce témoin secret et sûr, cette âme qui était en elle-même étrangère à ses désordres et en qui elle pouvait prendre foi pour continuer la vie.

Roland-Manuel, *Le Trille de Diable*, 93. Le soir, dans son lit elle [Florence] échafaudait des combinaisons extravagantes. La violence de son tempérament lui suggérait des inventions dont elle rougissait le lendemain.

Ibid., 257. "Prends-moi de force!" souffla-t-elle [Florence] tout bas. Les jeunes filles n'entendirent pas le tintamarre d'un réveil matin...

Ibid., 294. Tu comprends... *j'ai un homme*. C'est merveilleux.

Ibid., 394. On pouvait donc encore s'amuser avec Augustine!

Ibid., 392. Florence venait de lire un roman où il était question de deux femmes qui s'aimaient d'amour et qui entretenaient ensemble des rapports coupables. Depuis peu Florence savait que ces choses existaient. Après s'être enquise de maints détails, elle y avait longuement réfléchi pour conclure qu'elle n'aimait pas Augustine d'amour! Absolument pas! Cette seule idée lui donnait même un véritable fou rire!

Bertin, *La Dernière Innocence*, 190. une fille comme toi avec un homme...

Ibid., 293. Elle avait déjà pris le goût du bonheur, il lui fallait rentrer

Bertin, *Liens de famille*, 176. L'erreur que j'ai commise en couchant avec toi, je la regrette chaque jour. J'ai perdu ma liberté.

Ibid., 293. – Va-t-en! Je pourrais te tuer! La violence de Marie ne m'étonnait plus et j'imaginais clairement la scène [....]
    – Parce que tu m'aimes! hurla encore Clarice [...] N'avait-elle pas lu dans le regard de Marie tout l'amour-haine qui l'exaltait? Il n'y avait plus rien à faire mais elle ne pouvait l'accepter. Jamais elle n'avait éprouvé pareille douleur [...]
    – Voilà, c'est fini! murmura Marie me sentant approcher. Nous n'en parlerons plus parce qu'il n'y a rien à en dire. C'est la plus triste histoire de ma vie. Celle où j'ai le plus mal agi. Et elle se termine mal... On n'as pas le droit... Pas le droit.

Ibid., 310. Aimer une autre femme, quand on est femme et qu'on a le goût et la capacité n'offense personne.

Ibid., 359. J'étais toute entière préoccupée de Marie, obsédée par la vie affective de Marie qui cessa complètement après la rupture avec Clarice. Et c'est de cette rupture que Marie est morte!... Elle avait besoin de vibrer, de partager avec l'être aimé la vie qui affluait en elle. Il n'en pouvait être autrement pour elle et vivre sans amour ne l'intéressait pas. Je te le dis: Clarice avait raison de clamer que Marie l'aimait! Je l'ai compris trop tard!

Mallet-Joris, *Le Rempart des Béguines*, 81-2. Ce visage si froid bouleversé tout à coup, se défaisant, s'éparpillant en demi-sourires, en demi-sourires, en gémissements très légers, à peine perceptibles, en regards glissés sous la paupière et comme noyés tout de suite dans une tendresse liquide, ce cri intérieur que je sentais monter, ce ronronnement qui finissait en plainte, et ces canines aiguës mordant la lèvre inférieure si pâle, ne pouvant plus dissimuler une ivresse méchante et comme carnassière, c'était cela le centre brûlant et poignant et déchirant de mon amour pour Tamara.... cette lumière brûlante: le visage d'amour de Tamara.

Louvier, *Qui qu'en grogne*, 14–15. Je n'ai pas plus à t'apprendre du monde que tu n'as à m'apprendre. Je suis aussi ignorante que toi de cette joie que nous cherchons depuis notre naissance, aussi maladroite, aussi peu capable de me défendre contre une douleur qui me viendrait après un excès de bonheur aussi peu en état de défense contre un être qui me serait irremplaçable aussi neuve. Je n'ai pas envie d'un maître ni d'une servante: j'ai envie de mon égale.

Ibid., 151. Peu à peu me vint une immense pitié: Gabrielle ne me paraissait pire, ni meilleure que les autres. C'était une femme.

Et que pouvoir attendre d'une femme? Je les méprisais toutes d'être aussi peu capables de fermeté, de valeur, d'intelligence créatrice, et sans doute pour cela même je n'arrivais pas à les détester...

Et j'eus pitié de Gabrielle, beaucoup.

Ibid., 181. Je voulais m'offrir à elle, pour qu'elle soit au moins la première: pour la première fois, abdiquer tout, et dans ses mains à elle.

Ibid., 181. avec un sourire dur, des yeux moqueurs, rageurs... son regard qui s'emparait de moi sans broncher, sans faiblir, sans indulgence.

Ibid., 182. [...] qu'elle lise non seulement sur mon corps et mes tressaillements, mais encore sur mon visage, à quel point je deviens son vouloir. Jusqu'à la honte, jusqu'à l'indécence, l'impudeur, l'anéantissement total: après seulement je pourrais tendre à redevenir malléable. *A ce prix seulement.*

Et voulant lui crier les mots d'abandon, je me brisais en gémissant.

Mahyère, *Je jure de m'éblouir*, 115.
...je voudrais venger ma cousine. Elle est partie sur vos traces comme à la recherche du Saint-Graal et vous l'avez trahie.

– Ce que vous appelez ma trahison lui rappellera peut-être que Dieu ne souffre pas de partage. Je suis lasse de me partager entre cet atelier et Sainte-Thérèse, Sylvie et mon devoir, vos tangos et mes chants grégoriens...

Ibid., 195. Vous vivez de votre renoncement, je meurs de mon refus, mais l'enterrement sera le même, à quelques symboles près.

Monési, *Althia*, 28. J'entendais bien l'aimer en secret. Il allait de soi que même si un jour elle apprenait cet amour, elle ne m'en donnerait pas de retour: elle devait être tant aimée de personnes mieux aimantes que moi qui étais déjà mariée, avais des enfants, et, *je venais d'y songer, qui étais une femme*. Un amour partagé me paraissait impossible.

Ibid., 186. le soleil les rendait transparents, ils brillaient, dorés, doux et fauves comme un gâteau de miel.

Ibid., 181. déséquilibre physiologique ou glandulaire. N'importe quel psychiatre arrangera ça.

Francillon, *La Lettre*, 19. Il fait un vent fou, à croire que la maison va s'envoler. Je pense à toi sans cesse, je voudrais te prendre dans mes bras et je t'aime. Renée.

Ibid., 262. je ne crois pas que sans elle je m'en sorte

Ibid., 280. Elle l'aimait.

Ibid., 201. reculant le moment de toucher, d'écarter les lèvres basses avec ses doigts, d'aller plus avant, de chercher, de découvrir une pointe humide, de suivre le secret sillon, puis de pénétrer doucement avec d'infinies précautions dans les lieux plus secrets encore et d'y séjourner et d'atteindre les profondeurs lointaines qui lui offrent leur tiédeur, leur magie d'anémone de mer...

Dupont, *Le Cheroub*, 103. La sensualité n'était pas encore mon choix mais l'essence même de mon activité.

Ibid., 154. Vers elle, près de sa nuque, je me penchai comme si m'étourdissait la tentation d'y déposer mes lèvres. L'habitude avait créé en moi des réflexes de séducteur qu'il ne me venait même pas à l'idée de contrôler. Je leur cédais tout naturellement, espérant trouver au bout le climat de la passion que je croyais indispensable à ma vie.

Vilmont, *Les Drosères*, 213. Nous étions un couple authentique, indissoluble, imprudemment formé, alors que nous eussions dû fuir, trop faites
l'une pour l'autre...

Ibid., 213. Il me fallait convenir...que je formais un couple avec une femme;
qu'une enfance troublée de part et d'autre nous le valait et qu'enfin, sorties
de la quiétude aveugle où notre amour nous confinait, nous affronterions
peut-être pour la vie, le poids d'une difformité.

CHAPTER FOUR

Beauvoir, *La Deuxième Sexe*, II, 172. L'homosexualité peut être pour la
femme une manière de fuir sa condition ou une manière de l'assumer. Le
grand tort des psychanalystes c'est, par conformisme moralisateur, de ne
l'envisager jamais que comme une attitude inauthentique.

Ibid., 174. c'est une étape, un apprentissage et celle qui s'y livre avec le
plus d'ardeur peut être demain la plus ardente des épouses, des amantes,
des mères.

Ibid., II, 178. Parmi les artistes et écrivains féminins, on compte de nom-
breuses lesbiennes. Ce n'est pas que leur singularité sexuelle soit source
d'énergie créatrice [...] c'est plutôt qu'absorbées par un sérieux travail
qu'elles n'entendent pas perdre leur temps à jouer un rôle de femme ni à
lutter contre les hommes. N'admettant pas la supériorité mâle, elles ne
veulent ni feindre de la reconnaître ni se fatiguer à la contester; elles
cherchent dans la volupté détente, apaisement, diversion: elles ont meilleur
compte à se détourner d'un partenaire qui se présente sous la figure d'un
adversaire.

Ibid. contemplation

Ibid. chacune est à la fois le sujet et l'objet

Ibid. la dualité est complicité

Ibid., II, 185. dans la mesure où toutes deux sont narcissistes, caressant
dans l'enfant, dans l'amante, leur prolongement ou leur reflet.

Ibid., II, 192. En vérité l'homosexualité n'est pas plus une perversion délibérée qu'une malédiction fatale. C'est une attitude *choisie en situation*, c'est-à-dire à la fois motivée et librement adoptée.

Ibid., II, 13. On ne naît pas femme: on le devient.

Leduc, *Thérèse et Isabelle*, 8. – Mon amour.
  Isabelle arrivait du pays des météores, des bouleversements, des sinistres, des ravages. Elle me lançait un mot libéré, un programme [...]
  Elle m'attend mais ce n'est pas la sécurité. Le mot qu'elle a dit est trop fort. Nous nous regardons, nous sommes paralysées.
  Je me jetai dans ses bras.

Ibid., 90. Je la contemplais, je me souvenais d'elle au présent, je l'avais près de moi de dernier instant en dernier instant. Quand on aime on est toujours sur le quai d'une gare.

Ibid., 120. J'aimais Isabelle sans gestes, sans élans: je lui offrais ma vie sans un signe.
  Isabelle se dressa, elle me prit dans ses bras:
  – Tu viendras tous les soirs?
  – Tous les soirs.
  – Nous ne nous quitterons pas?
  – Nous ne quitterons pas.
  Le mois suivant ma mère me reprit. Je ne revis jamais Isabelle.

Duras, in *France-Observateur*, 5 Nov. 1964. C'est un livre à la fois admirable et très important parce qu'il est régi par une règle de fer, jamais enfreinte ou presque jamais, celle de n'utiliser qu'un matériau descriptif pur, et qu'un outil, le langage objectif pur. Ce dernier prend ici tout son sens. Il est celui-là même – mais porté au plain-chant par l'auteur – dont l'enfance se sert pour déblayer et dénombrer son univers.

CHAPTER FIVE

Galzy, *La Surprise de vivre*, 228–9. Vous me plaisez.

Ibid., 271. Une douceur jamais éprouvée la rendait plus sensible aux odeurs de la terre, à la clarté du jour, à la souplesse de son corps. Elle fit quelques pas pour sentir l'élasticité de ses mouvements, puis revint, tendit les draps du lit froissé, se pencha à la fenêtre.

C'était l'heure où la vie de la maison commençait avec les bruits de la cuisine, de l'écurie, de la noria du potager. Et ces bruits étaient autres, pleins d'une sorte d'allégresse.

Elle se tâta comme pour se reconnaître, se regarda dans son miroir et vit son visage resplendir. Une nuit avait suffi pour tirer d'elle une autre vivante.

Ibid., 278. Etait-elle aussi une sorte de monstrueuse exception? Elle en rougit dans la nuit, sur ce grand lit où, à présent, à la place du mort, elle évoquait le souvenir de la femme vivante.

Ibid., 227. Ne trouvez-vous pas que c'est délicieux d'être libre?

Rigal, *l'Envers des choses*, 31. Bien après, il y eut les hommes, la norma-lité. Jamais je n'ai retrouvé ce plaisir complet qui mettait à mort la douleur...

Toi [le père], tu aurais appelé ça homosexualité et tu aurais essayé de soigner.

Moi, j'ai nommé amour, simplement.

Ibid., 35. On ne danse pas avec son sexe, on danse avec son âme.

Ibid., 74. A certains moments, je m'étais demandée si je n'étais pas effe-ctivement "lesbienne". Mais aucune fille ne m'attirait. Je n'aimais pas les autres. Je n'aimais personne.

Ibid., 136. Ses yeux caressent mon corps, je frémis sous cette caresse, je fais l'amour pour la première fois complètement, sans qu'on me viole. Mon visage évolue dans un ballet infernal. J'ai envie de crier. Je hurle de bonheur.

Labarraque-Reyssac, *Lesbos à Poitiers*, 13. les amours entre filles s'af-fichaient sans pudeur, et, chose curieuse, sans crainte de sanctions.

Ibid., 36. Et toi, tu es facile à conduire. Légère, tu comprends tout de suite ce qu'on veut faire.

Ibid., 98. Moi ces caresses-là, entre filles, elles me dégoûtent.

Ibid., 131. C'est que son amour me paraissait hors nature, je l'ai repoussé de toute ma raison et contre mon instinct, peut-être!...

Ibid., 134. C'est l'obéissance à une mode due à l'influence de Gide, de Proust, de certaines femmes poètes ou romancières qui ont été à la mode au début du siècle. C'est aussi la sensualité qui veut s'assouvir et qui se contente de ce qu'elle trouve, comme ces pauvres épouses du harem qui leur maître unique ne peut satisfaire!

Ibid., 216–17. et cette fois, je ne lutte plus. Je suis fatiguée, curieuse aussi, tentée peut-être. Elle glisse un bras sous ma nuque. Ses baisers doux et légers caressent mes paupières, mes joues, mon cou tandis que sa main gauche effleure mes seins, s'attarde sur leur pointe qui durcit. Je suis parcourue de frissons et une étrange chaleur fait vibrer mon sexe qui attend, appelle peut-être. Et je trouve agréable sa bouche sur ma bouche, sa langue douce, vivante qui me fouille et à qui je réponds [...]
   [...] Et elle reprend la conquête de mon corps étendu, éveillé, curieux. Combien de fois ai-je rêvé de m'abandonner ainsi à Jean [...].

Ibid., 217. Mais avec Gladys il n'y a pas d'accident à redouter. On peut s'abandonner à la volupté qu'elle sait donner. Experte, elle me révèle à moi-même. Mais quand changeant de position, elle réclame de moi les mêmes caresses, une brusque nausée me saisit et je la repousse violemment.

Ibid., 218. je me suis sentie grotesque... Je nous ai vues grotesques.

Beck, *Noli*, 28. L'homophile masculine ne me déplaisait pas – tandis que, paradoxalement, le saphisme me faisait horreur. Et bien qu'en principe "homosexualité" et "homophilie" soient synonymes, le second terme me paraissait convenir beaucoup mieux à mes sentiments, parce que ne contenant pas le mot "sexe" qui, s'appliquant à deux femmes, me dégoûtait. Surtout relativement à Camille. Je pouvais même difficilement supporter l'idée, l'image qu'elle eût des fonctions naturelles, des organes internes, une nudité.

Ibid., 117. Le saphisme me dégoûte. Vous pouvez me faire un enfant? Alors vous ne m'intéressez pas.

Ibid., 117. Elle proposa que nous ayons chacune un enfant du même homme. L'idée, qui me parut affreuse, m'aurait peut-être séduite si Pilar me plaisait. Mais non.

Ferrié, *L'Accident d'amour*, 64. Il y avait Madame Dolls assise au bord du lit et Catherine agenouillée sur la couverture, les mains coincées entre ses cuisses pour empêcher les bras d'enlacer Madame Dolls et dans le coeur de Catherine une grande flamme d'amour qui éclairait le monde.

Madame Dolls n'osait plus bouger. La passion de Catherine l'épouvantait parce qu'elle ne savait pas quel nom lui donner. Un emballement... une affection pure... ou un amour plus violent rejoignant la catastrophe de l'accident...

[...] Parce que Catherine l'aimait ainsi, Madame Dolls ne pourrait pas la garder auprès d'elle. Et Catherine ne supporterait pas la séparation [...].

Ibid., 65. Vous êtes ma joie de vivre, dit-elle gravement. Ne croyez pas que je vous aime trop ou mal.

Ibid., 85. Etre là, près de vous, quand vous livrez le plus beau de vous-même au monde extérieur." La dernière phrase de Madame Dolls. La plus belle. Celle qui faisait oublier toutes les autres.

Catherine en comprit soudain le sens. La vérité était dans cette phrase et s'appelait amour.

Ibid., 97. Et puis brusquement, elle ne pense plus qu'à ce corps qui se blottissait contre le sien [...] ses bras se refermèrent sur Catherine endormie. Et elle écouta avec une épouvante de bonheur monter en elle cette volupté de tendresse qui lui venait de ce jeune corps accroché au sien.

Ibid., 100. Contempler le bonheur de Catherine hors du temps et de la réalité. Une joie si douce où se mêlait tant de plénitude qu'elle en devenait une douleur intolérable...

Ibid., 100. Le réflexe d'un amant qui s'endort après l'amour et cherche encore, dans le sommeil, la présence de son bonheur [...] Tout un corps lourd d'inconscience et qui parlait cependant. [...] Et elle avait aimé ce poids de chair qui avait fait d'elle une femme riche de tendresse, une femme comblée.

Ibid., 120. Elle embrassa Catherine comme elle respirait une fleur. Avec trop de tendresse. Avec trop d'amour. Presqu'avec respect. Parce que Catherine lui offrait un visage aux yeux clos, si empreint de pureté et de joie que Madame Dolls songea au visage d'un enfant qui communie pour la première fois.

Puis elle ne songea plus qu'à la fraîcheur de ces lèvres sous les siennes

[...] qu'à cette chaleur qui s'emparait d'elle avec tant de violence qu'elle en ferma les yeux.

Le grand vide était en elle. Il était en Catherine aussi. Elles se regardèrent quelques secondes sans parler, comme effrayées par ce qu'elles venaient de découvrir, par cette émotion partagée, par cette joie reçue.

Ibid., 172–3. À deux mètres il y avait le divan et sa couverture exotique. Le bras la halait doucement vers ces couleurs d'un autre monde et elle se laissait entraîner, les oreilles bourdonnantes, les yeux clos, le front moite, comme un être privé de conscience et livré à son instinct.

Il n'y avait plus d'autre solution. Il n'y en avait jamais eu d'autre [...].

Ce fut alors un torrent de passion, de fureur, de souffrance, de déchirement dans le bonheur qui en faisait deux êtres gémissants et torturés, jetés sur ce lit au sein d'un ouragan de délivrance et de sincérité.

Ibid., 177. Cette nuit-là, plus rien ne les sépara. Catherine connut le triomphe de l'amour, l'émerveillement de tenir un être vaincu entre ses bras, une faim commune et dévorante de se découvrir, de se retrouver plus encore, d'aller au-delà de leurs propres limites sans jamais connaître la lassitude.

Au petit matin, elles s'endormirent enfin, bras et jambes mêlés, comme un animal à huit membres [...].

Audry, *La Statue*, blurb. un roman romanesque, qui n'est pas romancé. L'aventure a eu lieu.

Aurivel, *L'Oiseau de Sapho*, 13. Tresses sur le dos, à genoux, Liliane se tenait le visage enfoui dans l'ouverture d'une culotte de cheval à demi baissée.

Ibid., 13. La discrétion qui entoura le scandale fut à la mesure de son énormité.

Ibid., 36–7. Elle déshabilla Eliane [...] Elle chercha immédiatement ce qui était pour elle la suprême jouissance: le contact actif des pointes des deux sexes exacerbés. Il ne fallut que peu de temps pour qu'elle plongeat dans ce trou noir et vermeil de quelques secondes où va se perdre l'amour. [...] aussi se reprit-elle, encore pantelante, pour achever de la langue la caresse, en même temps que ses doigts s'enfonçaient dans un ventre s'épanouissant [...].

Quotations on pages 178–95

Ibid., 39. Et, bien sûr, elles s'aimèrent avec fougue car leurs désirs se répondaient dans une véritable communion charnelle. La connaissance réciproque de leurs corps touchait à la perfection. Elles étaient jeunes, voraces, brûlantes. Tenues en bride, en quelque sorte, dans la journée [...].

Ibid., Preface. L'amour entre femmes se vit dans la tendresse, dans le quotidien face à la mort, face à l'autre, la troisième, face à l'habitude et en cela il ressemble à toutes les histoires d'amour.

CHAPTER SIX

François, *Les Bonheurs*, 12. La végétation, ainsi brouillée d'eau, ressemble à la vie qui ne se laisse pas aisément approcher quoique donnant sans cesse l'illusion de la proximité.

François, *Les Amantes*, 15. Dans la vie d'une femme, trop d'heures sont englouties dans l'irritante nécessité des choses.

Ibid., 32. C'est bien cet ami-là qu'elle veut. Il est son jumeau qu'elle reconnaît.

François, *Histoire de Volubilis*, 19. vit sur un sol peu sûr

Ibid., 23. Tout ce qui a dévié lui apparaît comme une métaphore vivante d'elle-même parce que le droit fil de sa vie elle l'a déchiré, elle le sait, et rien n'est sans conséquence.

Ibid., 179. quand elle regarde Elisabeth et qu'à son tour elle est regardée, cet échange où s'engouffre la mémoire mais aussi le présent, là, tout de suite dans sa brillance instantanée et, toujours contenue, l'espérance du futur.

François, *Joue-nous "Espana,"* Epigrams. J'écris pour voir (Bernard Noël).

Ibid. L'universel n'est pas une loi, qui pour être partout la même ne vaut vraiment nulle part. L'universel a son lieu. L'universel est en chaque lieu dans le regard qu'on en prend, l'usage qu'on en peut faire (Yves Bonnefoy).

Ibid. Un roman est une vie en livre (Novalis).

Ibid., 12. "Où sommes-nous allés la pêcher?"

Ibid., 149. J'ai acquis très tôt un besoin viscéral de silence et la solitude, contrepoint de l'amour, m'est indispensable.

Ibid., 158. L'ordre amoureux m'est inconnu mais c'est selon lui que je désire vivre. Peut-on faire un choix avant de savoir? Oui on le peut.

Ibid., 163–4. En moi tout s'accélère, j'ai le sentiment d'avoir acquis un trésor inestimable. L'air qui était léger est devenu mille fois plus léger. Je prends ta main, je la garde.

A partir de ce moment plus rien n'est pareil. Le lendemain c'est moi qui me lève et ce n'est pas moi. Ce vide aux contours brûlants qui s'est installé dans ma poitrine et qui respire à ma place, cette alerte de tout le corps, il me faut m'y ajuster et je ne sais pas. Il y a flottement, prises d'air, glissements. Une force me ramène chaque fois à un centre d'où je m'échappe à nouveau, non que je le veuille, mais ce centre trop plein ne se laisse pas ouvrir. Je me retrouve dans un état absolument inconnu. Ce qui s'est passé la veille m'apparaît comme une scène primitive, déjà éloignée dans le temps, une scène si parfaitement simple et complète que je reste sans pensée sur elle.

Ensuite chaque fois que je suis avec Marie-Claire, engagée avec elle dans les actes les plus quotidiens, dans l'ordinaire, je me dis "Elle est là." Cette sensation dépasse toute autre sensation.

Ibid., 188. Un territoire immense nous est accordé jusqu'au matin où la fatigue nous endort, nues dans la chaleur du lit que cerne le froid de la chambre. Mon ignorance n'a d'égale que la tienne, mon trouble n'a d'égal que le tien, la même passion nous dévore tarissant la salive, science non sue d'avance, lenteurs à perdre le coeur.

Ibid., 190. Jean Streiff est aujourd'hui évêque de Nevers. Peut-être cette histoire très ancienne émerge-t-elle en sa mémoire, parfois. Il a fait son devoir, il a dispensé le dogme, et, s'il l'a dispensé avec compassion, lui seul peut en répondre. Mais il a commis tranquillement un crime. Celui d'avoir utilisé le secret comme outil de séparation, comme levier de dislocation, et d'avoir regardé se disjoindre avec des craquements insoutenables le corps d'amour, car j'ai obéi.

Ibid., 192. Le mariage est indissoluble, disent les prêtres. Le mariage mais pas l'amour. L'amour on peut l'arracher comme du chiendent, surtout entre deux femmes. C'est un service à rendre au corps social.

La joie parfaite qui ne saurait s'enraciner dans le gâchis, la joie parfaite des renoncements libres, n'est pas venue. Parfois je te rencontrais, tu n'étais qu'une plaie vive. Et toujours, sur nous, ce silence mortel.

Ibid., 193. Pour rétablir l'unité ancienne et réparer l'injustice, pour réincorporer l'amour [...].

Best, *Hymne aux murènes*, 18–19. Le premier jour, Paule m'a souri. Mila? Mila quoi? [...] Elle a posé ses mains sur mes épaules. Des mains dures. Elle me parlait pourtant avec douceur, d'une voix qui venait de la poitrine et qui creusait un bizarre petit froid au centre de la mienne. Tu vas avoir mal.
Effectivement, j'ai eu mal. [...]
Encore ses mains dures. Mais ses yeux noirs riaient – hésitaient entre le rire et la volonté de ne pas rire – [...] elle avait un petit pli au coin gauche de la bouche – à peine un pli: une ombre, tout de suite effacée – dont la douceur constrastait avec la brutalité de ses mains. Brutalité volontaire. J'en suis sûre. Mais pourquoi volontaire? [...] De nouveau, nous nous sommes retrouvées face à face, et nos regards sont retombés dans les mêmes trous. C'était un peu comme si on avait emmêlé des outils: on ne savait plus très bien comment se dégager.

Ibid., 143. Ses mains encore dans mes cheveux. [...] Alors une brusque exhalaison de tout le corps – comme en ont les fleurs, par à-coups – venue on ne sait d'où, on ne sait de qui (peut-être à la fois de nous deux) nous inclut lentement dans le même remous, nous relie aux mêmes vibrations, comme si l'air entre nous les vêtements et jusqu'à la peau même tout avait disparu, abolissant jusqu'à la conscience claire d'être soi devant l'autre...
C'est seulement quand elle me repousse que je comprends que nous venons de nous embrasser. Complètement dépossédée de moi-même, évidée sur place de mes sens de mes tripes de mon souffle.

Ibid., 158. Infime désordre de cils, de petits plis autour des yeux, où l'arrogance en voie de se réinstaller soudain dérape et se disperse... Le regard de Paule brusquement me manque, comme on manquerait une marche, tandis que tous ses traits s'immobilisent dans ce sourire indéfiniment soutenu, devenu fixe, qu'on voit aux gens sur le quai des gares.

Ibid., 14. À croire qu'on leur a coupé la vapeur.

Best, *Il n'y a pas d'hommes en Paradis*, 197. hurlait aussi à l'intérieur en cherchant partout une sortie

Ibid., 284. un jour une amante s'éloigna de son amante, et celle-ci lui cria "Reviens!" Elle répondit "Je ne peux pas!" Alors l'autre lui dit "Ecoute, reviens aussi près que tu le peux, et c'est moi qui ferai le reste du chemin…"

Bibliography

A: FRENCH LESBIAN NOVELS

Alençon, Emilienne d'. *Sous le masque*. Paris: Sansot, 1918.

Allen, Suzanne. *Le Lieu commun*. Paris: Gallimard, 1966.

Arsan, Emmanuelle. *Emmanuelle*. Paris: Le Terrain vague, 1967.

Audry, Colette. *La Statue*. Paris: Gallimard, 1986.

Aurivel, Rolande. *Dans l'ombre et au soleil de Lesbos*. Paris: Walter Rauchenbusch, 1988.

– *L'Oiseau de Sapho*. Paris: Walter Rauchenbusch, 1989.

Balzac, Honoré de. *La Fille aux yeux d'or. Oeuvres complètes* vol. IX. Paris: P. Furne, 1842.

Beck, Béatrice. *Noli*. Paris: Le Sagittaire, 1978.

Belot, Adolphe. *Mademoiselle Giraud, ma femme*. Paris: E. Dentu, 1870.

Bernheim, Nicole-Lise, and Cardot, Mirelle. *Personne ne m'aime. Romance policière*. Paris: Ed. des autres, 1978.

Bertin, Célia. *La Parade des impies*. Paris: Grasset, 1946.

– *La Bague était brisée*. Paris: Grasset, 1947.

– *Liens de famille*. Paris: Grasset, 1977.

Best, Mireille. *Hymne aux murènes*. Paris: Gallimard, 1986.

– *Camille en octobre*. Paris: Gallimard, 1988.

– *Il n'y a pas d'hommes au Paradis*. Paris: Gallimard, 1995.

Bienne, Gisèle. *Douce amère*. Paris: Ed. des femmes, 1977.

Binet-Valner, Jean. *Sur le sable couchées*. Paris: Flammarion, 1929.

Borys, Daniel. *Carlotta Noll, amoureuse et femme de lettres*. Paris: A. Michel, 1905.

Bourget, Paul. *Un crime d'amour*. Paris: Lemerre, 1886.

Bud-Printems, Reine. *Lil*. Paris: Gallimard, 1985.

Cahun, Claire. *Aveux non avenus*. Paris: Ed. du carrefour, 1930.

Causse, Michèle. *L'Encontre*. Paris: Ed. des femmes, 1975.

– *Lettres à Omphale*. Paris: Denoël-Gonthier, 1984.

Causse, Michèle, and Lapouge, Maryvonne. *Écrits, voix d'Italie*. Paris: Éd. des femmes, 1977.

Champsaur, Félicien. *Dinah Samuel*. Paris: Ferenczi, 1882.

Chauveau, Sophie. *Débandade*. Paris: J.J. Pauvert, 1982.

Cim, Albert. *Les Bas bleus*. Paris: A. Savine, 1891.

Cixous, Hélène. *Ananké*. Paris: Ed. des femmes, 1979.

– *Souffles*. Paris: Ed. des femmes, 1979.

– *Illa*. Paris: Ed. des femmes, 1980.

– *Le Livre de Prométhéa*. Paris: Gallimard, 1983.

Colette. *La Retraite sentimentale*. Paris: Ollendorf, 1907.

– *Ces plaisirs* ... Paris: Ferenczi, 1932.

– *Le Pur et l'impur*. Paris: Aux Armes de France, 1941.

Colette (et Willy). *Claudine à l'école*. Paris: Ollendorf, 1900.

– *Claudine à Paris*. Paris: Ollendorf, 1901.

– *Claudine en ménage*. Paris: Ollendorf, 1902.

– *Claudine s'en va*. Paris: Ollendorf, 1903.

Cuisin, P. *Clémentine, orpheline et androgyne ou les caprices de la nature et de la fortune*. Paris: Davi et Locard, 1820.

D'Argis, Henri. *Gomorrhe*. Paris: Charles, 1889.

Deforges, Régine. *Pour l'amour de Marie Salat*. Paris: Albin Michel, 1986.

Delarue-Mardus, Lucie. *L'Ange et les pervers*. Paris: Ferenczi, 1930.

Diderot, Denis. *La Religieuse*. Paris: Buisson, 1796.

Dupont, Irma. *Le Cheroub*. Paris: Julliard, 1962.

Eaubonne, Françoise d'. *Le Satellite de l'Amande*. Paris: Ed. des femmes, 1975.

Estienne, Charles. *Notre-Dame de Lesbos*. Paris: Libraire des lettres, 1919.

Ferrié, Françoise. *L'Accident d'amour*. Paris: Ed. le Hameau, 1975.

Finas, Lucette. *Les Chaînes éclatées, roman*. Paris: Mercure de France, 1955.

Francillon, Clarisse. *La Lettre*. Paris: P. Horay, 1958.

François, Jocelyne. *Les Bonheurs*. Paris: Mercure de France, 1970 and 1982.

– *Les Amantes*. Paris: Mercure de France, 1978.

– *Joue-nous "España", roman de mémoire*. Paris: Mercure de France, 1980.

– *Histoire de Volubilis*. Paris: Mercure de France, 1986.

– *La femme sans tombe*. Paris: Mercure de France, 1995.

A: French Lesbian Novels

Galzy, Jeanne. *L'Initiatrice aux mains vides*. Paris: Ed. Rieder, 1929.

– *Les Démons de la solitude*. Paris: Ed. Rieder, 1931.

– *Jeunes Filles en serre chaude*. Paris: Gallimard, 1934.

– *La Jeunesse déchirée*. Paris: Gallimard, 1951.

– *La Surprise de vivre*. Paris: Gallimard, 1969.

– *Les Sources vives*. Paris: Gallimard, 1971.

– *La Cavalière*. Paris, Gallimard, 1974.

– *Le Rossignol aveugle*. Paris: Gallimard, 1976.

Garréta, Anne. *Sphinx*. Paris: Grasset, 1986.

Gautier, Théophile. *Mademoiselle de Maupin, double amour*. Paris: E. Renduel, 1835–36.

Gide, André. *Geneviève*. Paris: Gallimard, 1937.

Gourmont, Rémy de. *Le Songe d'une femme*. Paris: Mercure de France, 1899.

Hatvany, Claire Vallier. *Solitude à trois*. Paris: La Table ronde, 1961.

Hubert, Catherine. *Jessica ou l'île*. Paris: Geneviève Pastre, 1993.

– *Vers l'ouest*. Paris: Geneviève Pastre, 1996.

Hugues, Evelyne. *L'Insectueuse*. Paris: Ed. Tiresius Michel Reynaud, 1991.

Huré, Anne. *Les Deux moniales*. Paris: Julliard, 1962.

Huser, France. *La Maison du désir*. Paris: Seuil, 1982.

– *La Chambre ouverte*. Paris: Seuil, 1986.

Jaguar, Dorothé [sic]. *Un linceul de peinture bleue*. Clichy: Cavalières, 1994.

Kelen, Jacqueline. *Aimer d'amitié*. Paris: Laffont, 1992.

Labarraque-Reyssac, Claude. *Lesbos à Poitiers*. Paris: Amitié par le livre, 1978.

Lacretelle, Jacques de. *La Bonifas*. Paris: Gallimard, 1925.

La Vaudère, Jane de. *Les Demi-Sexes*. Paris: Ollendorf, 1897.

Leduc, Violette. *L'Affamée*. Paris: Gallimard, 1948.

– *Ravages*. Paris: Gallimard, 1955.

– *La Bâtarde*. Paris: Gallimard, 1964.

– *Thérèse et Isabelle*. Paris: Gallimard, 1966.

– *La Folie en tête*. Paris: Gallimard, 1967.

Lisa, Liu, and Gro. *Toutes trois*. Paris: Ed. du Seuil, 1975.

Loriot, Noëlle. *Les Méchantes Dames*. Paris: Julliard, 1995.

Lorrain, Jean. *Maisons pour dames*. Paris: Ollendorf, 1908.

Louvier, Nicole. *Qui qu'en grogne*. Paris: La Table ronde, 1954.

– *L'Heure des jeux*. Paris: La Table ronde, 1955.

Louÿs, Pierre. *Les Chansons de Bilitis*. Paris, 1894.

– *Aphrodite, moeurs antiques*. Paris: Mercure de France, 1896.

– *Les Aventures du Roi Pausole*. Paris: Mercure de France, 1900.

Mahyère, Eveline. *Je jure de m'éblouir*. Paris: Buchet/Chastel-Corrêa, 1958.

Mallet-Joris, Françoise. *Le Rempart des béguines*. Paris: Julliard, 1951.

Mansour, Joyce. *Rapaces*. Paris: Seghers, 1960.

– *Carré blanc*. Paris: Le Soleil noir, 1965.

Margueritte, Victor. *La Garçonne*. Paris: Flammarion, 1922.

Marion, Dominique. *La Chasse à l'orchidée*. Paris: Laffont, 1977.

Maupassant, Guy de. "La Femme de Paul." In *La Maison Tellier*. Paris: V. Havard, 1881.

Mendès, Catulle. *Méphistophéla*. Paris: Dentu, 1890.

Menteau, Odette. *Un chemin semé de graviers mauves*. Paris: Ed. Génevieve Pastre, 1994.

Michel, Anne. *La Dame noire*. Paris: Flammarion, 1992.

Monési, Irène. *Althia*. Paris: Seuil, 1957.

– *Une tragédie superflue*. Paris: Mercure de France, 1968.

– *La Vie d'une bête*. Paris: Mercure de France, 1972.

– *L'Amour et le dédain*. Paris: Mercure de France, 1974.

– *Les Mers profondes*. Paris: Mercure de France, 1977.

Monferrand, Hélène. *Les Amies d'Héloïse*. Paris: Ed. de Fallois, 1990.

– *Journal de Suzanne*. Paris: Nathan, 1991.

– *Les Enfants d'Héloïse*. Paris: Ed. Double Interligne, 1997.

Monfort, Charles. *Le Journal d'une saphiste*. Paris: Offenstadt, 1902.

Montegut, Maurice. "Don Juan Lesbos." In *Don Juan*, ed. Erich Fisbach. N.p.: Alfiléditions, 1993.

Pastre, Geneviève. *L'Espace du souffle*. Paris: Christian Bourgois, 1977.

– *7 14 17 ou Architecture d'Éros*. Rodez: Subervie, 1977.

– *Octavie ou la deuxième mort du Minotaure*. Paris: Les Octaviennes, 1985.

– *Flavie ou le voyage à Delphes*. Paris: Les Octaviennes, 1986.

– *Athènes et le péril saphique*. Paris: Les Octaviennes, 1987.

Peladan, Joséphin. *La Décadence latine, éthopée VIII: L'Androgyne*. Paris: E. Dentu, 1891.

– *La Décadence latine, éthopée IX: La Gynandre*. Paris: E. Dentu, 1891.

Pougy, Liane de. *Idylle saphique*. Paris: Librarie de la plume, 1901.

Proust, Marcel. "Avant la nuit." In *La Revue blanche*, Dec. 1893.

– *Du côté de chez Swann*. Paris: Gallimard, 1913.

– *Sodome et Gomorrhe*. Paris: Gallimard, 1921.

Rachilde [Marguerite Eymery]. *Madame Adonis*. Paris: E. Monnier, 1888.

– *Monsieur Vénus*. Paris: F. Brossier, 1889.

B: *Works Cited; Lesbianism in France* 257

Regnier, Henri de. "L'Amour et le plaisir." In *Couleur du temps*. Paris: Mercure de France, 1909.

Rigal, Muriel. *L'Envers des choses*. Paris: Ed. L'Athanor, 1977.

Rivière, Charles. *Sous le manteau de Fourvière*. Paris: Georges-Anquetil, 1926.

Rivière, Lucie. *La Soupe aux fruits*. Paris: Geneviève Pastre, 1994.

Rochefort, Christiane. *Les Stances à Sophie*. Paris: Grasset, 1963.

Roffinella, Martine. *Elle*. Paris: Phébus, 1988.

Roland-Manuel, Suzanne. *Le Trille du diable*. Paris: Ed. des deux rives, 1946.

Rousseau, Nita. *La Pluie sur la mer*. Paris: Flammarion, 1996.

Saint-Agen, Adrienne. *Amants féminins*. Paris: Offenstadt, 1904.

- *Charmeuse de femmes*. Paris: Offenstadt, 1906.

Saint-Ys, Andrée. *Au bord des eaux dormantes*. Paris: Sansot, 1919.

Sand, George. *Lélia* (1833). Paris: Classiques Garnier, 1960.

Sarrazin, Albertine. *L'Astragale*. Paris: J.J. Pauvert, 1965.

Sollers, Philippe. *Une étrange solitude*. Paris: Ed. du Seuil, 1958.

Tristan, Anne. *Histoires d'amour*. Paris, 1979.

V., Cécile. *Fréderique*. Paris: J'ai Lu, 1994.

Vergne, Anne. *La Somnambule*. Paris: Lattès, 1977.

Vilmont, Anne. *Les Drosères*. Paris: Tchou, 1968.

Vivien, Renée. *La Dame à la louve* (1904). Paris: R. Deforges, 1977.

- *Une femme m'apparut...* (1904). Paris: R. Deforges, 1977.

Wajsbrot, Cécile. *Une vie à soi*. Paris: Mercure de France, 1982.

- *Le Désir d'Equateur*. Paris: Calmann-Lévy, 1995.

Willette, Henriette. *La Femme et la faunesse*. Paris: E. Sansot, 1910.

Willy. *La Môme Picrate*. Paris: Michel, 1903.

Wittig, Monique. *L'Opoponax*. Paris: Ed. de minuit, 1964.

- *Les Guérillères*. Paris: Ed. de minuit, 1969.

- *Le Corps lesbien*. Paris: Ed. de minuit, 1973.

- *Virgile, non*. Paris: Ed. de minuit, 1985.

Zola, Emile. *Nana*. Paris: Charpentier, 1879–80.

B: WORKS CITED AND GENERAL WORKS ON LESBIANISM IN FRANCE

Allen, Jeffner. *Not a Passing Phase: Reclaiming Lesbians in History 1840–1894*. London: Women's Press, 1989.

- ed. *Lesbian Philosophies and Cultures*. Albany: State University of New York Press, 1990.

Allen, Jeffner, and Young, Iris Marion, eds. *The Thinking Muse: Feminism and Modern French Philosophy*. Bloomington: Indiana University Press, 1990.

Apter, Emily. *Feminizing the Fetish: Psychoanalysis and Narrative Obsession in Turn-of-the-Century France*. Ithaca, NY: Cornell University Press, 1991.

Baird, Deirdre. *Simone de Beauvoir*. New York: Summit Books, 1990.

Bartky, Sandra Lee. *Femininity and Domination: Studies in the Phenomenology of Oppression*. London: Routledge, 1970.

Beauvoir, Simone de. *Le Deuxième Sexe*. Paris: Gallimard, 1949.

– *The Second Sex*. New York: Alfred A. Knopf, 1952.

– *Journal de guerre, 1939–janvier 1941*. Paris: Gallimard, 1990.

– *Lettres à Sartre*. Paris: Gallimard, 1990.

– *Mémoires d'une jeune fille rangeé*. Paris: Gallimard, 1958.

Bechdel, Alison. *Lesbiennes à suivre, suivi de variations monogames*. Paris: Prune janvier, 1991.

Benstock, Shari. *Women of the Left Bank*. London: Virago, 1987.

Billy, André. *L'Epoque 1900*. Paris: Tallandier, 1951.

Bonnet, Marie-Jo. "Adieux à l'histoire." In *Stratégie des femmes*. Paris: Ed. Tierce, 1984.

– *Les Relations amoureuses entre les femmes du XVIe au XXe siècle*. Paris: Ed. Odile Jacob, 1995.

Boswell, John. *Same-Sex Unions in Pre-modern Europe*. New York: Villard, 1994.

Brassaï. *Le Paris secret des années 30*. Paris: Gallimard, 1976.

Brecourt-Vilars, Claudine. *Petit glossaire de l'érotisme saphique (1880–1930)*. Paris: J.J. Pauvert, 1980.

– *Écrire d'amour. Anthologie de textes érotiques féminins, 1799-1984*. Paris: Ramsay, 1985.

Broston, Paul, and Richardson, Colin. *A Queer Romance: Lesbians, Gay Men and Popular Culture*. London: Routledge, 1995.

Butler, Judith. *Gender Trouble: Feminism and the Subversion of Identity*. New York: Routledge, 1990.

Calle, Mireille, ed. *Du féminin*. Grenoble: Les Presses Universitaires de Grenoble, 1992.

Card, Claudia. *Adventures in Lesbian Philosophy*. Bloomington: Indiana University Press, 1994.

Castle, Terry. *The Apparitional Lesbian: Female Homosexuality and Modern Culture*. New York: Columbia University Press, 1993.

Cixous, Hélène. *L'Exil de James Joyce ou l'art de remplacement*. Paris: Grasset, 1968.

– *Dedans*. Paris: Grasset, 1969.

Colette. *Aventures quotidiennes*. Paris: Flammarion, 1924.

– *Mes apprentissages*. Paris: Ferenczi, 1936.

Conley, Verena Andermatt. *Hélène Cixous: Writing the Feminine*. Lincoln: University of Nebraska Press, 1984.

Coquillat, Michelle. *Romans d'amour*. Paris: Éd. Odile Jacob, 1988.

– *Entres elles*. Paris: Albin Michel, 1995.

Cossard, Michael de. *Une Américaine à Paris. La Princesse Edmond de Polignac et son salon (1865–1943)*. Paris: Plon, 1978.

Courtivron, Isabelle de. *Violette Leduc*. Boston: Twayne, 1985.

Daly, Mary. *Wickedary*. Boston: Beacon Press, 1986.

Dekker, Rudolf, and Pol, Lotte van de. *The Tradition of Female Transvestism in Early Modern Europe*. New York: St Martin's, 1989.

Delarue-Mardus, Lucie. *Mes mémoires*. Paris: Gallimard, 1938.

DeLauretis, Teresa. "The Female Body and Heterosexual Presumption." In *Semiotica* 67 nos. 3–4 (1987), 259–79.

– *Technologies of Gender*. Bloomington: Indiana University Press, 1987.

– *The Practice of Love: Lesbian Sexuality and Perverse Desire*. Bloomington: Indiana University Press, 1994.

Desthieux, Jean. *Femmes damnées (Renée Vivien, Sapho, Autour d'Elle, X, etc.)*. Paris: Ophrys, 1937.

Dijkstra, Bram. *Idols of Perversity: Fantasies of Feminine Evil in Fin-de-siècle Culture*. New York: Oxford University Press, 1986.

Dire nos homosexualités: Brochure faite par le groupe des femmes homosexuelles de Lille. Lille, 1978.

Doan, Laura. *The Lesbian Postmodern*. New York: Columbia University Press, 1994.

Dorenkamp, Monica, and Henke, Richard. *Negotiating Lesbian and Gay Subjects*. New York: Routledge, 1995.

Dottin-Orsini, Mirelle. *Cette femme qu'ils disent fatale, textes et images de la misogynie fin-de-siècle*. Paris: Grasset, 1993.

Duchen, Claire, ed. and trans. *French Connections*. Amherst: University of Massachussetts Press, 1987.

Eaubonne, Françoise d'. *Le Féminisme ou la mort*. Paris: Pierre Horay, 1974.

– "Violette Leduc et la condition féminine." In Paul Renard and Carlo Jansiti, eds., *Violette Leduc. Etudes réunies*, 23–9. Lille: Société de littérature de Nord, 1994.

Ettorre, E.M. *Lesbian Women and Society*. London: Routledge & Kegan Paul, 1980.

Faderman, Lilian. "The Morbidification of Love between Women by Nineteenth-Century Sexologists." *Journal of Homosexuality* 4 no. 1 (fall 1978), 73–90.

– *Surpassing the Love of Men*. New York: William Morrow and Co. Inc., 1981.

Farwell, Marilyn. "Toward a Definition of a Lesbian Literary Imagination." *Signs* 14 no. 1 (autumn 1988), 100–18.

– *Heterosexual Plots and Lesbian Narratives*. New York: New York University Press, 1996.

Femmes entre elles. "Lesbianisme." *Cahier de GRIF* 20 (1978).

Flanner, Janet. *Paris Was Yesterday (1925–1939)*. New York: Viking, 1972.

Flierger, Jerry Aline. *Colette and the Fantom Subject of Autobiography*. Ithaca, NY: Cornell University Press, 1992.

Foucault, Michel. *Histoire de la sexualité, tome 1: La Volonté de savoir*. Paris: Gallimard, 1976.

– *The History of Sexuality. Vol. 1: An Introduction*. Trans. Robert Hurley. New York: Random House, 1980.

– *The History of Sexuality. Vol. 2: The Use of Pleasure*. Trans. Robert Hurley. New York: Random House, 1985.

– *The History of Sexuality. Vol. 3: The Care of the Self*. Trans. Robert Hurley. New York: Random House, 1986.

Fourier, Charles. *Le Nouveau Monde amoureux* (rédigé vers 1820). Extraits présentés par Simone Debout-Oleszkiecwicz. Paris: J.J. Pauvert, 1967.

François, Jocelyne. *Le Cahier vert, Journal 1961–1989*. Paris: Mercure de France, 1990.

Gagey, Yvonne. *Lesbos, le culte de Sapho et les amours féminines*. Paris: Ed. Esprit et Joie, 1963.

Les Garçonnes. Suffragettes, MLF, bas rouges, panthères roses, lesbiennes, etc. *Le Crapouillot* special issue, Dec., 1972.

Gauthier, Xavière. *Dire nos sexualités*. Paris: Gallimard, 1976.

Gramont, Elisabeth de. *Mémoires*. Paris: Grasset, 1929.

Griffin, Gabriele. *Heavenly Love? Lesbian Images in Twentieth Century Women's Writing*. Manchester: Manchester University Press, 1994.

Grosz, Elizabeth A. "The Hetero and the Homo: The Sexual Ethics of Luce Irigaray." *Gay Information [Australia]* 17–18 (1988), 37–44.

Haddad, Michèle. *Des origines littéraires pour des "Demoiselles" bien réalistes. Courbet et George Sand*. Bulletin de la société de l'histoire et de l'art français, 1989.

Hirsch, Charles Henry. "De Mlle de Maupin à Claudine." *Mercure de France* 5 no. 42 (1902), 577–88.

Hughes, Alex. *Violette Leduc: Mothers, Lovers and Language*. London: W.S. Maney and Son Ltd., 1994.

Hyvrard, Jeanne. *La Pensée corps*. Paris: Ed. des femmes, 1989.

Jay, Karla. *The Amazon and the Page: Natalie Clifford Barney and Renée Vivien*. Bloomington: Indiana University Press, 1988.

Jullian, Philip. *Jean Lorrain ou le "Satiricon" 1900*. Paris: Fayard, 1974.

Kaplan, Gisela. *Contemporary Western European Feminism*. New York: New York University Press, 1992.

Kitzinger, Celia. *The Social Construction of Lesbianism*. London: Sage Publications, 1987.

Klaich, Dolores. *Femme et femme. Attitudes envers l'homosexualité féminine*. Trans. Martine Laroche. Paris: Ed. des Femmes, 1976.

Lacroux, Armand. *Amour 1900*. Paris: Hachette, 1961.

Lamblin, Bianca. *Mémoires d'une jeune fille dérangée*. Paris: Balland, 1993.

Laqueur, Thomas. *Making Sex: Body and Gender from the Greeks to Freud*. Cambridge, Mass.: Harvard University Press, 1990.

LeBrun, Annie. *Vagit-prop, Lâchez tout et autres textes*. Paris: Ramsay J.J. Pauvert, 1990.

Le Garrec, Evelyne. *Des femmes qui s'aiment*. Paris: Ed. du Seuil, 1984.

Lesselier, Claudie. "Le regroupement de lesbiennes dans le mouvement féministe parisien: position et problèmes, 1970–1982." In *Crise de la société, féminisme et changement*. Paris: Ed. Tierce, 1988.

– *Recherches sur l'homosexualité féminine en France. 1930–1960. Rapport de recherche ATP*. Paris, 1990.

Lorenz, Paul. *Sappho 1900. Reneé Vivien*. Paris: Julliard, 1977.

Martin-Fugier, Anne. *La Bourgeoise*. Paris: Grasset, 1983.

Mathieu, Nicole-Claude. *L'Anatomie politique, catégorisations et idéologies du sexe*. Paris: Côté-femmes, 1991.

May, Georges. *Diderot et "La Religieuse"*. New Haven, Conn., and Paris: Yale University Press and Les Presses Universitaires de France, 1959.

Mylne, Vivienne. *Diderot, La Religieuse*. London: Grant and Cutler, 1981.

– "What Suzanne Knew: Lesbianism and *La Religieuse*." *Studies in Voltaire and the Eighteenth Century* (Oxford: Voltaire Foundation) 207 (1981).

Paglia, Camille. *Sexual Personae*. London: Penguin, 1992.

Paramelle, France, and Lago, Maria. *La Femme homosexuelle*. Paris: Castermann, 1977.

Pelletier, Madeleine. *L'Emancipation sexuelle de la femme*. Paris: Girard et Brière, 1911.

Perrin, Elula. *Les Femmes préfèrent les femmes*. Paris: Ramsay, 1977.

– *Tant qu'il y aura des femmes*. Paris: Ramsay, 1978.

– *Coup de gueule pour l'amour des femmes*. Paris: Ramsay, 1995.

Picq, Françoise. *Libération des femmes*. Paris: Ed. du Seuil, 1993.

Pisan, Anne de, and Tristan, Anne. *Histoires du MLF. Préface de Simone de Beauvoir*. Paris: Calmann-Lévy, 1977.

Plante, Christine. *La Petite soeur de Balzac. Essai sur la femme auteur*. Paris: Ed. du Seuil, 1989.

Plat, Hélène. *Lucie Delarue Mardus. Une femme de lettres des années folles*. Paris: Grasset, 1994.

Plummer, Ken, ed. *Modern Homosexualities: Fragments of Lesbian and Gay Experience*. London: Routledge, 1992.

Porquerol, Elisabeth. "La Signification du saphisme à travers les âges." In *Le Crapouillot*, 10 (1950).

Pougy, Liane de. *Mes cahiers bleus*. Paris: Plon, 1977.

Quand les femmes s'aiment... Groupe des lesbiennes de Lyon, centre des femmes, 1978.

Querlin, Maryse. *Femmes sans homme*. Paris: J. d'Halluin, 1953.

Questions féministes. Eight numbers, including Monique Wittig, "La pensée straight," no. 7 (Feb. 1980); Emmanuelle de Lesseps, "Hétérosexualité et féminisme," no. 8 (— 1980); Monique Wittig, "On ne naît pas femme," (May 1980). Paris: Ed. Tierce, 1977–80.

Le Quotidien des femmes. Nine numbers from November 1974 to March 1976. Lille: Ed. Librairie des Femmes, groupe Psychanalyse et Politique.

Robinson, Christopher. *Scandal in the Ink: Male and Female Homosexualities in Twentieth-century French Literature*. London: Cassell, 1995.

Samuel, Pierre. *Amazones, guerrières, et gaillardes*. Brussels: Complexe/Presses Universitaires de Grenoble, 1975.

Sarde, Michèle. *Colette libre et entravé*. Paris: Stock, 1978.

Sarraute, Nathalie. *L'Ere du Soupçon*. Paris: Gallimard, 1956.

– *L'Usage de la parole*. Paris: Gallimard, 1980.

Schwatz, Gudrun. "L'Invention de la lesbienne par les psychiatres allemands." In *Stratégie des femmes*. Paris: Ed. Tierce, 1984.

Sedgwick, Eve Kosofsky. *Epistemology of the Closet*. Berkeley: University of California Press, 1990.

Shiach, Morag. *Hélène Cixous: A Politics of Writing*. London: Routledge, 1991.

Smith-Rosenberg, Caroll, and Newton, Esther. "Le Mythe de la lesbienne et la femme nouvelle." In *Stratégie des femmes*. Paris: Ed. Tierce, 1984.

Sohn, Anne-Marie. "La Garçonne face à l'opinion publique: type littéraire ou type social des années 20?" In *Le Mouvement social* (July–Sept. 1972).

Stambolian, G., and Marks, E. *Homosexualities and French Literature*. Ithaca, NY: Cornell University Press, 1979.

Stanton, Domna, ed. *Discourses of Sexuality: From Aristotle to AIDS*. Ann Arbor: University of Michigan Press, 1992.

Suleiman, Susan Rubin, ed. *The Female Body in Western Culture: Contemporary Perspectives*. Cambridge, Mass.: Harvard University Press, 1986.

– *Subversive Intent: Gender, Politics and the Avant Garde*. Cambridge, Mass.: Harvard University Press, 1990.

Sullerot, Evelyne. *Droit de regard*. Paris: Denoël-Gonthier, 1970.

– *Histoire et mythologie de l'amour. Huit siècles d'écrits féminins*. Paris: Hachette, 1974.

Tinayre, Marcelle. *Avant l'amour*. Paris: Mercure de France, 1897.

– *La Rebelle*. Paris: Calmann-Lévy, 1905.

Uzanne, Octave. "Du Saphisme en posie" and "Les Femmes damnées. Bensérade et Baudelaire." *Les Marges* 15 March 1921.

Valagrègue, Catherine. *Le Droit de vivre autrement*. Paris: Denoël-Gonthier, 1975.

Van Casselaer, Catherine. *Lot's Wife: Lesbian Paris 1890–1914*. Liverpool: Janus Press, 1986.

Vicinus, Martha, ed. *Lesbian Subjects*. Bloomington: Indiana University Press, 1996.

Vimaire, Charles. *Paris impur*. Paris: C. Dalou, 1889.

Viollet, Catherine. "Violette Leduc: écriture et sexualité." *Tangenee* no. 47 (March 1995), 69–83.

– "Violette Leduc, une 'sincerité intrépide'?" *Ecriture de soi au féminin*, special issue, *Dalhousie French Studies* 47 (summer 1999), 133–4.

Waelti-Walters, Jennifer. *Fairytales and the Female Imagination*. Montreal: Eden Press, 1982.

– *Feminist Novelists of the Belle Epoque*. Bloomington: Indiana University Press, 1990.

– *Jeanne Hyvrard: Theorist of the Modern World*. Edinburgh: Edinburgh University Press, 1996.

Waelti-Walters, Jennifer, and Steven C. Hause, eds. *Feminisms of the Belle Epoque*. Lincoln: University of Nebraska Press, 1994.

Waldberg, Patrick. *Eros Modern Style*. Paris: J.J. Pauvert/BIE, 1964.

Whitford, Margaret. *Luce Irigaray: Philosophy in the Feminine*. London: Routledge, 1991.

Wittig, Monique. *The Straight Mind and Other Essays*. Boston: Beacon, 1992.

Wittig, Monique, and Zeig, Sande. *Brouillon pour un dictionnaire des amantes*. Paris, 1976.

C: SOURCES OF FRENCH MEDICAL ATTITUDES TO LESBIANISM, 1870–1960

Bonaparte, Marie. *La Sexualité de la femme*. Paris: Presses Universitaires de France, 1951.

Caufeynon, Dr. *La Masturbation et la sodomie féminine. Clitorisme. Saphisme. Tribadisme. Déformation des organes*. Paris: Saint-Amand, 1925.

Charcot, J.M., and Magnan, C. "Pathologie mentale. Inversion du sens génital." In J.M. Charcot, ed., *Archives de neurologie (tome III)*. Paris: n.p., 1882.

Chevalier, J. *De L'Inversion de l'instinct sexuel*. Paris: Octave Doin, 1885.

Deutsch, Hélène. *La Psychologie des femmes*. Paris: Presses Universitaires de France, 1945.

Droui, Henri. *Femmes damnées. Essai sur les carences sexuelles féminines dans la littérature et dans la vie*. Paris: n.p., 1945.

Ellis, Havelock. *Etudes de psychologie sexuelle, tome II: L'Inversion sexuelle*. Paris: Mercure de France, 1908–9.

Fere, C. *L'Instinct sexuel, évolution, dissolution*. Paris: n.p., 1899.

Forel, A. *La Question sexuelle exposée aux adultes cultivés*. Paris: G. Stenheil, 1906.

Fouque, Dr C. *L'Amour qui n'ose pas dire son nom*. Paris: Coll. Etudes psychosexuelles, 1947.

Krafft-Ebing, Richard von. *Psychopatia sexualis* (16e et 17e éd. allemandes refondues par le Dr. Albert Moll). Paris: Payot, 1931.

Lereboullet, Dr, and Dechambre, Dr A., eds. *Dictionnaire encyclopédique des sciences médicales, t.XV, deuxième série: Onanisme*. Paris: Masson, 1881.

Lombroso, Cesare. *L'Anthropologie criminelle et ses récents progrès*. Paris: F. Alcan, 1890.

– *Les Applications de l'anthropologie criminelle*. Paris: F. Alcan, 1892.

– *La femme criminelle et la prostituée*. Paris: F. Alcan, 1896.

D: Bibliographies of Lesbian Fiction

– *Le crime: causes et remèdes*. Paris: Schleicher frères, 1899.

Martineau, Dr L. *Leçons sur les déformations vulvaires produites par la masturbation, le saphisme, la défloration et la sodomie*, collected by M. Lormand. Paris: Hôpital de Lourcine, 1884.

Moll, Albert. *Les Perversions de l'instinct génital. Etude sur l'inversion sexuelle*. Paris: n.p., 1893.

Porché, F. (Chagrin, F.). *L'Amour qui n'ose pas dire son nom*. Paris: Grasset, 1927.

Pouillet, T. *Essai médico-philosophique sur les formes, les causes, les signes, les conséquences et le traitement de l'onanisme chez la femme*. Paris: Vve A. Delahay, 1976.

Sérieux, Paul. *Les Anomalies de l'instinct sexuel*. Paris: n.p., 1888.

X (L. Martineau). "Déformations vulvaires produites par la défloration, la masturbation, le saphisme et la prostitution." In *Journal des sages-femmes*, 16 Aug. 1880.

Zambaco, Demetrius. "Onanism avec troubles nerveux chez deux petites filles." In *L'Encéphale* (Journal des maladies mentales et nerveuses), 1882.

NB: The Kinsey Report appeared in French in 1954; Freud's work on female homosexuality in 1973 and 1984; and Jung's *Psychologie du transfert* in 1980.

D: BIBLIOGRAPHIES OF LESBIAN FICTION

Bonnet, Marie-Jo. *Les Relations amoureuses entre les femmes du XVIe au XXe siècle*. Paris: Ed. Odile Jacob, 1995.

Damon, Gene, Watson, Jan, and Jordan, Robin. *The Lesbian in Literature. A Bibliography*. 2nd ed. Reno, Nev.: The Ladder, 1975.

Foster, Jeannette H. *Sex Variant Women in Literature*. New York: Vintage Press, 1956.

Gaber, Linda. *Lesbian Sources: A Bibliography of Periodical Articles 1970–1990*. New York: Garland Press, 1993.

Kuda, Mary J. *Women Loving Women: A Select and Annotated Bibliography of Women Loving Women in Literature*. Chicago: Lavender Press, 1974.

Index

This index comprises a list of proper names: authors, critics, literary movements, and literary references. It does not list titles or characters, as many of them will not be known in their own right. Titles appear under authors in the bibliography. There is no subject index, as all the novels in this study deal with overlapping, metamorphosing aspects of the same topic: lesbianism.

Abelard and Héloïse, 207
Alembert, Jean le Rond d', 217
Allen, Suzanne, 122, 123
Arsan, Emmanuelle, 122, 124
Audry, Colette, 127, 131, 152, 176–7, 214, 248
Aurivel, Rolande, 127, 152, 176, 177–9, 248–9
Avril, Jane, 4, 47

Baird, Deirdre, 220
Balzac, Honoré de, 3, 4, 20–7, 29, 32, 34, 36, 40, 46, 53, 74, 89, 163, 178, 211, 212, 214, 218, 226–7, 229
Barnes, Djuna, 186
Barney, Natalie, 4, 47, 73
Bartky, Sandra Lee, 217
Baudelaire, Charles, 3, 33–4, 40, 84, 101, 218, 229
Beauvoir, Simone de, 4, 7, 19, 53, 98, 127–32, 133, 138, 152, 163, 176, 185, 219, 220, 243–4
Beck, Béatrice, 167, 170–1, 246

Beckett, Samuel, 220
Belot, Adolphe, 34–7, 49, 66, 89, 212, 229
Benstock, Shari, 218
Benveniste, Emile, 146
Bernhardt, Sarah, 4, 47
Bernheim, Nicole-Lise, and Cardot, Mireille, 163
Bersianik, Louky, 151, 164, 222
Bertin, Célia, 102, 104–8, 125, 151, 161, 240
Best, Mireille, 5, 127, 152, 166, 180, 187, 199–205, 210, 212, 214, 251–2
Bienne, Gisèle, 164, 167, 180
Binet-Valner, Jean, 84–6
Bonnefoy, Yves, 195, 249
Bonnet, Marie-Jo, 5, 6, 98, 218, 219
Borys, Daniel, 63–4
Bosco, Monique, 166
Brossard, Nicole, 151, 166
Bud-Printems, Reine, 175
Butler, Judith, 185
Butor, Michel, 220

Cahun, Claire, 98–9, 239
Castle, Terry, 219
Causse, Michèle, 127, 151, 166, 222
Champsaur, Félicien, 46–7
Charcot, Jean Martin, 6, 50, 60, 219
Chauveau, Sophie, 174
Chevalier, Julien, 39–40, 46, 229–30
Christ, Jesus, 145
Christa, Emma, 185
Circe, 26
Cixous, Hélène, 5, 7, 98, 126, 127, 137, 138, 139–41, 143, 151, 166, 185, 210, 212, 214, 217, 221
Claudel, Paul, 197, 223
Colette, Sidonie-Gabrielle, 4, 47, 63, 64–72, 80, 108, 127, 212, 235–6
Conley, Verena Andermatt, 217
Constant, Benjamin, 108
Courtivron, Isabelle de, 136, 220, 221

Daly, Mary, 146
Dante Alighieri, 21
D'Argis, Henri, 56–7, 60, 234
Decadents, 49
Deforges, Régine, 179
Delamarre, Marguerite, 12
Delarue-Mardus, Lucie, 73–4, 163, 222
Delphy, Christine, 151
Diderot, Denis, 3, 11–20, 21, 34, 66, 121, 217, 218, 225–6
Dijkstra, Bram, 218
Duchamp, Marcel, 163, 222
Dupont, Irma, 122, 124, 242
Durand, Marguerite, 52
Duras, Marguerite, 138, 143, 220, 244

Eaubonne, Françoise d', 127, 151, 164–6, 212
Editions des femmes, 151

Editions Geneviève Pastre, 179
Edwards-Pilliet, Dr, 51
Ellis, Havelock, 6, 60
Encyclopédie, 17, 217
existentialists, 132

Faderman, Lilian, 98, 218, 219
Ferrié, Françoise, 152, 167, 171–4, 214, 246–8
Feydeau, Georges, 34, 37–8
Flach, Jacques, 52
Forrest, Katherine V., 185
Foster, Jeannette H., 98
Foucault, Michel, 7, 185
Francillon, Clarisse, 110, 117–19, 125, 152, 214, 242
François, Jocelyne, 5, 119, 127, 152, 166, 171, 187, 188–99, 204, 210, 212, 214, 223, 249–51
French Revolution, 3, 11, 19
Freud, Sigmund, 7, 60, 101, 219
Frick, Grace, 220
Fronde, La, 52
Front homosexuel d'action révolutionnaire (FHAR), 138

Gagnon, Madeleine, 166
Galzy, Jeanne, 98, 99–102, 105, 127, 151, 152–61, 167, 176, 187, 212, 239, 244–5
Garréta, Anne, 175
Gautier, Théophile, 3, 4, 20, 27–33, 34, 36, 46, 74, 76, 80, 89, 178, 211, 214, 218, 227–9
Genet, Jean, 131, 132, 221
Genette, Gérard, 7
Gide, André, 75, 97, 108, 219, 223
Goncourt, Edmond, and Jules, Huot de, 40

Hatvany, Claire Vallier, 120
Hause, Steven C., 219
Hubert, Catherine, 179, 180
Hugues, Evelyne, 183
Huré, Anne, 121

Huser, France, 175
Hyvrard, Jeanne, 134, 139, 146

Irigaray, Luce, 5, 7, 138, 185, 217

Jaguar, Dorothé, 185
Jaucourt, Louis, chevalier de, 217
Jay, Karla, 219
Joyce, James, 140

Kaplan, Gisela, 221
Krafft-Ebing, Richard von, 6, 50, 60, 219
Kristeva, Julia, 138

Labarraque-Reyssac, Claude, 167, 168–70, 245–6
Laclos, Pierre Choderlos de, 206–7, 223
Lacretelle, Jacques de, 4, 35, 53, 64, 66, 89–94, 167, 214, 219, 238–9
Lamblin, Bianca, 128, 220
Laqueur, Thomas, 219
LeBon, Sylvie, 220
Leduc, Violette, 4, 98, 108, 116, 120, 126, 127–37, 147, 176, 212, 214, 220, 244
Levay, David, 221
Lisa Liu Gro, 162–3
Lombroso, Cesare, 60
Lorde, Audre, 151
Loriot, Noëlle, 184–5
Lorrain, Jean, 63
Louvier, Nicole, 110, 111–13, 116, 241
Louÿs, Pierre, 62–3

Mahyère, Eveline, 110, 113–16, 152, 241–2
Mallet-Joris, Françoise, 98, 109–10, 152, 167, 240
Margueritte, Victor, 47, 81, 83
Marie-France, 163
Marmontel, Jean-François, 217
Martin-Fugier, Anne, 219

Maupassant, Guy de, 40–6, 58, 89, 212, 218, 231–3
Maupin, Madeleine de, 27
May, George, 13, 217
Medea, 26
Mendès, Catulle, 56–60, 63–4, 234
Menteau, Odette, 179, 180–1, 212
Merleau-Ponty, Maurice, 220
Mérode, Cléo de, 50
Michel, Anne, 184
Missy (Mathilde de Marny, duchesse de Belbeuf), 47, 218
Monési, Irène, 98, 110, 116–17, 122, 124–5, 151, 152, 162, 163–4, 167, 175, 183, 242
Monferrand, Hélène, 5, 127, 152, 166, 187, 205–10, 212
Monfort, Charles, 63–4, 235
Montegut, Maurice, 62–3
Montesquieu, Charles de Secondat, baron de, 13, 55, 217
Mouvement de la libération des femmes (MLF), 138
Mozart, Wolfgang Amadeus, 62
Mucha, Alfons, 4
Mylne, Vivienne, 217

Napoleonic Code, 3, 49, 52
Noël, Bernard, 195, 249
nouveau roman, le, 108, 132, 141, 143, 144, 220
Novalis, 195, 249

Orientalism, 23, 218
Osiris, 145

Paglia, Camille, 29, 218
Parshley, H.M., 220
Pastre, Geneviève, 212, 223
Peladan, Joséphin, 55–6, 60, 233–4
Pelletier, Madeleine, 53
Pert, Camille, 60
Phaedra, 26
Pickford, Mary, 163, 222
Pinget, Claude, 220

politique et psychanalyse, 138
Pougy, Liane de, 3, 50, 71, 72, 73, 74–7, 79
Proust, Marcel, 4, 74, 81, 86–9, 128, 219, 223, 237–8
Puccini, Giacomo, 50

Rachilde (Marguerite Eymery), 46, 163, 222
Racine, Jean, 117, 223
Radiguet, Raymond, 108
Raphael (Raffaello Sanzio), 29
Régnier, Henri de, 63
Reval, Gabrielle, 101
Rich, Adrienne, 151
Rigal, Muriel, 167–8, 171, 183, 245
Rivière, Charles, 81–3, 237
Rivière, Lucie, 180, 181, 212
Robbe-Grillet, Alain, 141, 220
Rochefort, Christiane, 98, 122–3, 152, 166, 214
Roffinella, Martine, 175–6
Roland-Manuel, Suzanne, 102–4, 239–40
Rousseau, Nita, 183

Sackville-West, Vita, 182
Said, Edward, 218
Saint-Agen, Adrienne, 71, 72, 73, 74, 77–81, 102, 103, 110, 214, 236–7
Saint-Exupéry, Antoine de, 113
Saint-Simoniens, 52
Salome, 26
Sand, George, 38
Sarraute, Nathalie, 108, 131–2, 138, 141, 220
Sarrazin, Albertine, 122, 123
Sartre, Jean-Paul, 130
Scève, Maurice, 144
second-wave feminism, 151
Shakespeare, William, 28
Shiach, Morag, 221
Simon, Claude, 143, 221
Smythe, Ethel, 182, 223
Sollers, Philippe, 97

Stein, Gertrude, 186
Streiff, Jean, 198
Sue, Eugène, 163, 222

Théoret, France, 166
Tinayre, Marcelle, 80, 223
Toulouse-Lautrec, Henri Marie de, 4

Ulysses, 145

Vaudière, Jane de la, 56, 61–2, 234–5
Vergne, Anne, 163
Verlaine, Paul, 33
Vian, Boris, 163, 185, 222
Vilmont, Anne, 122, 123–4, 243
Vivien, Renée (Pauline Mary Tarn), 73–4, 163, 222
Voltaire (François-Marie Arouet), 13, 217, 218

Waelti-Walters, Jennifer, 219, 221
Wajsbrot, Cécile, 6, 182
Whitford, Margaret, 217
Willette, Henriette, 73, 219
Willy (Henri Gauthier-Villars), 47, 63, 64–72, 80, 235–6
Wilson, Barbara, 185
Wings, Mary, 185
Wittig, Monique, 4, 5, 7, 53, 98, 112, 120, 126, 127, 134, 137–47, 164, 166, 180, 185, 196, 210, 212, 214, 219, 221
Women's Rights Congress, 51
Woolf, Virginia, 3, 6, 182, 186, 223

Yaffe, Deborah, 218, 222
Yourcenar, Marguerite (Marguerite Antoinette Marie Ghislaine de Crayencour), 127, 128, 130, 176, 220

Zeig, Sande, 146
Zola, Emile, 34, 40, 47, 69